Black Mask-ulinity

BLACK MALE MASCULINITY

Lemuel Watson, *Series Editor*

Rochelle Brock, Richard Greggory Johnson III,
and Cynthia Dillard
Executive Editors

Vol. 72

The Black Studies and Critical Thinking series
is part of the Peter Lang Education list.
Every volume is peer reviewed and meets
the highest quality standards for content and production.

PETER LANG
New York • Bern • Frankfurt • Berlin
Brussels • Vienna • Oxford • Warsaw

Black Mask-ulinity

A Framework for Black Masculine Caring

Edited by Lisa Bass

PETER LANG
New York • Bern • Frankfurt • Berlin
Brussels • Vienna • Oxford • Warsaw

Library of Congress Cataloging-in-Publication Data
Names: Bass, Lisa (Lisa R.), editor.
Title: Black mask-ulinity: a framework for Black masculine caring / edited by Lisa R. Bass.
Other titles: Black masculinity
Description: New York: Peter Lang, 2016.
Series: Black studies and critical thinking, Vol. 72 | ISSN 1947-5985
Includes bibliographical references and index.
Identifiers: LCCN 2016001477 | ISBN 978-1-4331-2655-0 (hardcover: alk. paper)
ISBN 978-1-4331-2654-3 (paperback: alk. paper) | ISBN 978-1-4539-1809-8 (e-book)
Subjects: LCSH: African American men—Education—Social aspects.
Masculinity—Social aspects—United States. | African American men—Race identity.
Classification: LCC LC2717 .B564 2016 | DDC 371.829/96073—dc23
LC record available at https://lccn.loc.gov/2016001477

Bibliographic information published by **Die Deutsche Nationalbibliothek**.
Die Deutsche Nationalbibliothek lists this publication in the "Deutsche
Nationalbibliografie"; detailed bibliographic data are available
on the Internet at http://dnb.d-nb.de/.

© 2016 Peter Lang Publishing, Inc., New York
29 Broadway, 18th floor, New York, NY 10006
www.peterlang.com

All rights reserved.
Reprint or reproduction, even partially, in all forms such as microfilm,
xerography, microfiche, microcard, and offset strictly prohibited.

Table of Contents

Foreword vii
    Vanessa Siddle Walker

Introduction 1
    Lisa R. Bass

Part One: Black Masculine Caring in Schooling

Chapter One: Black Masculine Caring in Educational Leadership:
    Introducing a Masculine-Centered Care Framework 11
    Lisa R. Bass

Chapter Two: The Risks of Cultivating Care in an Urban High School:
    Exploring a Black High School Principal's Experience and His Castigation.....27
    Mark A. Gooden and Daniel D. Spikes

Chapter Three: Who Cares? The Ethic of Care for Black Boys in School........... 45
    Julia Camille Ransom and James Earl Davis

Chapter Four: Unmasking Leadership: African American Male Scholars'
    Reflections on Critique, Justice, and Caring 59
    Floyd D. Beachum and Carlos R. McCray

Chapter Five: Masking Mentorship: Critical (Race) Care among
    Black Males in Special Education... 77
    Vonzell Agosto and Roderick Jones

Part Two: Black Masculine Caring: In Fatherhood, Spirituality, and Historical Traditions

Chapter Six: Black Fathers as Curriculum: Adopting Sons and Advancing Progressive-Regressive Black Masculinity 93
Ty-Ron M. O. Douglas

Chapter Seven: African American Men of Faith Care: The Intersection of Religion, Gender, and the Ethic of Care 113
Paul F. Bitting

Chapter Eight: Spirituality and Religion: The Foundation for Caring African American Males' Identity 131
Robert A. Horne

Chapter Nine: Manhood Development and Sustainable Institutional Care: John Hope at Morehouse College 143
Amber Jones

Conclusion: Honoring a Pedagogy of Caring for Black Males 153
Lisa R. Bass

Contributors 157
Postscript: A Reflective Essay on B(eing)-FREE: Lesson Learned from Gramp toward Transforming Mass Media Problems into Sustainable Solutions for Black Urban Youth 161
Brian Freeland
Index 175

Foreword

VANESSA SIDDLE WALKER

I probably should have been paying attention to the elliptical machine on which I was struggling to complete my assigned number of minutes. Instead, my gaze shifted to the muscular Black man a few feet away, who was walking threateningly toward a teenage Black male.

"Boy, I will bust you! Now get those rotations done!" The man's eyes showed no sympathy as he glared. Without resentment, the young man took a deep breath and complied.

Had I been of another cultural or age group, I might have understood the man's behavior to be verbal abuse. Instead, I smiled as I recognized a traditional form of interaction between Black men and youth, one in which Black men work up close in body and language as they encourage them to be the best they can be and refuse to accept anything less. His approach was direct, no-nonsense, and intolerant of noncompliance. He also gave the young man a warm, encouraging pat when he finished what had previously seemed impossible to him.

"He seems to enjoy working with you," I said later to the Black male trainer. Intrigued by the episode, I had watched the entire interaction while I peddled slower and slower on my own equipment.

"Yes m'am," the trainer said with a smile in my direction.

I had seen him work with teenage Black boys at other times and always with similar results. The young men called him "Mr. Rock"—a fitting title.

"You have to know how to measure caring and high standards," he explained as I smiled broadly. "They respond every time."

Perhaps if I had not spent the past twenty-five years writing about the segregated schooling of Black children, I might have been less intrigued by the interaction and felt no need to engage Mr. Rock about his work with the young Black men. Instead, the scene captured my imagination. I remembered seeing photographs of Black boys in Black schools with Black male principals leading student councils, excelling in language classes, and writing essays in student newspapers or yearbooks that spoke of their aspirations. I remembered conversations with Black men who talked about having no problem with Black boys in this earlier historical era. The boys looked up to the men, and the men took seriously their responsibility to mentor.

"If they had kept us working with Black boys, we would not be seeing the problems we are seeing today," I vaguely remembered an informant informally telling me once.

Interactions like the one I witnessed appear to have mostly faded in the current era, and few spaces address directly forms of interaction culturally congruent with a vaguely remembered past. I was thus delighted to review the important work of Lisa Bass and her colleagues. Considering both historical and contemporary examples, this volume examines an ethic of Black care in practice and introduces the concept of Black masculine caring. It demonstrates that images of the "tough man" actually are grounded in gendered and cultural practices. Whether evident in the mentoring style of the first Black college president of Morehouse, an adoptive father, or among leaders in faith communities, these chapters show the essential leadership role Black men play in the development of Black boys.

The chapters encourage us to face plainly the challenges faced by Black male leaders and the educational challenges Black boys encounter in varied school settings and to cease to denigrate the boys as originators of their own problems. Rather, they encourage us to understand that the difficulties begin with challenges outside themselves. As I consider the import of their suggestions, I am reminded of a statement made in 1914 at a conference of the National Association for the Advancement of Colored People in Baltimore. Coralie Cook described the circumstances of Negro children and considered explicitly the ways the circumstances the children confronted imprinted on their hearts a particular sensitivity to a hostile external environment. She postulated that the response should be to view the children with compassion. "It becomes us as guardians of their present to fortify them in every possible way to meet their future" (Cook, 1914).

Cook's challenge is recaptured one hundred years later in the effort of the authors in this volume to illuminate successful strategies to use in working with Black young men. Still, Black children are sensitive to their environments and they need adults who will train them to aspire. By considering examples of challenging circumstances and models of successful leadership both past and present, these authors give a new generation tools for a challenge to educate children sometimes forgotten in the midst of efforts to measure, rather than educate, them.

Often when I return to the gym, I look around to see whether I see Mr. Rock with no fanfare encouraging the Black male youth he encounters. I remain inspired by his unique brand of historically grounded and culturally sensitive motivation that causes the youth to look up to him. Perhaps the chapters in this volume will inspire others to go and do likewise with the ideas presented. Surely, the challenges facing the young men are no less real than when Coralie Cook encouraged listeners to accept the challenge of fortifying and inspiring the children one hundred years ago.

REFERENCE

Cook, C. F. (1914). *The problem of the colored child* (Box 1, F4). NAACP Proceedings, NAACP Collection, Library of Congress, Washington, DC.

Introduction

LISA R. BASS

The issue of Black administrators and caring appealed to me as I considered the ethic of care in educational leadership. I was particularly interested in the caring styles of Black administrators because of the increased incidences of violence and underachievement in schools with large populations of Black students, especially schools with populations of students living in poverty. Black leadership was of interest because Black leaders are disproportionately placed in high minority, high poverty schools, which is the target of reform for most districts (Bloom & Erlandson, 2003; Gooden, 2005). I began my investigation on this topic by studying how Black women school leaders demonstrated care utilizing the existing Black feminist caring framework (Collins, 1989) to frame my conversation (Bass, 2012). The findings from my study of Black women sparked my desire to discover whether Black men demonstrated care in similar ways.

As I began to investigate Black male principals' caring expressions and behaviors, I realized there was no existing theoretical framework to facilitate my exploration into the ways in which Black men care. The fact that caring, a very basic elemental aspect of humanity, had not yet explicitly been considered in Black males, was concerning. I posited this oversight occurred because of the tough-guy image placed on, and sometimes assumed by Black men choosing to act out this stereotype. In my research, I found that Black men are acutely aware of society's perceptions of them, and that these perceptions serve to burden and oppress Black men rather than to affirm or empower them. I was intrigued by my findings and wanted to dig deeper into the issue of Black masculinity and caring. For this reason, I began to gather expert, thoughtful scholars to discuss this topic from various perspectives, and through a variety of lenses in this book, because I believe the topic of Black masculine caring (BMC) is paramount, timely, and worthy of further investigation.

The prevailing negative image of Black men is gaining momentum and shapes the ways in which Black men are viewed and perceived by society. These perceptions subsequently shape the experiences, and moreover the futures of young Black males for better, but more often for worse. The most salient example of the detriment resulting from the negative images and stereotypes can be seen in the recent public slaughtering of Black males by police and self-proclaimed "well-meaning" citizens. These include Rumain Brisbon, 34, Phoenix, Arizona; Tamir Rice, 12, Cleveland, Ohio; Akai Gurley, 28, Brooklyn, New York; Kajieme Powell, 25, St. Louis, Missouri; Ezell Ford, 25, Los Angeles, California; Dante Parker, 36, San Bernardino, California; Michael Brown, 18, Ferguson, Missouri; John Crawford, 22, Beavercreek, Ohio; Eric Garner, 43, New York, New York; Jonathan Ferrell, 24, Bradfield Farms, North Carolina; Chavis Carter, 21, Jonesboro, Arkansas; Trayvon Martin, 17, Sanford, Florida; and, most recently, Freddie Gray, 25, Baltimore, Maryland. There are many others who could be named; however, the boys and men who qualify for this list were unfortunately too numerous to name in this introduction. I feel that the important issue of the senseless slaughtering of Black boys and men by police is worthy of its own research study and book.

Police and citizens alike have all claimed to feel threatened by the appearance, movements, and actions of these unarmed men to the point of using deadly force. Because of the strength and momentum of the negative stereotypes associated with Black males, officers and citizens who use deadly force on Black men and boys feel justified in doing so. Their instincts, shaped by years of social conditioning and media influence, indicate to them that if they do not attack, they themselves will be attacked. This is of concern to me not only as a citizen, but also as an educational researcher. This negative mind-set has infiltrated schools and has had an impact on the behavior of Black male students, teacher's perceptions of Black male students, and ultimately, the academic outcomes of Black males in school.

When the term *Black man* is uttered in the United States, it is usually associated with an image of a tough guy, and the connotation is often of negative stereotypes. As noted, this is largely due to the portrayal of Black men in the media as well as the negative stereotypes that have developed throughout years of racism (Coltrane & Messineo, 2000; Oliver, 2003). The writers of major motion pictures call for gentle spirits like Black actor Denzel Washington to play roles such as the bad cop in *Training Day* and the protagonist in *The Equalizer*—where throughout both films, he dispatches others either with weapons or with his bare hands. Further, the television media depicts Blacks negatively in general, and Black men are often cast as being criminal and dangerous (Coltrane & Messineo, 2000; Oliver,

2003). The news media are often similarly subjective, as Black men are generally depicted more negatively than White men who may commit the same offense, and are framed negatively for cases that have not yet been proved. This negative stereotyping has caused a great deal of frustration among Black men who reject these negative images and project positive, productive lifestyles. Unfortunately, they are often perceived and treated as thugs despite their choice to live productive mainstream lives (Oliver, 2003). Watkins, Green, Rivers, and Rowell (2006) focus on the impact of inequality, racism, violence, poverty, and health disparities. They note that Black men are more prone to depression because of the negative perceptions and inequalities they face on a regular basis. Black male school administrators are numbered among the Black men who live productive mainstream lives. They too, however, fall victim to stereotypes related to Black manhood. They are often looked to as the tough guy disciplinarian types, and expected to turn schools around—at least behaviorally (Gooden, 2005).

Black male administrators are often assigned to buildings that have higher numbers of Black students labeled at risk. They are generally expected to establish order with a strong hand, much like Joe Clark in the 1987 film *Lean on Me*. Black male leadership has been studied; however, caring is not generally associated with Black males or their leadership. The chapters in this book underscore the reality that Black males care, and that they need care. Authors further demonstrate some of the ways in which Black males care, and provide examples of effective caring practices for them.

Research has established the role of caring in the education of children and in securing their well-being (e.g., Cohen, McCabe, Michelli, & Pickeral, 2009; Noddings, 1984; Noddings & Slote, 2003) and emphasizes the role of socioemotional well-being in student achievement. In fact, Noddings and Cohen both assert that caring needs to be prioritized in the education of children. Cohen notes, "socioemotional skills, knowledge, and dispositions provide the foundation for participation in a democracy and improved quality of life" (p. 201). Preparing students for an improved quality of life is the overarching goal of education, and should consistently be the goal for all students. Unfortunately, many students enter schools and exit them without having improved life chances. In fact, researchers (e.g., Boyd, 2009; Darensbourg, Perez, & Blake, 2010; Dunn, 2013) have used the phrase "school-to-prison pipeline" to describe the negative aspects of schooling and the resulting outcome for some children—particularly African American children, with males being worse off than females.

The frustration felt by Black male principals stems from the negative stereotypes of Black men and the resulting expectations placed upon them as school leaders (see chapter 1 by Bass and chapter 2 by Gooden and Spikes). In a study conducted by Bass, shared in chapter 1, African American male leaders participated in a focus group in which they shared their feelings regarding care, and emerging themes indicated that they viewed themselves as caring fathers for their students; they believed that action must follow caring; they had a strong sense of spirituality that guided their actions; they practiced "rough love as care," when they deemed it necessary; and they took pride in their caring for students. In chapter 2 in a related study, Gooden and Spikes reported the value of the Black male is in his ability to demonstrate toughness in order to "whip a school into shape," according to district-level administration and teachers in the building. The men in the Bass study were caring; however, they felt they had to mask their caring instincts in order to be selected as principals and to be considered "effective" at managing their buildings. Study participants resented the fact that they had to mask their true caring character in order to become something the district wanted. Jesse Franklin, the principal highlighted in Gooden and Spikes's chapter, refused to concede to the expectations for him to implement uncaring practices. In fact, Franklin chose instead to demonstrate institutional and interpersonal care, and eventually lost his position for taking a stand. Unfortunately, his goal to demonstrate care by creating a system whereby he issued fewer referrals and suspensions was not popular with the teachers or the school district, and he paid the ultimate price for his choice to care.

Ransom and Davis continue the discussion of the plight of Black males in schools in chapter 3, arguing that the ethic of care is necessary for their proper development. Citing Nel Noddings's work (1992), they say that caring should be paramount in any educational setting, and should be included as a moral imperative for all those who wish to become teachers. In their chapter, caring for students is linked to increased expectations, academic efficacy, and student achievement. Ransom and Davis center their discussion on a study by Tyler and Boelter (2008), as they discuss the need for caring in terms of student achievement. In this study, Tyler and Boelter found that Black middle school children had higher levels of engagement and academic efficacy when they felt that teachers held high levels of expectations for them, but did not exhibit the same high levels of performance when they felt teachers' expectations were lower.

In chapter 4, Beachum and McCray discuss the plight of Black males in both K–12 and higher education as a result of the discrimination they face throughout their schooling experience. Their chapter confirms and underscores the need for Black male students to have exposure and access to positive Black male figures to help them negotiate their roles as Black men. There, they note, "African American males begin having even more such developmental experiences as they progress through the elementary grades (first through sixth), and head toward middle school and junior high school. As these Black boys are developing and cultivating self-identity, at the same time they are receiving messages from numerous sources, including television, the Internet, music, and peers, and reacting to interactions with teachers, school administrators, and other service providers" (Beachum & McCray, 2004; Tatum, 1997). They need more positive images to counteract the negative.

Agosto and Jones further address this point as they discuss the plight of Black males in special education in chapter 5. Constructing their discussion around Critical Race Theory, the situate institutionalized racism as an impediment to the success of Black males in special education, and provide a counternarrative about the need for mentoring and care of Black males in higher education. Unlike the authors of other chapters, Agosto also shares her own experiences in caring for Black males in the educational leadership program in which she is a professor, using her student and co-author as her case. Her expertise in the study of critical race theory, critical multicultural theory, and political clarity, along with her experiences as a secondary special education teacher served to help her develop political and ideological clarity about the intersection of relationships among youth, schools, and society. This knowledge, which represents a dominant part of her guiding intellectual capital, informs her as her own self-described personal experiences describe her, as "one who does not belong," and she folds her experiences into mentoring Black and Brown men.

Caring is indicated not only in the education of Black males, pre-K–20 education structure and beyond, but also in raising them. Care should be the guiding force behind each point of contact from the time children are born and throughout adulthood. Ty-Ron Douglas, in chapter 6, demonstrates this level of caring as a father, while bolstering the notion that Black men do care—both as fathers and as educators. In his chapter, he offers the emotive metaphor of 'Black children as systematic orphans,' and Black male educators as adoptive fathers. He situates himself in both the role of a natural adoptive father and as an academic one. This positioning of Black children and Black educators simultaneously acknowledges the injustices of the U.S. system of education and the role of Black male educators in protecting them. As any natural father, father educators serve as a compass to guide their "adopted children" to define purpose, cultural identity, and masculinity, suggesting that the role of the educator is much more dynamic than merely teaching the state-mandated curriculum. The act of adopting the disenfranchised is at the very heart of how Black administrators have been found to practice.

Bitting and Horne discuss the role of spirituality in Black men's caring, demonstrating care in their analyses. In chapter 7, Bitting begins his discussion with the development of a theory that describes the relationship between ethics, faith, race, and gender. He interviews subjects to further establish his theory by asking, 'What does it mean to be an African American male with a deep commitment to a faith community while serving in an educational environment?' His participants share stories of how to negotiate these two spaces that often have conflicting goals.

Horne, in chapter 8, seeks to understand the relationship between the role that the Black Church plays in the formation in Black men's caring identities. He includes a discussion of masking and cool pose that explains the tendency in

Black males to mask or hide their true feelings and emotions—including care—in order to maintain a strong and austere image to the outside world. These men do so because they succumb to the stereotypes and expectations placed on them by society. Horne provides a historical narrative of the placement of Black men in the context of slavery, the Black Church, and contemporary society. He uses this background to shed yet more light on the Black male experience and caring. Spirituality and religion are discussed as conduits through which Black men learn to express their ethic of caring.

Jones, in chapter 9, also discusses the need for care and mentoring of Black males, but at the institutional level. Jones notes the caring leadership of John Hope as he led Morehouse College. She notes his use of institutional and interpersonal care in his leadership and decision making to address the academic and moral needs of his students on both an interpersonal and institutional level. His leadership was hands on as he worked to meet the physical needs of his students, demonstrating interpersonal care, while he also demonstrated institutional care as he incorporated institutional structures that contributed to the building of Black manhood. He cemented his efforts by keeping the college connected to the greater community.

The postscript, by Freeland, represents a lived example of what it means to learn Black masculine caring from a Black male (his grandfather), then to pass it on as a father, as well as a mentor in his work as a teacher and coach. Brian Freeland shares personal accounts by exploring his relationships as a Black man and how this exploration of the role he perceives as his responsibility has led him to contribute to the development of other Black males. Freeland uses societal perceptions as a backdrop and discusses the role of popular culture in both challenging and shaping his message to the youth he serves. Freeland has continuously sought out solutions to improve the trajectory of the Black males in his care and framed a mentoring program as a result.

The chapters in this book demonstrate that Black men care and that black males need care, and examines the ways in which this caring is expressed. The authors support, and build upon the framework I began to generate as I analyzed their research on Black masculine caring.

Nel Noddings (1984, 1992), the principals in the Bass study (Bass), Ransom and Spikes, Beachum and McCray, Agosto and Jones, Douglas, and Freeland all bear witness to the notion that caring must be followed by actions. This notion is clearly espoused in the Black Masculine Caring Framework delineated in this text. Noddings says that caring should move the carer to action on behalf of the cared for. The Black male leaders in my study, as well as those in several of the other chapters in the book, noted how they took pride in their actions to help students as a result of their caring. The conclusion provides a brief overview of the chapters. The postscript, as noted above, represents an example of a Black man's proactivity as a result of his caring for Black males.

REFERENCES

Bass, L. (2012). When care trumps justice: The operationalization of Black feminist caring in educational leadership. *International Journal of Qualitative Studies in Education, 25*(1), 73–87.

Beachum, F., & McCray, C. (2004). Cultural collision in urban schools. *Current Issues in Education, 7*(4).

Bloom, C. M., & Erlandson, D. A. (2003). African American women principals in urban schools: Realities, (re) constructions, and resolutions. *Educational Administration Quarterly, 39*(3), 339–369.

Boyd, T. M. (2009). Confronting racial disparity: Legislative responses to the school-to-prison pipeline. *Harvard Civil Rights-Civil Liberties Law Review, 44*, 571.

Cohen, J., McCabe, L., Michelli, N. M., & Pickeral, T. (2009). School climate: Research, policy, practice, and teacher education. *Teachers College Record, 111*(1), 180–213.

Collins, P. H. (1989). The social construction of black feminist thought. *Signs*, 745–773.

Coltrane, S., & Messineo, M. (2000). The perpetuation of subtle prejudice: Race and gender imagery in 1990s television advertising. *Sex Roles, 42*(5–6), 363–389.

Darensbourg, A., Perez, E., & Blake, J. (2010). Overrepresentation of African American males in exclusionary discipline: The role of school-based mental health professionals in dismantling the school to prison pipeline. *Journal of African American Males in Education, 1*(3), 196–211.

Dunn, K. (2013). School-to-prison pipeline. *Faulkner Law Review, 5*, 115.

Gooden, M. A. (2005). The role of an African American principal in an urban information technology high school. *Educational Administration Quarterly, 41*(4), 630–650.

Noddings, N. (1984). *Caring: A feminist approach to ethics and moral education.* Berkeley: University of California Press.

Noddings, N. (1992). *The challenge to care in schools: An alternative approach to education: Vol. 8. Advances in contemporary educational thought.* New York, NY: Teachers College Press.

Noddings, N., & Slote, M. (2003). Changing notions of the moral and of moral education. In N. Blake, P. Smeyers, R. Smith, & P. Standish (Eds.), *The Blackwell guide to the philosophy of education* (pp. 341–355). New York, NY: Wiley-Blackwell.

Oliver, M. B. (2003). African American men as "criminal and dangerous": Implications of media portrayals of crime on the "criminalization" of African American men. *Journal of African American Studies, 7*(2), 3–18.

Tatum, B. D. (1997). *"Why are all the Black kids sitting together in the cafeteria?" And other conversations about race.* New York, NY: Basic Books.

Tyler, K. M., & Boelter, C. M. (2008). Linking Black middle school students' perceptions of teachers' expectations to academic engagement and efficacy. *The Negro Education Review, 59*(1–2), 27–44.

Watkins, D. C., Green, B. L., Rivers, B. M., & Rowell, K. L. (2006). Depression and Black men: Implications for future research. *The Journal of Men's Health & Gender, 3*(3), 227–235.

PART ONE

Black Masculine Caring IN Schooling

CHAPTER ONE

Black Masculine Caring IN Educational Leadership

Introducing a Masculine-Centered Care Framework

LISA R. BASS

STATEMENT OF THE PROBLEM

Students from high-poverty communities, African Americans, and other disenfranchised populations have been identified as at-risk groups in studies of student achievement in American schools. Research indicates that a persistent gap in achievement exists between African Americans and students who live in poverty and most other racial and ethnic groups (Weinstein, Schwartz, Bel Hadj Amor, & Stiefel, 2008). Ethicists have suggested that teachers who care about their pupils and take an active role in school leadership may be the missing piece in the unsuccessful reform efforts to close this achievement gap (Delpit, 2006; Noddings, 1984; Shade, 1997; Willis, 1995). Most school administrators know that African American, poor, and other disenfranchised students currently achieve at lower levels than most other groups (Ladson-Billings, 2006) because they have experienced structural inequities and received less support, not because they lack ability. Educational leaders also know that the care such disenfranchised students need must be expressed on multiple dimensions and at higher levels of intensity if they are to reach their potential. In short, administrators know that caring for traditionally disenfranchised students promotes student achievement. However, school leaders must move from knowing to doing if we are to see a positive change in the achievement of students who persistently perform at lower levels academically. We must implement leadership models that facilitate a climate of both interpersonal and institutional caring (Noddings, 1984; Siddle Walker & Snarey, 2004). Caring for students is a moral imperative that must underlie the leadership practices of both male and female principals of all racial demographics, so that all students can garner the maximum benefit from their schooling experiences. Then, and only then, will we begin to see persistent achievement gaps start to close.

INTRODUCTION TO THE STUDY

Care ethicists have discussed "care" as a verb (Gilligan, 1982; Mayeroff, 1971; Noddings, 1984, 2013), describing caring as the act of feeling enough passion or compassion about an issue to be moved to do something. Gilligan (1982) connected care to empathy rather than abstract ethical principles. It is out of this sense of connection and empathy that school workers seek to interrupt the inequitable educational practices they witness. Though Noddings (1984) referred to care as an ethic, she also purported that when people genuinely care about an unjust situation, they will spring to corrective action; in this sense, action means investigating and investing—investigating what the problem is, why it exists, and how one can act to remedy it, followed by investing the necessary resources to discover an appropriate solution and then acting on it (Bass, 2012). Gilligan (1982) framed the notion of care by pointing to the liberating qualities embedded in it when the needs of those cared for are met and their welfare is actively promoted. It can be argued that the caregiver experiences a sense of liberation as much as the person receiving the care, because the investment of people who care can be monumental, especially when the situations they wish to impact are dire, long-standing, and complex. The breakthrough is a great reward, not only for students receiving care, but also for the caregivers in complex cases. Therefore, the complexity of situations will not deter genuine caregivers from investing, as was evident in the men who participated in the current study. In fact, the more complex the situation, the more compelled some of the participating caregivers were to remedy it. Caring often means sacrificing one's personal comfort and preferences while pursuing the best interest of the person being cared for, which is consistent with the actions and experiences of the African American male leaders in this study.

The men in this study observed that the positive responses they wanted to see in the students they serve—such as positive identification with school, identity as a scholar, and increased academic achievement—are not seen in response to the simple spoken tokens of caring or expensive purchases, but in the type of caring that is evidenced by deeper action. Noddings (1984) referred to this type of genuine display of caring as *relational caring,* and further stated that the teacher should be the caregiver much of the time, caring for the child's physical, psychological, and academic needs. In a time when it is often said and believed that few people, including school workers, demonstrate genuine care, I found renewed hope as I sought out and found five contemporary, caring African American male educational leaders who exhibited the ethic of care in their practice.

District-level administrators often place African American principals in schools with a majority of high-poverty and high-need African American students. Arguably, such administrators hypothesize that African American students and their families will more closely identify with these leaders, and further assume that African American leaders will better understand the needs of the African American communities in which they are placed (Bloom & Erlandson, 2003; Pollard, 1997). Though this hypothesis often guides decision making in school districts, there is scant empirical research that validates this assumptive practice or investigates why the assumption may hold true. However, this is not to suggest that African Americans alone can care for African American and other disenfranchised groups. Instead, this study critically examined the leadership styles of African American male leaders who were placed in high-poverty settings, and resulted in the proposed conceptual framework of *Black masculine caring*.

Men have demonstrated the capacity to be caring leaders; however, the ethic of care has traditionally been viewed as a primarily feminist construct (Bass, 2009; Gilligan, 1982; Noddings, 1984). Typical American gender roles dictate that women leaders generally act from the heart and emotion, while men are believed to act more from a sense of logic. As a result, caring is rarely emphasized as a disposition within the context of male leadership (Lewis, 2000), though it is almost always included when discussing general feminist frameworks as well as feminist leadership frameworks. Consequently, many scholars have employed feminist caring frameworks exhaustively in describing the leadership styles of women, though not readily recognizing caring to be a prominent trait of male leadership (Gilligan, 1982; Strachan, 1999).

There are definite similarities and overlaps between masculine and feminine leadership styles, but the core values manifested in masculine approaches to leadership are incongruent to those emphasized in feminist theories and approaches to leadership. Scholars have argued that masculine-centered frameworks and theories, unlike feminist caring approaches, advocate for more linear, logical, and rational approaches to operations and decision-making (Stelter, 2002; Van Engen, Vander Leeden, & Willemsen, 2001). As such, masculine frameworks advance notions of pragmatism and efficiency, while feminist approaches generally employ a decision-making process viewed as more emotionally driven and guided by the needs of children or those they lead. Thus, leaders who employ what is considered to be a stereotypically masculine-centered approach are more likely to rely on logic, rules, and set structures as the primary basis for decision-making, while those who exemplify feminist caring theories of leadership advocate for prioritizing and responding to the needs of children.

THEORETICAL FRAMEWORK

Women have been studied at length with respect to feminist caring in leadership (Bass, 2012; Eagly, 2007; Gilligan, 1982; Stelter, 2002). Men, however, have not been studied as thoroughly through the lens of care, perhaps because the term *feminist* is often used to characterize and define caring. The relative absence of males in care literature may also be the result of those assumptions of male leadership in the foregoing discussion. Although feminist pedagogies are most often used in reference to advocacy for issues pertaining to women, there is no existing companion term or parallel concept that specifically delineates or celebrates the characteristics of caring men. This seeming definitional dissonance and lack of a conceptual framework may deter researchers from targeting males for studies pertaining to feminist care ethics, as well as hindering caring men's desire to understand and identify with feminist notions of caring. Thus, this work seeks to provide a language for men who care, specifically Black male leaders. When the caring of Black women is studied, the term "Black feminist caring" has been used because of the historical and cultural component that differentiates their caring styles from those discussed in the discourse on general ethics of caring. Notably, historical and cultural components were also evident in the data on African American males. For this reason, I introduce the concept of Black masculine caring as a basis for further conversation on this important issue in educational leadership.

STUDY SIGNIFICANCE

This study is essential because caring leadership is paramount to student achievement, particularly among African American students (Delpit, 2006; Dillard, 1995). Moreover, Wentzel (1997) found, in her longitudinal study with sixth through eighth graders, that when students believe their teachers and administrators genuinely care for them, they work harder to achieve. The focus of the current study was on the caring leadership of Black male leaders who work primarily with African American students and students from urban high-poverty backgrounds for four reasons:

1) African American students often underachieve in U.S. schools. Hence, the achievement gap persists between this group and their White and Asian peers, often making these students the target of school reform initiatives.
2) Students from high-poverty backgrounds underachieve when compared with students from middle- and upper-class backgrounds. Black men were of interest because they are often selected to lead buildings with a majority

of poor, high-need African American students, yet there is scant empirical data on the efficacy of this practice.
3) This study is a complement to a similar study conducted with African American women leaders using a Black feminist framework (Bass, 2012), which will be used in a comparative analysis with previously collected data.
4) African American children from high-poverty contexts generally have a dynamic need set, which calls for *intensive caring practices* in leadership. These practices mean that leaders who operate in high-need schools must often go above and beyond the expected duties of a building principal to better serve their students.

Overall, I lay the foundation for the concept of Black masculine caring on feminist caring as the standard for the ethic of care (Gilligan, 1982), because masculine approaches to caring have not yet been sufficiently explored. The purpose of this study is to examine the perception of caring leadership among African American male leaders with the goal of developing a framework for Black masculine caring. Black masculine caring is distinguished from masculine caring because the findings indicated that, similar to findings on Black feminist caring (Bass, 2012; Collins, 1990), culture and history impacted the participants' perceptions and executions of the caring ethic. Therefore, I conducted a study focused solely on the ethic of care among African American male educational leaders. The leadership styles of African American men and their manner of caring has not been closely examined in the educational leadership literature, and this study works to fill this gap.

RESEARCH DESIGN

This study investigated the phenomenon of interest using qualitative, exploratory multi-case study methodology (Merriam, 1998; Patton, 2002) to facilitate the collection of rich data that tell the stories of the participants. This study was designed to qualitatively examine the lived experiences of five African American male administrators. The sample was formed by the "snowball" sampling method: I asked an administrator who had a strong reputation for being caring and who was also familiar with the principals in the area for names of other male African American school leaders who also had reputations for caring. From him, I received the names of four other leaders who all agreed to participate in a focus group. I was specifically interested in how these men operationalized the ethic of care in their leadership practices. The participants in the study were from a large midwestern city and all worked in the same large urban school district. The multi-case study approach was selected to give voice to the study participants and to manifest their views in the findings of the study, specifically by including rich, descriptive narratives that would provide insight into the issue. Understanding the participants' actions via their stories was essential to addressing the line of inquiry put forward in this study—understanding ways in which Black men care for the students under their charge. As such, the use of the qualitative methodology accomplishes the goal of learning about a phenomenon of interest through the participants' perspectives (Merriam, 1998; Patton, 2002).

Study Sample and Data Collection

The study sample included five African American male school administrators working in the capacity of assistant principal or principal of middle schools and high schools. Notably, one of the five leaders served at the district level as associate superintendent.

Data were collected from email questionnaires, a focus group, and follow-up telephone calls for clarification as needed. All of the men were eager participants and were extremely open and forthcoming with their answers. Moreover, they seemed honored to have been selected to participate in the study and were grateful for the opportunity to connect with like-minded colleagues; they appeared to take comfort in knowing there were other men who operationalized an ethic of care in their leadership and decision-making. The men appeared comfortable during the focus group, seemed to be transparent, and responded honestly to questions as they made heartfelt comments. Participants were familiar with each other and were collegial and respectful during the focus group meetings. Overall, the group had excellent chemistry, and I did not notice any instances during which any of them attempted to outshine the others. During the focus group, the men provided thought-provoking and emotional responses to the questions, even above and beyond that which I expected as researcher.

Study Participants Table

Participant	Age Range	Position	Education Experience
Jonathan	35–40	Middle School Principal	12 years
Maurice	30–35	High School Principal	8 years
Frank	45–50	High School Assistant Principal	22 years
Brian	35–40	High School Principal	15 years
Rick	40–45	Former Principal, Assistant Superintendent	18 years

Data Analysis

The data from the focus groups, email interviews, and telephone calls were analyzed using the constant comparison and discourse analysis methods (Glaser & Strauss, 1967; Strauss & Corbin, 1998). Email interviews were read thoroughly upon receipt, and telephone calls were made for clarification as needed. From this initial round of data, I then developed a focus group protocol that was subsequently conducted in a comfortable, private conference room on a university campus. Participants were put at ease with snacks and small talk prior to the start of the focus group session. The men participating in this study viewed the handout containing the questions for the first time during the focus group. The recording of the focus group session was immediately transcribed. The email interview transcripts were also read and reread to create codes and to identify common themes (Patton, 2002; Strauss & Corbin, 1998). The themes that emerged were then used to generate topics for discussion used in this chapter.

Trustworthiness of the Data

Trustworthiness refers to the credibility of a study and the researcher's belief that the phenomena under investigation have been captured (Lincoln & Guba, 1985). In this study, credibility was sought by using member checking, a method in which the participants review the interpretations, findings, and conclusions to ensure reliability. Member checking was a joint endeavor between the researcher and the participants (Etter-Lewis, 1993). Participants provided detailed feedback both during the focus group and when contacted afterward. In follow-up with the participants, they each expressed gratitude and commented on how great it felt to be able to discuss a topic that is so rarely addressed. They also enjoyed each other's company and vowed to meet more often in the future.

EMERGENT KEY THEMES

The themes that emerged from this study did not support the stereotype that is set forth regarding male leadership. The major themes that emerged are described in brief below.

First, African American male leaders in high-poverty, majority African American contexts often demonstrate an ethic of care in their leadership. Despite the fact that caring is thought to be a feminist notion whereas men are said to be pragmatic, rational leaders, this shows that the ethic of care is also exhibited by African American men in their leadership practice.

African American male leaders are also compelled to step in as father figures for their students. This theme was pervasive, as can be seen in the participants' quotes below. One principal, Brian, boldly exclaimed: "I may be the only father that my students know." He went on to say:

> I've been a father to a thousand students. I'm their father pretty much, I mean, because the large majority of them do not have that ... and you can just look at them and tell that crave it. They want it. And who am I to deny it? And I'm actually proud that they consider me a father figure to them.

Other participants also addressed this topic of male leaders as father figures, including Jonathan:

> I can guarantee there's no one at this table that has not been labeled or called "daddy." That's the interesting thing ... regardless of whether they're Black, White, or Latino, you go into a kind of care mode, you know. Most of us are not only carers, but caretakers. It's the mentality that "I need to fix it." And we take this into the schools every day however we can fix it.

Another theme that emerged in this study is that the participants believed that action must follow caring. In short, they believed, as Noddings (1984) claimed, that if you care, your caring should move you to action. That is, caring must be demonstrated by actions. Most of the principals recounted a story about having to demonstrate their caring through their actions. In fact, they were very proud of how they acted on behalf of students without even giving it a second thought. One leader, Rick, summed it up aptly, and all agreed that: "Students will know that they are cared for by the actions of their leader."

As with Black feminist caring, the Black men in this study also identified strongly with spirituality on some level, and saw spirituality as a guiding force. Though all of the leaders found spirituality to be a driving force behind their caring style of leadership, they had varying experiences. Still, the focus group participants indicated a connection to spirituality as at least part of their motivation for caring. Participant Jonathan remarked:

> I was born to care; however, my religious experience has empowered why I care, if that makes sense. It's in me to care; however, because of my religious upbringing and all of that, it has empowered me to care even more ... how I care for others.

Rick, another of the principals in the group, concurred:

> I'd have to agree. It goes back, quite frankly, beyond me. It goes back to my roots. And my roots were grounded in what spirituality is and what it is to deal with the struggles and that's just the household many young Blacks grow up in. You know, hope is spirituality, and you know we dive off the shoulders of what that spirituality brings to the successes that we have and the failures that we have.

Perhaps the most surprising theme that emerged from the study was the idea of "rough love as care." In fact, the discussion surrounding this theme caught me off guard because it was not only unexpected, but also participants became very passionate and animated as they discussed this topic. Study participants indicated that they sometimes have to use "rough love" or force to demonstrate their care, particularly toward African American male students. They explained that such an approach is necessary to establish a basis for respect, and claimed that such "necessary roughness" is understood as paternal care between them and the African American male students, demonstrating to the students that they are reaching out and that they genuinely care. Each participant seemed to have a story to share of practicing "rough love" with students. There was a strong sense of brotherhood and agreement around the issue, whereas it does not appear extensively in the literature for feminist caring, indicating that this theme, unlike some of the others, definitely separated masculine caring from feminine caring. Because rough love is not usually associated with caring, it took me some time to grasp the notion of how "necessary roughness" demonstrates caring as the leaders in the focus group asserted. I believe this is where the influence of culture and gender dominates mainstream behavior and judgment. This theme sets the ethic of caring seen in African American women leaders apart from how African American men demonstrate caring. It was important to bring this theme out because it is absent in the literature as well as in my previous work with African American women wherein I explored Black feminist caring (Bass, 2012). Many of the principals commented on the behavior of rough love, including Maurice:

> Last year, as a first-year administrator, I actually went to the most behaviorally challenged school. The first day of school I was tested. This young boy was almost as big as me … he challenged me. But I cared enough to let him know that I would put my foot down … that I would "discipline" him if I needed to. I mean, because he challenged me, and really, you know, the typical response would have been to call security. "Let's get this boy out of here" is the normal reaction to such disruption; however, instead of me doing that, I looked to him man-to-man, like "here's the consequences for that action … and it might not be one that you are used to getting!"

A similar story was relayed by another participant:

> It's cultural … it's a cultural understanding. Yeah, I had an African American student when I was at a predominantly White school … an African American young man who kept getting everyone in trouble. And one day I told him, "Boy, if you don't sit your ass down and listen to me?" And he immediately sat down. (Brian)

Although the student was clearly being addressed in a way that he was not accustomed to, another participant commented on the need to approach the students in this way:

> Sometimes we understand that with our caring, you just have to leave us alone and let us do what we know works with particular children. The norm is becoming using strategies by, what's her name … Ruby Payne? Well for some of ours, we need to make them think that there is going to be some pain! We know how to get their attention, and still do it in a respectful way. Our care showing could be different, and probably is a little bit different than those outside this door. (Jonathan)

One focus group participant noted how often rough love shown to students would transfer to the home, after some concerted effort by the leader:

> I could name story after story, kid after kid, where I did have to, you know, put him in my car or put her in my car and take her home and look grandma in the eye and let her know that we're either going to handle it this way or a way that might have a less favorable outcome. I could bring him back to school and he could see that I have your support to discipline him in a particular manner that's not allowed in the public school system right there on the spot. And then you develop a relationship over time with the kid and see what the cultural norms and expectations are going to be not only in the school, but also roll over into the household. (Frank)

The cultural norms that Frank spoke of were addressed by other participants:

> There are differences in cultures and norms, and we have an inert ability as African American males to figure out African American students more quickly. I think society recognizes that piece but won't necessarily recognize some of the expectations and some of the practices that go along with that piece. I think that's why [other participant] mentioned that he was sought out to be a role model for a particular student that needed guidance. (Rick)

Brian also commented on the importance of "rough love":

> Along the lines of what everyone else is saying, once you build that relationship, there are times when you've got to shut the door and let that kid know that "that's the way it is gonna be. It's gonna be that way in no uncertain terms." It's almost like all you have to do is give them a certain look. You look at them a certain way and they'll know from across the room. You could be in an auditorium full of people, and you give them that look … it's a done deal.

All of the foregoing comments indicate that the Black male leaders in this study had found past success in building caring relationships by any means necessary, even if they used unconventional methods.

The idea of past success affecting future actions was the basis of another theme that emerged from the study—the leaders were motivated to care by past success in relationship-building. The participating male leaders in this study all had a story to share in which they had demonstrated care and it worked miracles in turning situations around for disenfranchised, high-risk students with whom they had built relationships. The following accounts discuss relationship-building and how the resulting successes motivated the leaders to continue to demonstrate caring in their practice:

> I've been working with this young lady, and something happened over the weekend. She came back and said, "Mr. W., I've just got to tell you this, um, this girl had some friends who over the weekend got into trouble." When I asked her why she didn't go and participate, she said she didn't want to disappoint me. Those are the types of relationships that we do build, and when they're built correctly with a student, they'll go through a brick wall for you. I was proud of the student for staying out of trouble in this particular incident; however, I had to exercise tough love as I discussed with her how I thought she was still too close to the troublemaker. (Jonathan)

Similarly, the participant in the next account indicates the influence of an aunt's care on his own caring practices. He recalled a very compelling story of the relationship between him and his aunt and how her caring encouragement still motivated him to care for others:

> I remember when I was about four or five, and I was about ready to quit, give up. It was my aunt who sat down and for the first time there was somebody that actually showed me that they cared about me. And she said, "We can do this, baby, we can get through this." I will never forget how that influenced my decision to become a math teacher. And that's why I went into education. I was four years old and when I got through, she looked at me and she said, "Boy, you're smart. Don't ever forget that." And from that day forward, I was more confident. "I'm like the smartest dude in here, right?" (Rick)

Another theme that emerged was that study participants felt the struggle between societal expectations, those of the school districts, and their desire to be caring leaders. They felt that society expected them to *always* be big tough guys, while they wished to temper that toughness and use it as they deemed necessary. They sometimes wanted the choice of being nurturing and gentle when it was appropriate, but did not see this as a real option. As a researcher, I experienced the male leaders as strong and passionate, yet gentle. The men in this study did not present themselves as purposely antiestablishment mentors, or even as "tough guys." However, they made it apparent that they ruled with mission and purpose, and that this guided their leadership, including how they demonstrated care. If a rule came between them doing what they knew to be right, they would break it, though they did not boast or take pleasure in it. This philosophy might also be described as "care trumps justice," which I also discussed in the study I completed with female administrators (Bass, 2012). A number of the study participants commented on this notion:

> I'm being real; the vast majority of folks don't think we even care, as men. They don't think that Black men give a damn about too much of anything because there are so many masks that we have to wear. So outside of this context—I mean, this is probably the most Blacks that I've met from the profession at the same time with sitting right here. I mean, we

can't go into a meeting and be this way because we have to wear so many masks. We do. I mean, it's almost hypocrisy the way we have to live with so many masks on caring because, you know, you just have to. And kids can be ripping your heart out, and right there before everyone, you just have to sit there and stay composed. And also perhaps maybe it's some of our fault, because that's what's been built for us as Black men. (Brian)

Jonathan chimed in with his thoughts, which were not all that different from Brian's:

> There is a perception that Black men don't care at all. So there is a perception … there is a gap between the projection and the perception. And why? It's just [said in frustration], I don't know. It's just a negative stigma that we have, you know. It's just like we are non-caring people or don't have the ability to do it.

As the energy built in the room, Brian began again:

> When you are working with people not of your racial background, the label they perceive you as is being a big, Black male. The coach … I am a coach, but I hate being labeled as *just that*. And also an enforcer. They look at me like "you're clearing these halls out. You take care of this." I mean, you're not respecting my intellect or my ability; in a few situations, I've heard, "You go over here and clear this out. You take care of that by any means necessary." It's insulting [with an increasingly frustrated tone]. I mean, it's insulting. And I'm just like, I can do other things. I can do this role, but for you to think that's what I'm here for, and probably the reason why you hired me, it's insulting.

A final theme revealed in the study was the idea that the leaders took pride in their caring role and needing to be needed. Study participants were very proud to be among those who cared about students. They enjoyed telling their stories in the company of other caring leaders and discussing how they knew their caring made a difference in the lives of their students. They clearly enjoyed knowing that their students needed them, as reflected in their comments:

> You know, I remember that I was a grown man the first time I saw my dad even cry. And I was like a little baby because I was just like, "Should I just go over and crawl in the corner and cry? I mean, what do I do? I'm not supposed to see this?" Although this was the first time I saw my dad display this level of emotion, there was never a minute that I thought that my dad did not care. But because of the way he presented himself, you know, this sturdy, this broad shouldered, you know … I take on the world of caring. It's also an interesting thing, and really good for me to hear the other guys here saying what they do, because that's what we all do. Because that's who we are. (Brian)

Frank, getting in the last words for the session, summarized the sentiment of the group as he discussed the many hats that men wear as they care:

> We are all dad, we are all uncles, we become cab drivers, medics, probationary officers … we do it all, I mean, but I think a lot of times it's because as men, we know. We know the challenges and the feelings that some of these young men have. We know what it feels like

to feel marginalized or underrepresented. So caring, for us, is a lot different, I think, than most people would ever imagine.

Thus, a number of marked themes emerged from the study.

IMPLICATIONS FOR RESEARCH AND CONCLUSIONS

The core foundational principles of Black masculine caring include a framework that acknowledges Black men have the capacity to care, and often care deeply; Black men's capacity to care is dependent upon their prior experience; caring is often demonstrated by Black men as much as it is demonstrated by others; the caring exhibited by Black men is influenced by culture; and caring demonstrated by Black men is often misunderstood or misinterpreted.

After embarking on this work, it is clear that further empirical studies of scale on the direct effect of caring on student achievement need to be implemented in order to better understand the impact of caring on student learning. Furthermore, additional work needs to be done toward understanding the notion of caring from a variety of perspectives, rather than assuming one "blanket" approach on behalf of all teachers and administrators. Implications for this research support the development of the grounded theory framework for Black masculine caring. Moreover, the findings of this study suggest that African American male leaders may identify with the ethic of care as it is currently framed less readily than female leaders, because it has heretofore been viewed as a feminist notion in the literature and fails to acknowledge the dynamic nature of the style of Black masculine caring.

Given the emergent themes of this study, I will use this research to inform further studies on male leadership and caring on a grander scale. As the central goal for this work was to promote more caring schools by inspiring and training caring administrators from all backgrounds, I believe that this training should be built into educational leadership and policy programs and taught in both leadership and ethics classes.

REFERENCES

Bass, L. (2012). When care trumps justice: The impact of black feminist caring in educational leadership. *International Journal of Qualitative Research in Education, 25*(1), 73–87.

Bloom, C. M., & Erlandson, D. A. (2003). African American women principals in urban schools: Realities, (re)constructions, and resolutions. *Educational Administration Quarterly, 39*(3), 339–369.

Collins, P. H. (1990). *Black feminist thought: Knowledge, consciousness, and the politics of empowerment.* New York, NY: Routledge.

Delpit, L. (2006). *Other people's children: Cultural conflict in the classroom.* New York, NY: New Press.

Dillard, C. B. (1995). Leading with her life: An African American feminist (re) interpretation of leadership for an urban high school principal. *Educational Administration Quarterly, 31*(4), 539–563.

Eagly, A. H. (2007). Female leadership advantage and disadvantage: Resolving the contradictions. *Psychology of Women Quarterly, 31*(1), 1–12.

Etter-Lewis, G. (1993). *My soul is my own: Oral narratives of African American women in the professions.* New York, NY: Routledge, 1993.

Gilligan, C. (1982). *In a different voice: Psychological theory and women's development.* Cambridge, MA: Harvard University Press.

Glaser, B., & Strauss, S. (1967). *The discovery of grounded theory.* Chicago, IL: Aldine.

Ladson-Billings, G. (2006). From the achievement gap to the education debt: Understanding achievement in U.S. schools. *Educational Researcher, 35*(7), 3–12.

Lewis, K. (2000). When leaders display emotions: How followers respond to negative emotional expression of male and female leaders. *Journal of Organization Behavior, 21*(2), 221–234.

Lincoln, Y., & Guba, E. (1985). *Naturalistic inquiry.* New York, NY: Sage.

Mayeroff, M. (1971). *On caring* (Vol. 43). New York, NY: Harper & Row.

Merriam, S. B. (1998). *Qualitative research and case study applications in education.* San Francisco, CA: Jossey-Bass.

Noddings, N. (1984). *Caring: A feminine approach to ethics and moral education.* Berkeley: University of California Press.

Noddings, N. (2013). *Caring: A relational approach to ethics and moral education.* Berkeley: University of California Press.

Osler, A. (1997). *The education and careers of Black teachers.* Buckingham, England: Open University Press.

Patton, M. Q. (2002). *Qualitative research & evaluation methods* (3rd ed.). Thousand Oaks, CA: Sage.

Pollard, D. S. (1997). Race, gender, and educational leadership: Perspectives from African American principals. *Educational Policy, 11,* 353–374.

Shade, B. (1997). *Creating culturally responsive classrooms.* Washington, DC: American Psychological Association.

Siddle Walker, V., & Snarey, J. R. (Eds.). (2004). *Race-ing moral formation: African American perspectives on care and justice.* New York, NY: Teachers College Press.

Stelter, N. Z. (2002). Gender differences in leadership: Current social issues and future organizational implications. *Journal of Leadership & Organizational Studies, 8*(4), 88–99.

Strachan, J. (1999). Feminist leadership: Locating the concepts in practice. *Gender and Education, 11*(3), 309–322.

Strauss, A., & Corbin, J. (1998). *Basics of qualitative research: Techniques and procedures for developing grounded theory* (2nd ed.). Thousand Oaks, CA: Sage.

Thompson, A. (2004). Caring and color talk: Childhood innocence in White and Black. In V. Siddle Walker & J. R. Snarey (Eds.), *Race-ing moral formation: African American perspectives on care and justice* (pp. 23–37). New York, NY: Teachers College Press.

Van Engen, M. L., Vander Leeden, R., & Willemsen, T. R. (2001). Gender, context and leadership styles: A field study. *Journal of Occupational and Organizational Psychology, 74*(5), 581–598.

Wentzel, K. R. (1997). Student motivation in middle school: The role of perceived pedagogical caring. *Journal of Educational Psychology, 89*(3), 411.

Willis, A. I. (1995). Reading the world of school literacy: Contextualizing the experience of a young African American male. *Harvard Educational Review, 65*(1), 30–50.

WORKS CONSULTED

Casella, R. (2003). Zero tolerance policy in schools: Rationale, consequences, and alternatives. *Teachers College Record, 10*(5), 872–892.
Collins, P. H. (1986). Learning from the outsider within: The sociological significance of Black feminist thought. *Social Problems, 33*(6), S14–S32.
Dunbar, C., & Villarruel, F. (2002). Urban school leaders and zero tolerance policies: An examination of its implications. *Peabody Journal of Education, 77*(1), 82–104.
Freire, P. (1970). *Pedagogy of the oppressed*. New York, NY: Continuum.
Larson, C. L., & Murtadha, K. (2002). Leadership for social justice. In J. Murphy (Ed.), *The educational leadership challenge: Redefining leadership for the 21st century* (One hundred and first yearbook of the National Society for the Study of Education, pp. 134–161). Chicago, IL: National Society for the Study of Education.
Lincoln, C. E., & Mamiya, L. H. (1990). *The Black church in the African American experience*. Durham, NC: Duke University Press.
Murphy, S. E., Zewdie, S., & Reichard, R. J. (2008). The strong sensitive type and leadership prototypes on the evaluation of male and female leaders. *Organizational Behavior and Human Decision Processes, 106*(1), 39–60.
Pounder, J. S. (2002). Women better leaders than men? In general and educational management it still "all depends." *Leadership and Organization Development Journal, 23*(3/4), 122.
Skiba, R. (2000, January 14). No to zero tolerance. *The New York Times*, p. 27.
Skiba, R., & Peterson, R. (1999). *The dark side of zero tolerance: Can punishment lead to safe schools?* Retrieved from www.pdkintl.org/kappan/kski9901.htm
Swanson, R. A., & Holton, E. F. (2001). *Foundations of human resource development*. San Francisco, CA: Berrett-Koehler.
Weinstein, M., Schwartz, A. E., Bel Hadj Amor, H., & Stiefel, L. (2008). Closing the black-white achievement gap in high school: An assessment of evidence on interventions to improve test scores and college prospects of African American students. NYU Wagner Research Paper No. 2011-12.

CHAPTER TWO

The Risks OF Cultivating Care IN AN Urban High School

Exploring a Black High School Principal's Experience and His Castigation

MARK A. GOODEN AND DANIEL D. SPIKES

The so-called achievement gap in education refers to "the disparity in academic performance between groups of students" (Education Week, 2011). Specifically, it is most often used to point to academic disparities between Black or Hispanic students and their White peers. Academic performance is usually based on standardized test scores, dropout rates, and college enrollment rates (Education Week, 2011). American students who are Black or African American, used interchangeably herein, do not perform as well as their White peers with regard to these performance indicators. They also face additional challenges, including disproportionate suspension and expulsion rates and special education placement (Gooden, 2005; Lomotey, 1993). For example, research found that 9- and 13-year-old Black students, on average, scored about 23 points lower than White students on the National Assessment of Educational Progress (NAEP) reading assessment of 2012 (National Center for Education Statistics [NCES], 2013). On average, 17-year-old Black students scored 26 points lower than did White students on the NAEP reading assessment. For the NAEP math assessment, when compared with their White peers, averages showed that 9-year-old Black students scored 25 points lower, 13-year-old Black students scored 28 points lower, and 17-year-old Black students scored 26 points lower (NCES, 2013).

Like test scores, graduation rates differ markedly between Blacks and Whites. The graduation rate for White students from the 2009–2010 cohort, for example, was 78%, but it was just 52% for Black students, a difference of 26% (Schott

Foundation, 2012). Moreover, there were more than 13 states that reported graduation rates of less than 50% for Black students, with half of them reporting gaps of more than 30% between Black and White students. A majority of Black students in these states are concentrated in schools that are predominantly Black and located in underresourced districts (Schott Foundation, 2012).

There has been a tremendous amount of focus on the achievement and attainment gaps, but the discipline gap, which we argue is directly related to teaching and the curriculum, receives less attention (Gregory, Skiba, & Noguera, 2010). To be clear, if students are not in the general classroom, then there is a high likelihood that they are not learning. Yet it must be noted that students of color are disproportionately suspended or expelled from school at a higher rate than other students, and Black students are often given harsher penalties than Whites for the same infractions (Bryan, Day-Vines, Griffin, & Moore-Thomas, 2012; McFadden, Marsh, Price, & Hwang, 1992; Wallace, Goodkind, Wallace, & Bachman, 2008; Wehlage & Rutter, 1986). Researchers have argued that such varying discipline measures can have a direct impact on the so-called academic achievement gap (Gregory et al., 2010). The argument is simply that schools must focus less on disciplining students and more on teaching, nurturing, and developing an engaging, culturally centered curriculum for them.

Similarly, literature also suggests that Black students are disproportionately referred to special education classes (Thrasher, 1997). Achievement is a major predictor of being referred for special education, with the presence of a learning disability being the most prevalent and subjective category. When controlling for several characteristics, though, researchers have found that response to the student's race is also a significant predictor of special education referrals (Hosp & Reschly, 2004). However, although the crisis has been in place for more than four decades, recent research is just starting to move from identifying the issue to actually taking action and responding to it positively with the intention to change it (Hosp & Reschly, 2004). Thus, if research has found that being referred to special education is a strong predictor of placement, it follows that if instruction is lacking, which is indisputably related to student achievement, then students, particularly Black students, suffer the consequences by being referred to special education more often.

Despite this educational crisis facing so many Black children in urban schools, there is hope. One line of research confirms that effective school leaders, who operate using culturally centered approaches, have been found to provide stability in urban educational environments (Gooden, 2005; Lomotey, 1989) and ultimately make a significant impact on the academic achievement of their Black students (Gooden, 2005; Lomotey, 1989). Since Black principals are more likely to be placed in schools where a majority of the students are Black (Dillard, 1995; Fiore & Curtin, 1997; Gooden, 2005; Jones & Montenegro, 1985), it is fitting to examine the leadership approaches of successful Black principals in urban schools.

This chapter reviews some of the existing literature that chronicles the culturally centered leadership approaches of Black principals who have made a significant impact on the learning and general schooling experiences of Black youth. We then present a vignette based on the personal experiences of Jesse Franklin, a Black male principal at Kingston Career Technical High School, an urban school in a large midwestern urban school district. When Franklin became principal of the high school, the school was struggling on academic performance indicators and working to find how best to teach and relate to its predominantly African American student population. During the four years of Franklin's leadership, the school began to see improvement on a number of indicators, particularly those that focus on nurturing and developing a culture that supports children of color, thus making the school a destination for the urban neighborhood's students. The chapter concludes with a brief discussion of the strategies that leaders can use to make a similar impact.

LITERATURE REVIEW

Research findings have suggested the importance of a principal's relationship with the community. For example, Khalifa (2012) explored the relationship between a school principal's community involvement and student academic performance; he found that being a community leader who advocated for the community's concerns enabled a principal to establish trust with the parents of his students. Greater trust between a principal and the students' parents led to an improved relationship among the community and the school, which in turn resulted in better academic performance by the students (Khalifa, 2012). Other scholars have similarly found that urban schools are more successful when the school leader is able to establish a strong partnership with the community (Bryant, 1998; Horsford, 2009; Morris, 2008).

It is also suggested that *caring* leadership practices can lead to improved academic outcomes for students in urban schools (Bass, 2012). In examining how an ethic of care is used by African American women in particular, researchers have noted a Black feminist caring leadership style (Bass, 2012; Thompson, 2004). Noddings (1984) adds to this idea, suggesting that because of the oppressive and discriminatory experiences that Black women have faced as a result of their race, gender, and social class, they often demonstrate care out of empathy rather than merely moral obligation.

While they may differ slightly from women leaders, Black male principals also demonstrate ways of caring for students. Lomotey (1993) interviewed two African American female principals of successful elementary schools serving large percentages of Black students, and found that these leaders did not focus solely on their administrative role. Thus, Lomotey (1993) determined that effective school leaders are those who are able to successfully and fluidly navigate their roles as both bureaucrat-administrator and ethno-humanist. A bureaucrat-administrator is adept at developing goals and harnessing energy, as well as facilitating communication and managing instruction. However, according to Lomotey (1993), the ethno-humanist goes further and is "[committed] to the education of all students, [has confidence] in the ability of all students to do well; and [has] compassion for, and understanding of, all students and the communities in which they live" (p. 396). Such ethno-humanist principals are not only concerned about the academic progress of their students but they are also invested in the long-term quality of life of the individual and the prosperity of Black people as a whole.

Specifically, the principals in Lomotey's (1993) study were able to harness the energy of the school staff so that they could work together to establish and implement goals. Moreover, they were skillful in articulating these goals and in creating a culture where everyone felt empowered to share ideas and participate in authentic discussions that would result in a shared vision and direction for the school. The two female campus leaders were excellent instructional managers and were heavily involved in curriculum planning and teacher supervision but, at the same time, each principal maintained a culture in her school that ensured special attention was paid to Black students. They led and demonstrated a concerted effort to ensure that their Black students felt important and valued, a notable departure from what, too often, is the plight of Black children in schools as represented well in research literature. Moreover, the staff whom Lomotey (1993) studied at these schools worked to implement African and African American curricula at their campuses through the Curriculum Integration Project, which the principals felt required full staff commitment in order for the project to be successful. As Black women, the principals in Lomotey's study also empathized with and felt connected to their Black students because of a shared cultural background; they also felt a sense of responsibility to transmit the African American culture from one generation to the next (Lomotey, 1993).

Gooden (2005) used a similar theoretical construct when examining the leadership style of Thomas Grant, an African American male principal who worked in a successful information technology high school located in a large urban district in the Midwest. Like Lomotey (1993), he found that Grant also "demonstrated aspects of the bureaucrat-administrator and the ethno-humanist in his leadership style" (p. 637). Defining the bureaucrat-administrator role as involving the normal everyday ascribed responsibilities of the principal, he spent numerous hours observing how Grant developed goals and harnessed the energy of his staff to work toward the school's vision and published mission statement. Gooden also noted how Grant communicated to his staff through an organized teaming structure that provided for a more effective and efficient way for pertinent information to be disseminated throughout the staff. Grant also managed the organization through his efforts to motivate the teachers to focus on improving student outcomes by supporting the teachers' professional development and classroom instruction.

However important the business or managerial side of his work, though, it was Grant's ethno-humanist role that made his approach to leadership unique and culturally centered, going beyond the common rigidity of bureaucratic responsibilities. Such an ethno-humanist role seemed, in fact, to be interwoven in all Grant's work, even as he performed his more necessary and routine duties as a principal (Gooden, 2005). Black principals, as ethno-humanists, fulfill a critical role in helping to improve the educational experiences of Black students by focusing directly on their specific needs. Hence, Grant's ethno-humanist approach was revealed again and again through his commitment to his students and their learning. When meeting with teachers, for example, Grant always questioned their plans by asking, "Is it good for kids?" and "How is it good for kids?" Gooden's findings also revealed that Grant knew most, if not all, of his students by name; arguably, such a connection made the children feel like he was engaged with and cared for them as people. Equally helpful was the fact that he was a product of the neighborhood in which he worked. He constantly interacted with his students, and even instituted Saturday school to support their success and help them recover lost academic credits. Grant also showed compassion for and confidence in his students. He understood their challenges but believed in their abilities, and he knew they were capable of being successful with the school's support.

Research has shown that Black children face difficult situations multiplied by years of neglect and being undereducated or miseducated, even as they put forth real effort to be successful in schools. Though the difficulties and challenges Black students face may at times manifest in behavioral issues within the educational environment, research strongly suggests that it is counterproductive to further exclude them from education. In the following section, we provide another example of a Black leader who understood the root of the issue and sought to disrupt the "culture of counter productivity" in his role as principal of a predominantly African American school. In the current study, researcher Gooden worked with the principal as an external cognitive coach striving to help him build his internal leadership capacity. The bulk of those conversations, while confidential, served as the basis for the interview upon which this chapter is based. Additional information regarding the principal, the school history, the school environment, and school achievement were retrieved from two publicly available documents (one produced by an educational foundation and the other by the school district) and other publicly accessible websites. These sources are unnamed in order to protect the anonymity of the principal who is the focus of this study.

PRINCIPAL FRANKLIN AND KINGSTON CAREER TECHNICAL HIGH SCHOOL

Jesse Franklin (a pseudonym) first arrived as principal of Kingston Career Technical High School (KCTHS) in the fall of 2005, at the beginning of the second year in a newly designed school, and he was preparing to enter a new, $41 million, 271,000-square-foot facility the following year. The previous principal had relocated back to her hometown, and Franklin, who was a graduate of one of the local high schools in the city, applied to be the interim principal when she left. Franklin, who began his teaching career as an athletic coach, was offered the interim principal position and was subsequently hired as principal soon thereafter.

At the beginning of his tenure, Franklin was faced with numerous challenges in his quest to raise the academic performance of his students. By the end of his first year, only 52% of Kingston students scored proficient or better on the state test for reading, and only 68% did so on the writing test. Proficiency or better was achieved by only 48% of students on the math test, and only 23% and 13% of students scored proficient or better on the social studies and science graduation tests, respectively. Notably, more than 30% of the students at Kingston had special needs, almost twice the district average of 15% to 18%. According to Franklin, most of these students were categorized as learning disabled and/or emotionally disturbed, and 95% of the school's students were eligible for free or reduced-priced lunch, a factor suggesting financial issues at home. In addition to academic concerns, there were also questions regarding the safety of the school based on numerous violent incidents in the school's past. In fact, during Franklin's first year, two Kingston students were shot at a gas station directly across the street from the school, a locale known as a morning hangout spot for many of the school's students.

State academic rating was also an issue of concern for the school. The rating system is based on several factors: the percentage of students passing the state test; students' scores on state tests; attendance rates; high school graduation rates; and whether or not the school meets Adequate Yearly Progress (AYP) as defined by the No Child Left Behind (NCLB) Act. The state ratings, in order from lowest to highest, are: academic emergency; academic watch; continuous improvement; effective; excellent; and excellent with distinction. When Franklin arrived, KCTHS was on "academic emergency" status because of poor academic performance, high dropout rates, low graduation rates, and low attendance rates; its school rating was the lowest of six ratings given by the state. After Franklin's first year, the school had shown little improvement and remained on "academic emergency" status. His goal was to move the school to "academic watch" and then ultimately to "academic improvement." To do so, however, would require some drastic changes and a strong leadership approach that could meet the challenges of an urban school like KCTHS.

THE SCHOOL: KINGSTON CAREER TECHNICAL HIGH SCHOOL

Kingston Career Technical High School, once simply Kingston High School, has had a long and storied past. Kingston High School was built in the early 1800s to provide free schooling for poor families. Because of shifts in population, in the early 1950s the school moved to a suburb. By the turn of the next century, Kingston High School was considered one of the lowest performing high schools in the city.

In 2002, the school district approved a plan to build new schools and renovate many others within the district, and Kingston was one of the schools chosen to receive a new building. Additionally, as a result of several years of community and school district discussions, it was determined that the school district needed to create its own career-oriented technical school that would prepare students for both college and careers. Hence, Kingston Career Technical High School was born. Renamed because of its new focus, the newest building is much different from the original small, two-story school. Notably, the district took the small-schools approach when designing the school and constructed three separate learning communities: Advanced Manufacturing Technologies; Building Technologies; and Health Technologies and Entrepreneurship.

THE PRINCIPAL: JESSE FRANKLIN

Jesse Franklin has been in education for more than twenty-five years. He graduated from Madison High School, located in the same city as KCTHS. After high school, Franklin went on to attend a major university in the Midwest, where he subsequently graduated with a BS in Health and Physical Education. He began his professional educational career as a coach and eventually transitioned into a position as a classroom teacher. Later, he returned to another major university in the Midwest to pursue a master's degree in Education Administration. After receiving his graduate degree, Franklin became an assistant principal at Kingston High School, where he served for six years until he became the interim head principal and subsequently took on the role of head principal of the newly reconfigured and renamed Kingston Career Technical High School.

Being named principal at KCTHS was not a given for Franklin, even with his experience and capacity as assistant principal. As a matter of fact, when a school is reconfigured, district protocol held that the previous administration would not usually be retained, let alone given a promotion. However, there was a departure from that way of operating when it came to Franklin. He explained, revealing why he believes he was promoted:

> Kingston had been a historically low-performing school, and usually when they reconfigure things, they don't bring in people of that current administration. I was lucky enough to be

able to be one of those people that they looked at and allowed to be interviewed and ended up being promoted. I think the thing that allowed me to do that was my relationship with kids—getting kids to respond and to basically get them to be motivated to be ready to learn. (J. Franklin, personal communication, June 20, 2013)

For Franklin, his relationship with the students was just as important as any curriculum, and he seemed to hold firm belief in the popular adage "People don't care how much you know until they know how much you care." He elaborated on his views:

I think a lot of times we don't put emphasis on [the relationship with the students]. I think we put more and more emphasis on curriculum and not enough emphasis on relationship-building, looking at the culture and addressing, you know … addressing the culture of the school. (J. Franklin, personal communication, June 20, 2013)

Such a balanced emphasis on caring and pedagogy is similar to the emphasis placed on the bureaucrat-administrator and ethno-humanist roles described in the research by Lomotey (1993) and Gooden (2005), who noted these characteristics in the successful principals they each studied.

Franklin as the Bureaucrat-Administrator

Instructional management

As Lomotey (1993) noted, the bureaucrat-administrator is committed to the educational progress of his or her students and therefore is heavily involved in curriculum planning and teacher supervision. Franklin's commitment to high-quality teaching and instructional management suggested his comfort in the role as bureaucrat-administrator.

Specifically, a primary focus of Franklin's to provide high-quality instruction for his students. He stated that, "I think we put more and more emphasis on curriculum" (J. Franklin, personal communication, June 20, 2013). Additionally, he worked to improve teacher quality and to make KCTHS a place where good teachers wanted to work.

Now as time went on, [when] you start getting into that third and that fourth year, [the] culture started to change. We got a lot of press about what we were doing—we were taking kids down to New Orleans—doing things there. More and more of those veteran teachers [started] to say, "Well look, it seems like Kingston is a decent place now. I wanna go to Kingston." (J. Franklin, personal communication, June 20, 2013)

Developing goals

The bureaucrat-administrator is also skillful at developing goals and works collaboratively with staff to develop these goals and garner support for the work. At

KCTHS, the goals were made clear, consistently addressed, and regularly accomplished through their campus improvement plan, also known as the One Plan. Franklin spoke directly to the improvement plan:

> [We address goals through] the school improvement plan. Basically [it states] what you're going to do. It's just a measurable document that says I'm [going to] do this. This is what the outcomes are going to be. (J. Franklin, personal communication, June 20, 2013)

Harnessing energy

An effective bureaucrat-administrator is also able to harness the energy of his staff in order to meet the school's goals, and such energy harnessing was evident at KCTHS. As the culture started to change and as the school's vision was being implemented, Franklin created momentum and helped make the school a place that more students wanted to attend. He remarked:

> See, at first it was a school that nobody wanted to go, even though we had this big, nice, pretty building. Now, the culture's changing, [and] they wanted to start coming. (J. Franklin, personal communication, June 20, 2013)

Franklin used this positive momentum to create an environment where the faculty began to understand the need for articulating a mission. As a result, he motivated people to contribute and take ownership:

> Now they're looking at [KCTHS] like this can really work. At first it was, "we don't want to touch it," but now when [they're] like, "this can really happen," everybody wants to get on board and bring in their own ideas. (J. Franklin, personal communication, June 20, 2013)

However, even as Franklin inspired some faculty at the school to get on board, he crossed and upset detractors who disagreed with his approach. Many insisted that he needed to be tougher with those students who broke the rules and suspend them for even minor infractions. Franklin himself made, and recognized, his own mistakes and missteps in the process, but he denied the need for harsher penalties. It was through this resistance that Franklin was able to convince all teachers and leaders that a more compassionate approach was needed in a school with a predominantly African American, high-poverty student body.

Franklin as the Ethno-humanist

Compassion

A commitment to Black children and complete confidence in their abilities were strikingly evident in Franklin's leadership philosophy. For instance, part of his approach involved hosting numerous assemblies where guest speakers would come to the school to motivate the students to do well. What was unique about the speakers, though, is that they presented a culturally based message that resonated with the students' lived experiences. The speakers could relate to the students, either because they shared similar backgrounds or because they were closely connected to someone who did. Franklin felt that this was important because he believed that students would respond better to people who could understand and relate to them. Likewise, Franklin believes that his own similar background helped him establish trust with students. He felt that recognition of the students' backgrounds, lived experiences, and hardships showed the students that the school understood and cared:

> I was bringing people in that really talked about life issues and that really talked about where they were at, you know, people that talked about real-life issues that they're dealing with—didn't sugarcoat [anything], you know, about what was going on. I mean, I've been there ... I'm one of those kids. You know what I mean? I'm one of those kids that's an inner-city kid, and if it wasn't for athletics I would be one of those statistics, you know, that you hear about Black, you know, African American males. (J. Franklin, personal communication, June 20, 2013)

The idea that leaders who come from similar backgrounds as their students have a greater propensity to show care is not a novel concept. In fact, the findings in Bass's (2012) study, as discussed earlier, confirmed such an idea, as the leaders in her study often exhibited an empathetic core because of the shared understanding of the experiences and challenges that their students faced. Similarly, Franklin would often refer to his background and his past experiences as the foundations for his philosophy. He frequently spoke of his great passion for his job, which he explicitly noted came from his belief that he could provide his students with greater opportunities to learn and achieve. In addition, Franklin's understanding of the community he served and his compassion for these students demonstrate his qualities of the ethno-humanist, a role that researchers like Lomotey (1993) have found in successful Black principals of urban schools.

Confidence

Franklin believed caring for his students also meant setting high expectations for them and believing that they could succeed, so much so that the belief that every student had the ability to succeed became the culture of the entire school. As Franklin shares, "It was just a matter of setting expectations. What are we talking about? What are we doing? And constantly staying in their face and [not giving] up on them" (J. Franklin, personal communication, June 20, 2013). Instilling confidence in the young student body in this way, through high expectations and devotion, was an important element of Franklin's role as principal.

Commitment

Being committed to the students and having confidence in their abilities is another attribute of the ethno-humanist principal. Not only do effective leaders show concern about the academic success of children, but they are also dedicated enough to be concerned about their overall well-being. Franklin was committed to creating a culture at KCTHS where students felt safe and like "normal" children. This became especially clear and more critical for him during his first year, after a shooting occurred near campus, injuring two of his students. According to Franklin, one of the students was critically injured, leaving him a quadriplegic who was, unfortunately, not able to return to school.

Obviously, this early ordeal became an extreme test of Franklin's leadership. Franklin's immediate concern was for the students who were injured, those who witnessed the incident, as well as the Kingston student body in general. Through reflection, he concluded that he must first and foremost assure the students that they were safe at school and that the school was a good place to be:

> I don't even know how you handle something like that, but to just try to make sure that kids understand that they are safe, and if there's a silver lining, [it] is that it was outside of the building. It wasn't inside the building. We want to make sure that the kids understand that hanging out in front of, you know, hanging out at stores and all of that when you get off the bus, you know—get off the bus and come into the building. You wanted to get kids to be in the building and understand that this was a safe place. (J. Franklin, personal communication, June 20, 2013)

To address the emotional well-being of students and remind them that their school was a safe place, Franklin brought in special counselors and social workers to meet with students and provide support for those who were especially adversely impacted by the incident.

Franklin's clear concern for the students drove him to explore ways to prevent the recurrence of a similar tragedy, if possible. For the benefit of the entire student body and staff, Franklin investigated and sought to address what he felt was one of the key issues that allowed an incident like the shooting to occur—idle time. He discovered that students were being dropped off early by the city bus and would hang out in an unsafe area off campus until school began. In response, he worked with the school and community to find ways in which to remedy this issue. Franklin's response to the shooting and dedication to addressing the matter underscored his deep commitment to his students.

Dress code

When Franklin took over as principal of Kingston Career Technical High School, he instituted a dress code. There are various reasons schools require students to wear uniforms, from trying to curtail bad behavior to creating a less threatening environment (Gottfredson & Gottfredson, 2001). With uniforms, students do not have to worry about what their peers are wearing or whether or not they can afford what the "cool kids" have. Requiring a dress code, then, can eliminate some of the stress and peer pressure that students from urban schools face daily.

It has also been argued that implementing a dress code contributes to a safe learning environment (Wingert, 1999) by reducing the likelihood that students can represent gang affiliations, and it provides an easy way for school personnel to identify their students and recognize potentially threatening strangers on campus. Further, a dress code enables school leaders to differentiate between groups of students on campus; for example, freshmen students may be required to wear a certain color while sophomores wear another.

Franklin's rationale for requiring a dress code incorporated all of these reasons, but, most important, he wanted to be able to quickly identify the students of each academy. Continuing with the theme of establishing high expectations for students, he also wanted to create a workplace-like culture wherein students dressed for success. He hoped the higher standards would better prepare students for success after graduation:

> Well, it was twofold. The first fold was [to] put them in uniforms to make sure that we could tag kids and find out what programs they're in, and if we knew that we had kids in different programs, they had different uniforms. They can take pride in the programs that they were in. Secondly, [it allowed] us to change the culture in a way. It's just like when you take over a new office or something and you might want to paint your office, just to show that this is a new person in here. There's a new, for lack of a better word, a new flavor. (J. Franklin, personal communication, June 20, 2013)

Franklin emphasized that a dress code was not about punishing students, nor was it about making them feel as though they were being institutionalized. Some teachers wanted a dress code because they were concerned with how the students were dressing and critical of general styles popular with the Kingston students like hats and sagging pants. However, Franklin insisted that such criticisms were not why he instituted or enforced a dress code at KCTHS:

> We were missing the focus here, and I've seen it all the time in inner-city schools. We are institutionalizing kids that are in the inner-city schools. We want them to walk a straight, disciplined line, but if I would carry myself to a suburban school of kids of the same age, [those] kids would be able to be lax. They would be able to have different types of T-shirts on. They would be able to wear flip-flops. So, my thing is [that] I did not want a school that was an institution that was preparing kids to be institutionalized, and I see it all the time in inner-city schools. We have to really understand what we're doing when we do that and understand that we're not trying to prepare kids for jail. We're trying to prepare kids for society and to be productive in the community. (J. Franklin, personal communication, June 20, 2013)

Franklin clearly understood how his philosophy behind instituting dress codes could be misinterpreted and poorly implemented, even when he thought he had communicated it effectively. At times, it seemed even the school's faculty did not understand the rationale behind instituting a dress code. He realized it could counteract his efforts to build students' self-esteem, but he believed it was important nonetheless. In the end, the dress code remained in place at KCTHS, but was supported by people for different reasons.

Community partnerships

Successful Black leaders of urban schools have also been instrumental at creating and fostering positive relationships with the community (Khalifa, 2012). When Franklin first became principal of KCTHS, the relationship between the school and the community was strained. Negative perceptions of the school made it difficult to garner support from the local organizations within the immediate community. Franklin recognized, however, the importance of involving key community leaders if the school and its students were going to be successful, and as an ethno-humanist principal, he strived to do just that.

Franklin worked to establish new relationships and cultivate existing ones with the corporations and institutions in the immediate and larger community. He remarked, "We had other people that were coming that I cultivated. These are business partners that I cultivated so it was more about dealing with that now" (J. Franklin, personal communication, June 20, 2013). Through his efforts, local businesses continued to fund or began funding many of the school's programs.

Franklin and his team also partnered with others in the community to gain additional academic and discipline support. He recalled:

> We implemented truancy programs where we brought a consultant company in to come and build relationships as a wraparound service, where they would deal with the kids that were truant. We brought in community. We had an unofficial magistrate that would deal with the truant officers. We had a freshmen transition coordinator so we built in capacity for that type of relationship to be expanded. (J. Franklin, personal communication, June 20, 2013)

Thus, Franklin sought support from various constituents to help him empower and provide for the school and its students, with the clear goal of preparing his high school students for college, the world of work, or other post-secondary opportunities. To achieve his objective, he worked to build multiple networks of groups focused on his goal of caring for students and increasing their chances for success.

DISCUSSION AND CONCLUSION

Franklin served as principal at Kingston Career Technical High School for four years. Over that time, the academic performance of the school's students increased significantly:

> We went from being in [a state of] emergency to continuous improvement within that four-year span. Our performance index went from, like, 33 to 76. A [score of one] hundred is perfect. I mean, we were really on the move. We were really on the move. (J. Franklin, personal communication, June 20, 2013)

During Franklin's time at KCTHS, then, there was a marked improvement in the school culture, student safety, and academic performance, all of which must be credited in part to his leadership philosophy and direct efforts.

While academic achievement is undoubtedly important, at the same time we know that students cannot achieve their best in cold and unwelcoming environments. Thus, an overemphasis on single indicators like standardized achievement test scores is myopic. Benchmarks of a successful principal, as they have been defined through the literature and Franklin himself, must also be achieved. Throughout this chapter, we have tried to demonstrate and explain that "necessary" components of bureaucracy are just that in urban schools with predominantly Black, poor populations—necessary, but not sufficient. The research reviewed herein, along with the vignette that we have presented of Franklin, offers a cogent argument that what is needed in conjunction with the everyday business of schools is a caring, nurturing educator who understands the importance of fostering positive relationships.

Moreover, we were particularly interested in how Franklin, who focused boldly on building a relationship with his students in the face of resistance, defined the concept of care. After a moment's reflection, Franklin defined a caring educator or leader as one who is concerned about and focused on the vision of the school, remarking, "I think you have to be passionate about the vision and the mission of the school, and you have to really buy in to what you're trying to do" (J. Franklin, personal communication, June 20, 2013). Franklin's vision was to prepare Kingston Career Technical High School's students for college and careers, or, more specifically, to ensure that students had the ability to choose one or the other after graduating. For Franklin, education was the great equalizer for these African American students growing up in the inner city. He viewed a caring educator or leader as one who equips students to be prepared for college and/or a career, an outlook that was consistent with what we had seen and heard from Franklin throughout our time with him. He shared:

> That was the main thing, [for] kids [to have] a choice. They weren't funneled. We provided the educational foundations for them, a choice to either go into college, some type of post-secondary education, or to go into some type of career. (J. Franklin, personal communication, June 20, 2013)

It became apparent to us that Franklin drew from his personal experiences and accomplishments to inform his role as an ethno-humanist.

Inherent in the notion of the ethno-humanist is an ethic of care that finds the individual committed to serving in the urban environment. Such commitment was patently evident in Franklin. For example, when working in the school's environment became difficult during his first year, Franklin did not make plans to exit. He instead redoubled his efforts, focused on asking the difficult questions, and strongly considered the best ways to support his students. In his commitment, Franklin also displayed confidence in both his students and himself to make a meaningful change in the school. Finally, as he encouraged his students to achieve, he never lost his deep sense of empathy and compassion for their condition (Bass, 2012). Considering all of this, we must then recognize that his thinking about leadership and support of the students likely stemmed from the fact that he came from the same neighborhood and cultural background as they did. Gooden (2005) found the same attributes in Thomas Grant, also a principal of an urban inner-city high school.

Though it was apparent that Franklin made some effective changes at the school, we want to return briefly to the point that he did have a number of detractors. This became a very difficult aspect of leadership for Franklin, who worked hard to sell his ideas to the leadership and faculty of the school. While there are a number of complexities around his arguments for his approach and other aspects of his leadership, suffice it to say that many of the teachers on the faculty disagreed with Franklin's view that children should remain in school and suffer suspension only as a last resort. Though his methods align with suggested solutions for the issue of over-suspending Black students, he lamented the many times when some of his African American teachers disagreed vehemently with his approaches. Their criticisms even led him to question whether he should be tougher and suspend more kids.

Some of the more influential teachers in the school began a whisper campaign against Franklin, questioning his leadership abilities and, specifically, his ability to deal with disciplinary issues. In Franklin's view, this amounted to unfair accusations that he was not controlling the children because he was not suspending them for some minor infractions. Eventually, the growing disagreement between Franklin, his supporters, and the disgruntled teachers and their supporters led to school visits by the superintendent. According to Franklin, though, the superintendent found himself pleasantly surprised and felt that the school was operating well, and the immediate district supervisor agreed. Moreover, as noted previously, there were several gains made during Franklin's four years at the school. However, in the end, Franklin was released from his position as principal of Kingston Technical Career High School.

Doing great work for children of color and advocating for them are not without their risks. The status quo and mainstream thinking support the notion that many of these children misbehave and thus should be excluded from the regular classroom, and much of the available research has concurred. What we have offered here, though, contains lessons that strong leaders can adopt if they wish to support such children with care, youth who are often traumatized by oppression, their school and neighborhood environments, and years of substandard education. We hope willing leaders will take on this important task and work to support them with nurturing and principles of care.

REFERENCES

Bass, L. (2012). When care trumps justice: The operationalization of Black feminist caring in educational leadership. *International Journal of Qualitative Studies in Education, 25*(1), 73–87.

Bryan, J., Day-Vines, N. L., Griffin, D., & Moore-Thomas, C. (2012). The disproportionality dilemma: Patterns of teacher referrals to school counselors for disruptive behavior. *Journal of Counseling and Development, 90*(2), 177–190.

Bryant, N. (1998). Reducing the relational distance between actors: A case study in school reform. *Urban Education, 33*, 34–49.

Dillard, C. B. (1995). Leading with her life: An African American feminist (re)interpretation of leadership for an urban high school principal. *Educational Administration Quarterly, 31*(4), 539–563.

Education Week. (2011). *Achievement gap*. Retrieved from http://www.edweek.org/ew/issues/achievement-gap/

Fiore, T. A., & Curtin, T. R. (1997). *Public and private school principals in the United States: A statistical profile, 1987–88 to 1993–94*. Washington, DC: U.S. Department of Education, National Center for Education Statistics, Office of Educational Research and Improvement.

Gooden, M. A. (2005). The role of an African American principal in an urban information technology high school. *Educational Administration Quarterly, 41*(4), 630–650.

Gottfredson, G. D., & Gottfredson, D. C. (2001). What schools do to prevent problem behavior and promote safe environments. *Journal of Educational and Psychological Consultation, 12*(4), 313–344.

Gregory, A., Skiba, R. J., & Noguera, P. A. (2010). The achievement gap and the discipline gap: Two sides of the same coin? *Educational Researcher, 39*(1), 59–68.

Horsford, S. D. (2009). From Negro student to Black superintendent: Counternarratives on segregation and desegregation. *The Journal of Negro Education, 2*(78), 172–187.

Hosp, J. L., & Reschly, D. J. (2004). Disproportionate representation of minority students in special education: Academic, demographic and economic predictors. *Exceptional Children, 70*(2), 185–199.

Jones, E. H., & Montenegro, X. P. (1985). *Women and minorities in school administration*. Arlington, VA: American Association of School Administrators. Retrieved from ERIC database (ED273017).

Khalifa, M. (2012). A re-New-ed paradigm in successful school leadership: Principal as community leader. *Educational Administration Quarterly, 48*(3), 424–467.

Lomotey, K. (1989). *African-American principals: School leadership and success*. New York, NY: Greenwood.

Lomotey, K. (1993). African-American principals: Bureaucrat/administrators and ethno-humanists. *Urban Education, 27*(4), 395–412.

McFadden, A. C., Marsh, G. E., Price, B. J., & Hwang, Y. (1992). A study of race and gender bias in the punishment of handicapped school children. *Urban Review, 24*(4), 239–251.

McIver, M. A., & Farley, E. (2003). *Bringing the district back in: The role of the central office in improving instruction and student achievement* (Unpublished manuscript). Johns Hopkins University, Baltimore, MD.

Morris, J. (2008). Research, ideology and the Brown decision: Counter-narratives to the historical and contemporary representation of black schooling. *Teachers College Record, 110*(4), 713–732.

National Center for Education Statistics. (2013). *The nation's report card: Trends in academic progress 2012* (NCES 2013 456). Institute of Education Sciences, U.S. Department of Education, Washington, DC.

Noddings, N. (1984). *Caring: A feminine approach to ethics and moral education.* Berkeley: University of California Press.

Schott Foundation for Public Education. (2012). *The urgency of now: The Schott 50 state report on public education and Black males.* Cambridge, MA: Author.

Thompson, A. (2004). Caring and colortalk: Childhood innocence in White and Black. In V. Siddle Walker and J. R. Snarey (Eds.), *Race-ing moral formation* (pp. 23–37). New York, NY: Teachers College Press.

Thrasher, J. F. (1997). *Teacher-student ethnicity, suspension/expulsion, and referrals to special education: Implications for African American males* (Unpublished doctoral dissertation). University of the Pacific, Stockton, CA.

Wallace, J. M., Jr., Goodkind, S., Wallace, C. M., & Bachman, J. G. (2008). Racial, ethnic, and gender differences in school discipline among U.S. high school students: 1991–2005. *Negro Education Review, 59*(1–2), 47–62.

Wehlage, G. G., & Rutter, R. A. (1986). Dropping out: How much do schools contribute to the problem? *Teachers College Record, 87*(3), 374–393.

Wingert, P. (1999, October 4). Uniforms rule. *Newsweek,* 72–73.

CHAPTER THREE

Who Cares?

The Ethic of Care for Black Boys in School

JULIA CAMILLE RANSOM AND JAMES EARL DAVIS

INTRODUCTION

The ethic of caring is not readily associated as a philosophy among Black males or applied as practice with Black boys in schools, though statistical data suggest that it should be. For example, literature has shown that Black males are labeled most "at risk" in educational settings (Thomas & Stevenson, 2009), and have the highest high school dropout rate in the United States, just ahead of Latino males (Schott Foundation for Public Education, 2012). Additionally, Black males are more likely to score below proficiency in key subject areas on standardized tests (Howard, 2008) and to be placed in remedial and special education courses (Howard, 2008; Noguera, 2003; Thomas & Stevenson, 2009). Such low achievement can lead to eventual departure and disengagement from schooling. In fact, researchers have noted that Black students are overrepresented in discipline practices such as school expulsion and suspension (Fenning & Rose, 2007), and that Black boys, in particular, receive a disproportionate share of disciplinary measures (Thomas & Stevenson, 2009).

However, teacher expectations and student perceptions of caring can have an impact on academic engagement, academic self-efficacy, student behavior, and student-teacher relationships (Fowler, Banks, Anhalt, Hinrichs Der, & Kalis, 2008; Thomas & Stevenson, 2009; Tyler & Boelter, 2008). Given the importance of student-teacher relationships and how they affect the academic and behavioral outcomes for students, examining these relationships and the ethic of care that teachers display toward Black males—arguably our most vulnerable school population—is essential for allowing us to find successful models and strategies that teachers can use to show these boys that they care. When teachers and school communities display positive interest in and care for Black males, then engagement with schooling and academic performance may increase.

This chapter discusses the impact of teacher care on the education of Black males. First, we examine the nexus of race, gender, and class that many Black male students experience, followed by a review of the literature on the ethic of care. In addition, we explore the effect of teacher perceptions, expectations, and student-teacher relationships on the academic performance of Black male students to ascertain the influence of relationships on the ethic of care. We then identify successful caring strategies and models that have been used by teachers in schools and classrooms to engage Black male students. Finally, we suggest implications for research and practice-based caring strategies on our review of the literature.

EXISTING AT THE INTERSECTION

Black males embody an intersection of multiple identities within our society, including race, gender, class, and sexuality. Moreover, the gender of a person of color often determines the way that he or she is accepted or rejected in school settings (Thomas & Stevenson, 2009). Gender also affects which parts of his or her identity the student may choose to privilege over others. Given that Black males exist at the intersection of identities or social categories, it is essential to consider all dimensions of Black maleness, since membership within the Black racial group as well as the male gender group can often lead to marginalization within institutional settings in varying ways. For this reason, it is equally important to examine Black males' experiences within institutional settings. Analyses conducted using the concept of the intersection, or intersectionality, have sought to "demonstrate the racial variations with gender, and the gender variations within race" (Nash, 2008, p. 2) when examining the influence of differentiated identities on systems of power. Interestingly, such examinations of the nexus of race and gender arose out of the critiques of feminism and critical race theory taken from Black feminist scholars, who have noted that the racial, gender, and class forms of oppression were not separate and additive, but multiple, dynamic, and interactive (Chafetz, 1997). Thus, understanding Black males' simultaneous existence in subordinate and dominant subject positions requires a framework with wider conceptions of identity and categorical analysis (McCall, 2005).

The intersectional analysis of the institution of schooling is crucial because, as mentioned, Black male students form the most disadvantaged group in educational settings. Being Black and male becomes a dynamic, interactive experience in school, particularly as students encounter various teachers in the classroom. When socioeconomic class is added to the dynamic interaction of race and gender, low-income Black males in schools have yet another experience of differentiation to be examined. Low-income Black males, even though they are males, do not have access to the same privileges of hegemonic masculinity, such as quality education, as do middle class and wealthy White males in society (hooks, 2000). As hooks (2000) noted, low-income Black males may experience contradictions between the ideological assumptions of the privileges of masculinity and the reality that they do not hold these privileges because of their race. Within the classroom, this may translate into students' assumption that the teacher should always care, but this is not always the case for the Black male students. Since school settings are places where Black male adolescents will develop emerging gender and racial identities (Davis, 2006), the presence of nurturing, caring relationships during this time can encourage or hinder positive development for these young men. To aptly explore the experiences or lack of care that Black males encounter in schools, the analysis cannot be performed through the lens of race, class, or gender alone. It must also include analysis from the perspective of membership across all of these groups. In order to experience the ethic of care, though, it is first essential to understand the meaning of care in the context of schooling and the classroom.

THE ETHIC OF CARE

The theory of the ethic of caring that will guide this chapter has been examined in the fields of education, philosophy, and youth development, and expanded upon to include a theoretical basis as well as caring in practice in school settings. In her 1996 work, Noddings defined caring as "a set of relational practices that foster mutual recognition and realization, growth, development, protection, empowerment, and human community, culture, and possibility" (as cited in Owens & Ennis, 2005, p. 393). Additionally, according to Noddings (1984, 1992), caring should be paramount in any educational setting, and should be included as a moral imperative for all those who decide to become teachers. The foundation of Noddings's ethic of care theory consists of the notion that there is one who is cared for and one who is caring. In the school setting, the teacher is the person who fulfills the *one-caring* role while the student fills the *cared-for* role. Teachers who possess the ethic of care feel responsible for empowering their students; they believe that they are charged with both doing something and being personally responsible for them (Owens & Ennis, 2005).

To establish a successful ethic of care relationship between teacher and student, several characteristics must be present. Noddings (1984, 1992) claimed that the one-caring teacher must be engrossed in and committed to the student, and should experience a shift from a focus on the self to focusing on the student other. The student also has a role in the ethic of care relationship in that he must be receptive and open to the efforts of the teachers, and must respond in a caring way (as cited in Owens & Ennis, 2005). The first characteristic of the one-caring teacher is engrossment, which occurs when teachers both accept and acknowledge the relevancy of student feelings and experiences. Teachers become engrossed when they begin to understand and value their students, and, in response to the engrossment, students are receptive and responsive to the teacher, all of which works to better enhance the ethic of care relationship.

The second characteristic of teachers' one-caring role is commitment to the students. Commitment means that the teachers hold the belief and actually demonstrate that caring for their students is a priority, and work diligently to stay involved with their students. The ethic of care relationship is further enhanced when the students realize that the teacher is strongly committed to their needs. Finally, the one-caring teacher must move from self-focus to a focus on the student other, which means that the teacher is able to view the world through the eyes of the student. Teachers who have experienced such a shift of focus are even able to make course material more engaging by using what motivates their students. Furthermore, the ethic of care relationship is strengthened by the student's responsiveness when the teacher demonstrates that his or her motives are based on commitment to the student and not the self (Owens & Ennis, 2005). According to Noddings (1984, 1992), caring teachers demonstrate ways of interacting with other people to their student, and work to embody their most ideal ways of caring for others in order to convey this to their students (Owens & Ennis, 2005).

Noddings's original characterization of the ethic of care in the student-teacher relationship has received research support and attention from various fields, including psychology and philosophy (Roberts, 2010). However, these characteristics do not address the fact that those students who have been disenfranchised in the educational setting may need different types of care from their teachers and might also respond in varying ways to the care teachers provide. Notably, however, difficulties can arise when the actors in a caring relationship are a group who has been historically disenfranchised and a group with whom all of the power has rested (Roberts, 2010). Much of the extant research related to teacher care and Black students, in fact, focuses on culturally relevant pedagogy. In her work exploring culturally relevant critical teacher care, Roberts (2010) illustrated the different nature of care that Black students may desire if care is being offered in the educational setting; she examined teacher care between African American teachers and African American secondary school students, and found that African American teachers communicated with political clarity on the issues of race and class that students might need to overcome in the future. Specifically, the teachers in Roberts's (2010) study went beyond the known ethic of care to provide a counternarrative to students that combatted the false message generated by White teachers that there is a color-blind society with equal opportunities awaiting all students. Teachers also showed care by explicitly communicating to students that they cared about their future beyond schooling, into the larger context of society. When examining Black males and culturally relevant pedagogy, Lynn and Jennings (2009) indicated that Black male teachers can demonstrate care for Black boys by being role models or father figures and by using critical pedagogical practices.

In demonstrating the importance of the removal of focus on self, deemed by Noddings as one of the characteristics of care, Tosolt (2010) found that students who identify with a minority group such as Black or Latino were more likely to perceive a teacher as caring if the teacher complimented their academic performance. While White students found teachers more caring if they related to them interpersonally or treated them as friends, academic caring was more important for Black students than interpersonal closeness with teachers. However, when looking at within-group differences, male Black students preferred academic caring to be given in conjunction with interpersonal caring, particularly behaviors from teachers like hugs and compliments; this type of caring preference notably contradicts the stereotype Black male aggressiveness (Tosolt, 2010). Altogether, these findings point to variations in the ethic of care provided by teachers, and differences in the caring desired by racial minority students.

STUDENT-TEACHER RELATIONSHIPS (WHO CARES FOR BLACK MALE STUDENTS?)

The ethic of care and the student-teacher relationships that students of color, and specifically Black males, experience in schools will often have an impact on achievement and engagement in the classroom. Although student-teacher relationships and feelings of care are crucial to future aspirations and success for students, ethnic minority children often face negative student-teacher relationships, lack of care from teachers, and low teacher expectations. As Noguera (2003) stated, "if students do not believe that their teachers care about them and are actively concerned about their academic performance, the likelihood that they will succeed is greatly reduced" (p. 449). Several researchers addressing this issue have examined gender, race, and the quality and outcomes of student-teacher relationships. For example, a meta-analysis of studies examined whether teachers' expectations, referrals for other educational services, and speech, both positive and negative, differed toward minority students when compared with White students. Tenenbaum and Ruck (2007) found that minority students received less positive feedback from teachers and were held to lower expectations than White students. Teachers also gave minority students more negative referrals, such as to special education, whereas they gave White students more positive referrals, such as to gifted classes (Tenenbaum & Ruck, 2007). These findings of negative speech, low expectations, and disparate referrals are important when considering the fact that, as previously stated, Black males are disproportionately referred for special education services in schools.

Arguably, the negative speech and referrals are often the result of biases that teachers hold against Blacks and other racial minorities. Teachers consciously and subconsciously bring their biases with them to the classroom, and these notions can be highly racialized. In her study of inner-city Black and Latino high school students, Carter (2005) found that both male and female students cited feeling a lack of support and affirmation from teachers in their school. Students also reported feeling that teachers had lower expectations of them because of their appearance and cultural racial backgrounds—they distinctly felt the presence and effects of the biases the teachers held. Similarly, using data from the *National Education Longitudinal Study of 1998* (National Center for Education Statistics, 1998), Oates (2003) examined how teacher perceptions of diligence and expectations of students have an impact on achievement in standardized tests, finding that White teachers had substantially lower academic expectations of Black students and lower perceptions of Black students' diligence. Lower performance from Black students in the study was correlated to teacher bias regarding expected lower performance, perceptions of lack of diligence, and lowered expectations overall.

The poor student-teacher relationship experienced by minority students is pervasive at all levels of schooling. Further demonstrating the influence that student-teacher relationships can have on academic performance, Tyler and Boelter (2008) found that Black students at the middle grade levels had higher academic engagement and academic efficacy when they felt that teachers held high expectations for them, but did not have the same high levels of academic performance when they felt teachers' expectations were lower. Besides academic perceptions, teachers' behavioral perceptions of Black students are also important to examine, since they can influence the ways that students and teachers foster classroom relationships. In a study that explored the quality of student-teacher relationships and perceptions of behavior, Fowler et al. (2003) found that Black students were rated lower in pro-social or emotional behavior by White teachers than they were by Black teachers. The lower rating of pro-social behavior, moreover, was significantly related to poor student-teacher relationships. Fowler et al. (2003) noted the salience of the finding because differences in the way teachers read or perceive low pro-social, emotional behavior can have an impact on how they decide to refer a child for special education services.

Preconceived notions, perceptions of bad behaviors, biases, and poor student-teacher relationships can be gendered as well as racialized. These biases and preconceived notions are especially harmful for Black male students who exist at the intersection of these identities. Poor student-teacher relationships result in decreased potential for the development of the ethic of caring in the classroom. Fenning and Rose (2007) asserted that Black male students do not fit the perceived norm of schooling. Although Black males are the students in most need of academic assistance, they are also the most likely to be removed from the educational setting because of negative student-teacher relationships (Fenning & Rose, 2007). Thomas and Stevenson (2009) argued that teacher bias or negative teacher perceptions of African American male students can lead to punitive classroom strategies, unnecessary disciplinary actions, and increased referrals. According to Skiba, Michael, Nardo, and Peterson (2002), the "racial disproportionality in exclusionary discipline is common, with African American male students receiving punishments (e.g., suspensions and expulsions) harsher than those of their European counterparts; in fact, those harsher consequences tend to be administered for less severe offenses" (as cited in Thomas & Stevenson, 2009, p. 163). Black male students are acutely aware of the ways they are perceived by teachers in classrooms, leading to a lack of responsiveness from the student, which is one of the core characteristics of the ethic of care. Isom (2007) found that Black male middle school students, when asked how their teachers would describe them, pointed to the fact that they are good students but anticipated teacher perceptions including deviant behavior and lack of academic ability. It seems, then, that these male students were reminded by interactions with teachers in the school that in the educational setting "whiteness equates with knowledge, while 'Blackness' is not only oppositionally constructed, but criminal to boot" (Isom, 2007, p. 421).

Ferguson (2001) conducted an ethnographic study of African American male students in elementary school that examined the nexus of race, identity, masculinity, school behavior, and punishment. She discovered that Black male students labeled as "at risk" of failure became more visible to teachers in their classrooms, and as such were more likely to be singled out for punishment for rule breaking. She therefore asserted that a child being labeled as "at risk" becomes a predictor of the future at school for that student (Ferguson, 2001). Comparably, Black males are also often given attention for the wrong reasons, or the focus on other, which is important in the ethic of care, is a negative focus. Noguera (2003) also pointed to a distinct lack of support and positivity from teachers of Black male students. In a study of Black male student opinions of teacher perceptions in Northern California high schools, Noguera (2003) noted that less than a quarter of the respondents (18%) thought that their teachers treated them fairly. Noguera (2003) found similar results in a study of Black male students attending a magnet high school; they were least likely to agree with the idea that they were "supported by their teachers," or to believe that teachers cared for their success. The results suggested that teachers in Noguera's (2003) study demonstrated a blatant lack of engrossment and commitment, both of which are important in the ethic of teacher care. Although there are many examples of poor student relationships that lead to the absence of the ethic of care, there are models and strategies that can begin to repair the relationship between Black males, teachers, and schooling.

SUCCESSFUL MODELS AND STRATEGIES IN CARE

While Black male students regrettably encounter a lack of care, poor student-teacher relationships, and biases in the classroom throughout the United States on a daily basis, there are some models and strategies that teachers and schools should use to provide a caring environment for racial minorities—or, more specifically, for Black males, our most disadvantaged group in the classroom. Lewis, James, Hancock, and Hill-Jackson (2008) maintained that becoming familiar with culturally responsive teaching practices is the best way that teachers, especially White teachers, can begin to connect with Black students. Lewis et al. (2008) went on to suggest that teachers follow suggestions offered by Landsman (2006), including becoming engaged in the community and getting to know individuals on a personal basis; placing themselves in environments where they are in the minority to understand that they have their own culture and realize this impacts the ways they interact with Black students; and increasing their knowledge of all diverse groups. Implementing these suggestions will work to build the ethic of care, because students will begin to feel a commitment and a focus on the other from the teacher, and will thereafter become more responsive to the teachers' efforts.

Fenning and Rose (2007) contended that a way for teachers to build positive student-teacher relationships to stem the rate of disproportionate disciplinary action is through gaining knowledge of institutional racism. The authors stressed that teachers should feel a sense of responsibility for actively helping ensure that racial inequality does not exist in any area related to students, such as in the instructional setting, in disciplinary action, and in the larger school environment. By exhibiting knowledge of racism and making efforts to combat it, teachers will show Black male students that they can see the world from the students' point of view. Moreover, through demonstrating this knowledge, the teacher shows movement from a focus on the "self" to a focus on the student, which is one of the key components of creating the ethic of care. Cassidy and Bates (2005) illustrated a model of an entire school that uses care as an integral way to engage at-risk student populations, a group that Black males are often associated with in schools. In the model school, the ethic of care began at the top with the administration and ran through all of the teachers and students. "The administrators see care as being embedded in the culture of the school, and they frequently use the metaphor of 'the soil' to describe an environment rich in nutrients that allows each youth to flourish" (Cassidy & Bates, 2005, p. 77). The teachers built relationships and demonstrated care by using flexible curricula, showing respect for students, and creating a familial atmosphere wherein students felt emotionally, socially, and academically safe. Even more, teachers and the principal in Cassidy and Bates's (2005) model school made themselves available to students to talk about personal as well as academic issues. The ethic of care was important to teachers and administrators at the school, and it was clearly important to them that the students recognized that they were being cared for.

When considering the high school level specifically, establishing the ethic of care will support and encourage Black males through what can be a turbulent time. For Black male students, excelling in school and participating in school activities can be seen as out-of-bounds because some may view those activities as inconsistent with who they think they are as people. Black males may also be deterred from schooling at this age because there are no peers or role models who participate in those activities without compromising their sense of self (Noguera, 2003). The presence of a teacher who is caring and committed to these students at this time may allow students to believe that they can achieve in school. Thus, creating more caring high school environments could help Black male students' academic success as much as their personal sense of self and worth.

The mounting evidence of the prevalently negative student-teacher relationships that Black males face suggests that communities of care in high schools similar to the program that Ellerbock and Kiefer (2010) investigated would be beneficial to ensure that Black male students experience the ethic of care. They examined a high-school program called Freshman Focus, established within a small ninth-grade learning community in a larger high school setting. The researchers found that care was established through teacher commitment to the program, developmentally responsive care traits in the teacher-student relationships, and a program environment that addressed students' personalized learning needs. Teacher commitment to the program meant that teachers who might originally have objected to working with freshmen felt that these students had value and held positive beliefs about the students, which then promoted a sense of care among both teachers and students. The developmentally responsive care traits included teachers knowing adolescent psychological and emotional developmental needs, and showing students that they were there to guide and support them through these changes. A feeling of belongingness fostered a program environment committed to the learning needs of the students. Additionally, everything in the program was tailored to the freshmen in the program, including events, classes offered, and instruction, which made the students feel as though the program was a special community exclusively for them (Ellerbock & Kiefer, 2010). Such a model of a whole caring community would serve to cultivate relationships among Black males, their fellow students, and their teachers.

Finally, establishing mentoring or role-modeling programs is a winning strategy to encourage more caring for Black boys in schools. Noguera (2003), as well as Clark, Lee, Goodman, and Yacco (2008), elucidated the benefits that Black males can gain through successful mentoring programs. Clark et al. (2008) noted that male role models, in particular, serve as examples of possible future selves for Black male students, and have been shown to enhance the academic performance of Black males. Arguably, then, the presence of positive role models who display a level of commitment to Black male students will enhance the potential for the ethic of care to develop in their mentor-to-mentee relationships and further contribute to the students' success.

IMPLICATIONS FOR FUTURE RESEARCH, POLICY, AND PRACTICE

In the face of overwhelming evidence of the absence of care, the existence of successful models like those discussed in the previous section has several implications for research, policy, and practice. It should be noted here that the issue of care for Black male students is complicated by the fact that the teachers in their classrooms are more likely to be female (Thomas & Stevenson, 2009), and the assumption is that these teachers, as women, are compelled to nurture their students no matter what. The issue of care for Black boys in school is further complicated by the stereotype of Black males as tough, criminal, and academically inferior (Ferguson, 2001; Isom, 2007; Thomas & Stevenson, 2009). The review of literature has shown that Black male students are more likely to suffer teachers' negative perceptions of them, have poor student-teacher relationships, and experience biases that impact behavioral and academic outcomes. The negative perceptions and biases teachers hold prevent them from committing to and therefore helping their Black male students, which are essential aspects of the ethic of care. Hence, the literature points to several implications for research, policy, and practice. The first implication is the need for further research using the ethic of care as a framework to examine student-teacher relationships. Further investigations into the ethic of care should include Black male students as a unit of analysis. These students continue to experience disproportionately negative educational outcomes; therefore, it is essential to examine and better understand the ways that they are or are not being extended the ethic of care through positive student relationships and classroom environments with minimal levels of bias.

The second implication for research in the field of care should investigate the differences in care that occur in critical teacher care, which infuses some aspects of critical race considerations within the ethic of care. The type of care explored in Roberts's (2010) study, for example, could enhance the ethic of care for Black male students by showing them that there is a future for them, and that there are teachers who care about that future. Finally, future research studies conducted to explore teacher bias and the impact of poor student-teacher relationships should include teacher information that is aggregated by gender and race congruence with students. Understanding the differences in attitudes between male and female teachers of varying races would help to elucidate the discrepancy in the impact of gender and race congruence on student-teacher relationships.

Infusing the key principles of the ethic of care into teacher practice and enacting a practice of care within schools must begin with teacher preparation at the teacher education stage. In fact, the ethic of care should be considered along with other core competencies for successful teachers. Teachers must also be made aware of their biases and how these influence student-teacher relationships in order to then understand and move beyond them. Additionally, teachers should continually receive professional development designed to cultivate their ethic of care for Black male students. Schools should incorporate role-modeling programs and entire communities of care to enhance caring for Black male students and all students in the learning environment.

Finally, the implications for policy include the need for policy makers to acknowledge that the ethic of care exists, and that this ethic is a direct result of student-teacher relationships. Discipline and punitive policies must recognize the human element of perception that is invariably involved in teachers' decision-making processes. If there is no care in the student-teacher relationship for Black males, then they are more likely to receive more severe forms of punishment. Once this is acknowledged, policy makers will be better prepared to create fair and equitable disciplinary policies that move away from zero tolerance toward restorative policy.

REFERENCES

Carter, P. L. (2005). *Keepin' it real: School success beyond Black and White*. Oxford, England: Oxford University Press.

Cassidy, W., & Bates, A. (2005). "Drop-Outs" and "Push-Outs": Finding hope at a school that actualizes the ethic of care. *American Journal of Education, 112*(1), 66–102.

Chafetz, J. S. (1997). Feminist theory and sociology: Underutilized contributions for mainstream theory. *Annual Review of Sociology, 23*, 97–120.

Clark, M., Lee, S. M., Goodman, W., & Yacco, S. (2008). Examining male underachievement in public education: Action research at the district level. *NASSP Bulletin, 92*(2), 111–132.

Davis, J. E. (2006). Research at the margin: Mapping masculinity and mobility of African American high school dropouts. *International Journal of Qualitative Studies in Education, 19*(3), 289–304.

Ellerbrock, C. R., & Kiefer, S. M. (2010). Creating a ninth-grade community of care. *Journal of Educational Research, 103*(6), 393–406.

Fenning, P., & Rose, J. (2007). Overrepresentation of African American students in exclusionary discipline: The role of school policy. *Urban Education, 42*(6), 536–559.

Ferguson, A. A. (2001). *Bad boys: Public schools in the making of Black masculinity (law, meaning, and violence)*. Ann Arbor: University of Michigan Press.

Fowler, L. T. S., Banks, T. I., Anhalt, K., Hinrichs Der, H. H., & Kalis, T. (2008). The association between externalizing behavior problems, teacher-student relationship quality, and academic performance in young urban learners. *Behavioral Disorders, 33*(3), 167–183.

hooks, b. (2000). *Feminist theory: From margin to center* (2nd ed.). Cambridge, MA: South End Press.

Howard, T. C. (2008). Who really cares? The disenfranchisement of African American males in PreK–12 schools: A critical race theory perspective. *Teachers College Record, 110*(5), 954–985.

Isom, D. (2007). Performance, resistance, caring: Racialized gender identity in African American boys. *Urban Review: Issues and Ideas in Public Education, 39*(4), 405–423.

Landsman, J. (2006). Being White: Invisible privileges of a New England prep school girl. In J. Landsman & C. Lewis (Eds.), *White teachers/diverse classrooms: A guide to building inclusive schools, promoting high expectations, and eliminating racism* (pp. 1–26). Sterling, VA: Stylus.

Lewis, C., James, M., Hancock, S., & Hill-Jackson, V. (2008). Framing African American students' success and failure in urban settings: A typology for change. *Urban Education, 43*(127), 127–153.

Lynn, M., & Jennings, M. E. (2009). Power, politics, and critical race pedagogy: A critical race analysis of Black male teachers' pedagogy. *Race Ethnicity and Education, 12*(2), 173–196.

McCall, L. (2005). The complexity of intersectionality. *Signs: Journal of Women in Culture and Society, 30*(3), 1771–1800.

Nash, J. C. (2008). Re-thinking intersectionality. *Feminist Review, 89*, 1–15.

National Center for Education Statistics. (1988). *National Education Longitudinal Study of 1988 (NELS:88)*. Washington, DC: U.S. Department of Education. Retrieved from http://nces.ed.gov/pubsearch/getpubcats.asp?sid=023

Noddings, N. (1984). *Caring: A feminist approach to ethics and moral education*. Berkeley: University of California Press.

Noddings, N. (1992). *The challenge to care in schools: Alternative approaches to education*. New York, NY: Teachers College Press.

Noguera, P. A. (2003). The trouble with Black boys: The role and influence of environmental and cultural factors on the academic performance of African American males. *Urban Education, 38*(4), 431–459.

Oates, G. L. (2003). Teacher-student racial congruence, teacher perceptions, and test performance. *Social Science Quarterly, 84*(3), 508–525.

Owens, L. M., & Ennis, C. D. (2005). The ethic of care in teaching: An overview of supportive literature. *Quest, 57*(4), 392–425.

Roberts, M. A. (2010). Toward a theory of culturally relevant critical teacher care: African American teachers' definitions and perceptions of care for African American students. *Journal of Moral Education, 39*(4), 449–467.

Schott Foundation for Public Education. (2012). *The urgency of now: The Schott 50 state report on public education and black males*. Retrieved from http://www.schottfoundation.org/urgency-of-now.pdf

Skiba, R. J., Michael, R. S., Nardo, A. C., & Peterson, R. L. (2002). The color of discipline: Sources of racial and gender disproportionality in school punishment. *Urban Review, 34*(4), 317–342.

Tenenbaum, H. R., & Ruck, M. D. (2007). Are teachers' expectations different for racial minority than for European American students? A meta-analysis. *Journal of Educational Psychology, 99*(2), 253–273.

Thomas, D., & Stevenson, H. (2009). Gender risks and education: The particular classroom challenges for urban low-income African American boys. *Review of Research in Education, 33*(1), 160–180.

Tosolt, B. (2010). Gender and race differences in middle school students' perceptions of caring teacher behaviors. *Multicultural Perspectives, 12*(3), 145–151.

Tyler, K. M., & Boelter, C. M. (2008). Linking Black middle school students' perceptions of teachers' expectations to academic engagement and efficacy. *The Negro Education Review, 59*(1–2), 27–44.

CHAPTER FOUR

Unmasking Leadership

African American Male Scholars' Reflections on Critique, Justice, and Caring

FLOYD D. BEACHUM AND CARLOS R. MCCRAY

As the United States forges into the twenty-first century, it unfortunately carries with it the "baggage" of the preceding century's "problem of the color line" (Du Bois, 2003). Du Bois eloquently identified the problem of race, which still blinds, holds, and binds us in the new millennium. Since American schools have the potential for igniting the fire of change, which could shine as a beacon light for all of society, the task of preparing educators in American K–12 schools falls largely on colleges and universities. Thus, they become places of great promise as well as paradox owing to the irony that higher education has the ability to elicit change or reinforce the preexisting hegemony.

The purpose of this chapter is to highlight the plight of African American males throughout the educational pipeline (K–16), as well as to unmask the challenges, difficulties, and obstacles these men face—not only as a result of what they do, but of who they are. Specifically, three themes that emerge from the literature will be addressed: critique, justice, and caring (Starratt, 1991). Scholars have noted that effective educators should have a critical and discerning eye that questions people, policies, practices, and perspectives (Beachum, 2011; McCray & Beachum, 2014; Ryan, 2006; Villegas & Lucas, 2002). Moreover, the scholarly emphasis on justice highlights the importance of fairness and equality, both of which are constant struggles in K–12 education (Starratt, 1991; Siddle Walker & Snarey, 2004). Caring, too, has been recognized as a crucial component in the learning and leading process (Beck, 1994; McCray & Beachum, 2006; Noddings, 1992), but we will place additional emphasis on this notion of caring with regard to African American males. While the extant literature seems to aptly address the importance of critique and justice, a detailed examination of caring has been largely unexplored.

REVIEW OF LITERATURE

Following is an examination of the educational and psychological plight of African American males from their K–12 experience through their interactions in higher education. This comprehensive view will provide insight into the complexity, contradictions, and challenges African American males face throughout the educational pipeline.

African American Males in Early Schooling and Elementary School

For our purposes, the early schooling grades include kindergarten to approximately the fifth grade. Although the available research on African American males during these grades is limited, it is nonetheless useful for describing the context for African American males in these early years of their education. Slaughter-Defoe and Richards (1994) noted that African American male students receive treatment different from that of other males and female students, beginning as early as kindergarten. Carter (2003) indicated that African American males' disengagement from school and related activities begins in the early schooling years and continues as they matriculate to higher grades. Similarly, Davis (2003) asserted, "By all indicators, Black males consistently fall behind other students in early school performance and lead their peers in school infractions and other negative outcomes" (p. 521). Unquestionably, these early developmental experiences are critical to the future educational trajectory of African American males (Best, 1983).

African American males begin having even more such developmental experiences as they progress through the elementary grades (first through sixth), and head toward middle and junior high school. As these Black boys are developing and cultivating their self-identity, at the same time they are receiving messages from numerous sources, including television, the Internet, music, and peers, and reacting to interactions with teachers, school administrators, and other service providers (Tatum, 1997). All of these factors influence African American males' development of identity. According to Isom (2007):

> Students of color then, male and female, find themselves shifting identities between various social setting and external expectations. Moving between projected selves and other constructed versions of one's self, while fighting against often internalized distorted views of the self, within a social context often hostile to one's self, the African American youngster finds her/himself on an ever shifting playing ground for authentic identity development. (p. 411)

Here, Isom (2007) points to the existence of an internal/external conflict for African American children, especially for Black boys. Isom (2007) conducted a qualitative research study of fifth, sixth, and seventh grade African American males in a community-based after-school program; when she asked the boys to define what it meant to be a male, they responded with "funny," "sports," "rough," "like to fight a lot," and "think they cool" (p. 411). These comments provide but a small glimpse into the internal perceptions of African American boys. While they are trying to sort out the complexities of masculinity, the external perceptions of them by others may impact their experiences and judgments and affect their understanding of their role as men. hooks (2004) wrote, "Even before black boys encounter genocidal street culture, they have been assaulted by the cultural genocide taking place in early childhood educational institutions where they are simply not taught" (p. 38). As an example, she reflected upon her own schooling experiences in the early grades, remembering instances of Black boys who were under-taught by White teachers. She also recalled cases in which a selected African American male was placed in gifted and talented classes, but then almost always proved to be subordinate and docile so he did not challenge the status quo in the classroom (hooks, 2004). Cose (2002) similarly described a third or fourth grade teacher who told the class that Blacks had "lazy tongues." Likewise, in McCall's (1995) autobiography, he wrote about his experiences as an eleven-year-old boy attending a predominantly White school, remembering efforts by teachers to avoid eye contact with him and, in one case, an instance when he sat down with a group of students who then got up and moved away from him; these kinds of encounters fueled his withdrawal from educational endeavors. In addressing McCall's story, hooks (2004) wrote, "McCall saw his turning away from education as rejecting a world wherein he had been given the message that he did not belong and would not belong no matter the degree of his intelligence" (p. 37). Beachum (2013) reflected upon his similar experiences of prejudice and rejection in sixth grade while attending a predominantly White school:

> In sixth grade, I moved to a majority White school where I had my first experiences with overt racism. I recall many instances of race-based harassment and mistreatment. I did not know how to handle such treatment or why I was being singled-out. All I knew is that I was being made to feel inferior and this brought great disappointment and sadness. My reality had been crushed as I began to understand that there were other realities and not just my own. Even though I was struggling to deal with racism, I tried not to let it negatively impact my grades. I still strived to do the best job I could. (p. 124)

Accounts like these of the early schooling experiences of African American males make it apparent that as Black boys are trying to figure out who they are and how to succeed academically, they are also at times burdened with the additional stress of dealing with low expectations and/or mistreatment from White peers or teachers. In the early years of schooling, teachers and administrators are still able to impose a physical presence on African American males as well as other students, and young Black males are still viewed as boys; however, as they grow up, receive more social messages, and become young men, they are sometimes treated much differently (Kunjufu, 2002; Tatum, 1997).

African American Males in Secondary School

For many African American males, secondary school is a period of complexity, self-discovery, and multiple, often conflicting, messages. They must first deal with the overarching pressure to conform to traditional notions of masculinity. "Society has historically suggested that boys should play sports, suppress outward displays of emotion, and compete rigorously against each other" (Harper, 2004, p. 92). Literature further indicates that traditional identity development among boys includes notions of independence, mastery, dominance, competence, and competition (Connell, 1993; Gilligan, 1982; Harper, 2004; hooks, 2004). Furthermore, such notions are negotiated and validated by other males (Connell, 1993). According to Morrison and Eardley (1985):

> Boys grow up to be wary of each other. We are taught to compete with one another at school, and to struggle to prove ourselves outside it, on the street, the playground and the sports field. Later we fight for status over sexual prowess, or money, or physical strength or technical know-how … the pressure is on to act tough. We fear humiliation or exclusion, or ultimately the violence of other boys if we fail to conform. (p. 19)

In addition, parents are not immune to these kinds of messages from the broader society. In fact, these kinds of messages are part of our socialization process. Harro (2000) explained that society, friends, and loved ones give us messages about "what rules to follow, what roles to play, what assumptions to make, what to believe, and what to think" (p. 18). Thus, Harper (2004) aptly summarized societal influence upon parents when he noted:

> Parents have also been influenced by these societal indices of masculinity, as many communicate messages of power, toughness, and competitiveness to their young sons. No father wants his son to grow up being a "pussy," "sissy," "punk," or "softy"—terms commonly associated with boys and men who fail to live up to the traditional standards of masculinity in America. Masculine identity is largely impacted by societal messages that say men should be the breadwinners for and protectors of their families; should be legends in college and professional sports; and should be leaders and executives in the organizations by which they are employed. (p. 92)

Notably, such traditional conceptualizations of masculinity are sometimes altered and acted out differently by African American males, especially in their adolescent years.

In the United States, there is a widely accepted standard of manhood, a standard largely characterized by men assuming the roles of financial provider, protector, disciplinarian, and emotional "rock" of the family (Harris, 1995; hooks, 2004). Many African American men are unable to attain this standard, however, so they opt instead for alternative expressions of manhood. Harris (1995) wrote:

> For those who are unable to meet traditional standards of masculinity, manhood has been redefined to be consistent with their alienation from mainstream values and institutions. This alternative definition also differs from that adhered to by low-income European American men because of historical and ongoing discrimination and prejudice. (p. 279)

This reconceptualization of Black manhood frequently promotes hyper-masculine perceptions of the "tough guy," "hustler," and/or "player of women" (Oliver, 2006; Prier & Beachum, 2008). The "tough guys" are those who "are good at fighting, are not afraid to defend themselves, and incite fear in others" (Harper, 2004, p. 93). The "hustler" is one who uses his street knowledge, instincts, and smooth talk to make money and steer situations to his advantage; Oliver (2006) noted that hustlers are frequently revered as men who "used their wits to transcend ghetto poverty and achieve a measure of material success unattainable to most ghetto residents" (p. 925). Perhaps the most unsettling perception of Black men, though, is the term "player," which describes the man who has multiple girlfriends or women. Maleness is often expressed in the ability to date, manipulate, use, and/or control females (Beachum & McCray, 2011; Kitwana, 2002). Moreover, the image of the Black man as "player" is reinforced by television and other media. Harper (2004) agreed, stating, "Media and commercial images overwhelmingly depict, popularize, and celebrate certain types of African-American men—namely pimps, rappers, and athletes, who are surrounded by attractive women (usually more than one at a time) and appear to be financially prosperous" (p. 93).

These expressions of manhood are further complicated by similar mannerisms that can include "distrust of organizations and authority, need for approval and support from peers, disdain for feminine qualities, predominant heterosexual focus, and denial of vulnerability" (Harris, 1995, p. 280). Similarly, Black male masculinity has been defined as "an emphasis on physical strength, an expectation of both submissiveness and strength in women, angry and impulsive behavior, functional (and often violent) relationships between men and between men and women, and strong male bonding" (Franklin, 1984, p. 140). Others have described African American males' performance-orientation, speech patterns, posture, greetings, and dress as "cool pose" (Majors & Billson, 1993). Though the elements of this persona are not necessarily problematic in themselves, they are often different from mainstream notions and can be misinterpreted, particularly in school settings.

At the secondary school level, however, these expressions of masculinity can cause several problems. Males of color, in general, are experiencing problems in American schools. A report by the College Board Advocacy & Policy Center

(2010) stated, "Even within the limited framework of official data definitions, the educational crisis facing young African American, Hispanic, Native American and, among Asian-Americans, particularly Southeast Asian and Pacific Islander men, is formidable at the K–12 level" (p. 22). For African American males, disparities in the enforcement of disciplinary policies are particularly troubling, as the Schott Foundation for Public Education (2010) reported:

> To add insult to injury, Black Male students are punished more severely for similar infractions than their White peers. They are not given the same opportunities to participate in classes with enriched educational offerings. They are more frequently inappropriately removed from the general education classroom due to misclassifications by the Special Education policies and practices of schools and districts. By Grade 8, relatively few are proficient in reading and, finally, as a consequence of these deficiencies in educational practice, less than half graduate with their cohort. (p. 37)

Another study noted that the demeanor of African American males was frequently misinterpreted by White middle-class teachers to be defiant, aggressive, and intimidating (Kunjufu, 2002; Majors, Tyler, Peden, & Hall, 1994). In addition, subjective impressions and perceptions can lead to over-identification for special education, which is evident in negative teacher attitudes and low expectations for African American male students (Kunjufu, 2005; Obiakor, Harris, & Beachum, 2009). These misperceptions and negative attitudes surely come into play as teachers and school administrators engage in disciplinary procedures. "More than 30 years of research has consistently demonstrated the overrepresentation of African American youth in the exclusionary discipline consequences of suspension and expulsion" (Fenning & Rose, 2007, p. 536). In addition, Day-Vines and Day-Hairston (2005) reported that African American students constitute 16.9% of the entire student population in the United States; however, they make up 33.4% of all students who are subject to disciplinary actions resulting in suspension from school. Thomas and Stevenson (2009) noted that boys, in general, represent 71% of all suspensions, adding:

> a closer analysis shows that African American boys represent a disproportionate percentage of boys overall who are subjected to exclusionary disciplinary action. The overrepresentation of African American boys in school discipline referrals and exclusionary consequences has been well documented since the 1970s. (p. 165)

This is particularly troubling for African American males, especially when combined with other research noting that "out-of-school suspensions may be linked to several negative educational outcomes including continued academic failure, grade retention, negative school attitudes, and increased dropout rates" (Nichols, 2004, p. 409). Additionally, African American males receive mixed messages about their value and worth at school. For example, Davis (2003) wrote, "We do know that Black boys are both loved and loathed at school. They set the standards for hip-hop culture and athleticism while experiencing disproportionate levels of punishment and academic failure" (p. 520). Davis's comment further establishes the premise that African American males are valued more for their physical attributes, such as playing sports, than for their academic abilities. Thus, at the secondary school level, Black male masculinity can be wrongly interpreted, resulting in aggressive discipline by teachers and administrators such as in increased suspensions and expulsions, referrals to special education based on subjective criteria (Yawn & Obiakor, 2013), and the overvaluing of athletics to the detriment of academic emphases. Despite these prejudices in youth, one might surmise that African American males who successfully navigate K–12 and college to then obtain positions as faculty members would be shielded from much of the bias, low expectations, and inequity, but such is not the case.

African American Male Professors

Harold Cruse's (1967) *Crisis of the Negro Intellectual* explained the challenges that African American academics face. Cultural leaders as well as African American scholars, he argued, were "just as trapped by the system as the poor" (p. 94). Truly, the environments for African American men working in teacher education and leadership preparation present a number of challenges. According to Cleveland (2004), African American men "inhabit an unsafe space" (p. xiv) in colleges of education. He further notes that their mere presence in some classrooms brings about a sense of fear, dread, and anxiety in White students. Unfortunately, many of these students have had little or no contact with Black men and have been inundated by negative media messages to the point that they believe most Black men to be violent, over-sexed, and/or anti-intellectual (Gordon, 2002). In addition, African American male faculty members are often feared by both colleagues and students and, in other cases, are more frequently challenged, because it is assumed that they are underprepared (Smith, 2004). According to Smith (2004), White students use a number of subversive tactics such as "inappropriately and uncivilly challenging the lesson, question the professor's capabilities, using defiant or disengaged body language ... [and] reporting their dislike of the class to the department chairperson or the dean" (p. 180), actions which are aimed at actively disintegrating and undermining Black professors' authority in the classroom. This results in many Black male scholars experiencing "racial battle fatigue" or suffering from a debilitating stress as a result of racism's persistent daily onslaught. Moreover, the scholarship of people of color is often viewed as "biased and non-rigorous" (Delgado Bernal & Villalpando, 2002, p. 169). Such an "apartheid of knowledge" is reflected in the culture of institutions of higher education. Even worse, faculty of color tend to work at less prestigious universities, are relegated mostly to the rank of lecturer or instructor, and are likely to focus in ethnic studies and education, which offer few rewards in terms of pay (Delgado Bernal & Villalpando, 2002). The available literature therefore reveals that the struggle within African American males to develop and enact a sense of masculinity can lead to self-destructive behaviors or less-desired consequences, as well as evoke negative responses from teachers, administrators, peers, students, and society in general. At this point, we will revisit the notions of critique, justice, and caring to provide some additional insight.

CRITIQUE, JUSTICE, AND CARING AND AFRICAN AMERICAN MALES

Critique, Not Criticize

Starratt (1991) proposed an ethical framework to help guide practicing educational administrators. His first tenet, called the ethic of critique, is based in Critical Theory, which asks bold, broad, and insightful questions such as "Who defines?" "Who controls?" and "Who dominates the arrangements?" According to Starratt (1991):

> An ethic of educational administration appropriately begins with the theme of critique, a critique aimed at its own bureaucratic context, its own bureaucratic mind-set. ... By uncovering inherent injustice or dehumanization imbedded in the language and structures of society, critical analysts invite others to act to redress such injustice. ... The point the critical ethician stresses is that no social arrangement is neutral. It is usually structured to benefit some segments of society at the expense of others. (p. 189)

Thus, the position of African American males throughout their schooling and in society is not a neutral arrangement, but rather one that is structured to benefit some segment of society. If we carefully examine their experiences, we note that African American males are generally not taught critique as a value. Instead, they are criticized and stigmatized throughout their lives. This criticism and stigmatization happens in the early years of schooling (Beachum, 2013; Davis, 2003; Morris, 2009); in secondary schooling (Majors et al., 1994; McCray & Beachum, 2011; Nichols, 2004); and in society (Dyson, 2004, 2007; Ferguson, 2001; Gordon, 2002; Noguera, 2009). This criticize-over-critique dynamic has catastrophic results for African American males.

The true value of critique is that it can foster a critical consciousness, and the development of a critical consciousness is extremely important for African American males. Such thinking would give them the insight to better examine and challenges the forces that create their environments, as opposed to accepting their situation as reality or settling on survival tactics, as by, for example, adopting a code of the street mentality. Ryan (2006) remarked:

> Being critical means becoming more skeptical about established truths. Being critical requires skills that allow one to discern the basis of claims, the assumptions underlying assertions, and the interests that motivate people to promote certain positions. Critical skills allow people to recognize unstated, implicit, and subtle points of view and the often invisible or taken-for-granted conditions that provide the basis for these stances. (p. 114)

On the one hand, when youth constantly hear and experience the message that they are outcasts, different, unworthy, uneducable, and uncontrollable, they can internalize these messages and then act them out as a self-fulfilling prophesy (Beachum & McCray, 2011). On the other hand, having a critical consciousness allows them to better analyze their predicament rather than adopting a manufactured or false persona (Dyson, 2007). Furthermore, as they interrogate their own situations, they can begin to understand how their individual plight connects to the broader society. "The ethic of critique implores the individual to question personal motives, beliefs, and values" (Beachum, Obiakor, & McCray, 2007, p. 272). This kind of critique and questioning is also advocated by West (2004), who noted, "The Socratic commitment to questioning requires a relentless self-examination and critique of institutions of authority, motivated by an endless quest for intellectual integrity and moral consistency" (p. 16). One of the great benefits here is the latter part of West's assertion. Too often, African American males, in particular, "fall prey to the seductive lure of bravado, patriarchy, and hyper-masculine identities" (Beachum, 2011, p. 66). Valuing critique instead of constant criticism is a way to guide African American males down the path toward greater "intellectual integrity" and "moral consistency."

And Justice for All?

When discussing justice, we must recognize the issue of fairness. From the information provided thus far, it would seem that much of the treatment that many African American males receive is not fairly enacted. Starratt (1991) discussed an ethic of justice that highlighted governance, fairness, and balance. According to Cunningham and Cordeiro (2003), "Justice involves equity and fairness in relation to individual and community choice" (p. 194). Siddle Walker and Snarey (2004) added to this in noting, "Justice means liberating others from injustice and orientating oneself away from biases and partial passions and toward universal ethical principles" (p. 4). Together, these notions have important implications for African American males in terms of their treatment and how they perceive themselves and their situations.

Additionally, it is important to understand one's position with regard to forms of responsibility. Beachum and McCray (2008) provided a foundation for conflating justice with ideas about responsibility. Individually, we all have a responsibility to make sound decisions to benefit ourselves, foster our intellectual growth, advance our careers, and improve our lives. At the same time, though, we are connected to a broader community responsibility that forces each of us to make decisions that support our community, assist our families, help the disadvantaged, and take up causes beyond our immediate surroundings. Dyson (2005) added another level of complexity to the discussion of responsibility when he introduced the concepts of immediate and ultimate responsibility, stating:

> Immediate responsibility involves persons and societies acting accountably to address issues, ideas and problems in the present time and environment. Ultimate responsibility involves persons and societies acting accountably to address issues, ideas and problems with an eye on their personal and social impact in the long run. (p. 214)

For African American males, their treatment, experiences, and perceptions of themselves may very well lead them to overemphasize ideas of individual and immediate responsibility. This could explain their susceptibility to materialism, misogyny, and violence, as well as the devaluing of education in certain situations (Beachum & McCray, 2011; Dyson, 2007). To clarify, this is not that other populations are not impacted by the same problems, but certain segments of society are even more vulnerable. Responsibility has many facets and is not singular or even just dichotomous. Dyson (2005) provided further insight:

> To speak of immediate responsibility without figuring in ultimate responsibility ... is to minimize the role of more distant and daunting factors that shape the choices at hand. To speak of ultimate responsibility ... without understanding how immediate responsibility may still alter personal and social outcomes is to posit a determinism that dishonors individual effort and social transformation. (p. 214)

West (1994) likewise connected individual concerns with broader community and cultural connections, writing, "How people act and live are shaped—though in no way dictated or determined—by the larger circumstances in which they find themselves. These circumstances can be changed, their limits attenuated, by positive actions to elevate living conditions" (p. 19). Therefore, African American males view their responsibility in context and, if this context is one of limited opportunities, persistent barriers, and negativity, then the emphasis on immediate and individual responsibility is understandable. As West suggested, these situations can be altered or changed and responsibility can be viewed in larger terms of community responsibility and ultimate responsibility.

Similarly, the idea of balance is within the framework of justice. This side of the justice coin allows certain groups, like people of color, to levy a critique in the interest of fairness. A primary way to do this is by deconstructing social situations in order to unearth bias. Jacques Derrida was instrumental in the understanding of deconstruction as he emphasized the notion of de-centering (as cited in Powell, 1997).

He viewed Western thought as based on some center, a primary point, truth, idea, or measure for normality. These centers grab attention, credibility, support, devotion, and/or allegiance (as cited in Dantley, Beachum, & McCray, 2008). By doing this, they also exclude their opposites and anything that is not the norm. Hence, Derrida noted that a situation of binary opposites is created, such as man/woman, White/Black, wealthy/poor, written word/spoken word (as cited in Powell, 1997). In each of these pairs, the first term is centered, the second is marginalized, according to Derrida, and he recommended a mental shift in the two terms wherein the marginalized term temporally became dominant or highlighted. Such a subversion of the previously dominant term would recognize more fundamental fairness and justice. Derrida added, "But eventually, one must realize that this new hierarchy is equally unstable, and surrender to the complete free-play of the binary opposites" (as cited in Powell, 1997, p. 28). This free-play of the binary opposites underscores the inherent value of both sides and seeks to eliminate the hierarchical process that allows one to oppress the other. African American males, as well as others, use this deconstruction process to highlight many instances of unfairness.

African American males have levied significant critiques of policies, practices, and outcomes using deconstruction for fairness. With regard to aggressive policing and the mass incarceration of African American males, Miller (1996) wrote:

> With the marriage of electronic news to entertainment consummated in the early 1990s, no set of social conditions better lent itself to the manipulation by claims-makers than crime. Crime became a political game of bait and switch. The bait was violent crime—more money and resources were necessary to fight it. The switch occurred when the newly acquired criminal justice armamentaria were brought to bear. Because relatively few violent offenders could be found among the millions of underclass citizens of color who received the brunt of the newly energized justice system—from police to prosecutors—the definitions of dangerousness were twisted and stretched to include as many among them as possible, as often as possible. (p. 3)

Not surprisingly, African American males were those who were disproportionately searched, detained, arrested, prosecuted, and incarcerated. Deconstruction forces one to ask, Why are the incarceration rates for African American males so high, especially when compared with their White male counterparts? Some writers have noted that today's mass incarceration is a continuation of the usage and disenfranchisement of African American males in U.S. society (Alexander, 2012; Wacquant, 2001).

Similarly, African American males face a comparable situation in K–12 schools that can be connected to the history of Blacks in America. Lewis and Erskine (2008) noted that African American males "are at or near the bottom of every major academic barometer as it relates to academic achievement" (p. 67). In schools, they are overwhelmingly disciplined more, tracked into lower-functioning classes than their White male peers, and are expelled, suspended, and drop out at higher rates (McCray & Beachum, 2006; Obiakor, 2001; Skiba & Knesting, 2001; Skiba & Peterson, 1999; Thomas & Stevenson, 2009). On balance, if this were happening to White males, what would be the societal response, and why? Deconstruction helps us to reimagine the situation and suggest other responses that we know to be likely, but many may not want to acknowledge these reasons. This deconstruction dimension of justice allows African American males to examine situations in the interest of greater fairness.

Who Cares?

The final component of Starratt's (1991) ethical framework was an ethic of caring. He asserted that "caring recognizes that it is in the relationship that the specifically human is grounded; isolated individuals functioning only for themselves are but half persons. One becomes whole when one is in relationship with another and with many others" (Starratt, 1991, p. 195). Others have similarly noted that "care means liberating others from their state of need and actively promoting their welfare; care additionally means being orientated toward ethics grounded in empathy rather than dispassionate ethical principles" (Siddle Walker & Snarey, 2004, p. 4). With these definitions in mind, African American males must deal at times with the notion that they do not care. In fact, the hyper-masculinity associated with Black males can operate in ways that devalue an emphasis on feelings, concern for others, and strong relationships (Beachum & McCray, 2011; Harper, 2004; Oliver, 2006). Beachum, McCray, Yawn, and Obiakor (2012) expanded on Starratt's ethic of caring in claiming that it also entails compassion (Gilligan, 1982); sincere dialogue (Freire, 1973; Shields, 2004); modeling (Kunjufu, 2002); and practice.

The four aforementioned aspects of caring are critically important to the plight of and possibilities for African American males. As "compassion is the capacity for sharing the interests of another" (Beachum & McCray, 2011, p. 60), it is based on sympathy and concern for others. As noted earlier, hyper-masculine identities for African American males can overvalue the opposite, displaying a lack of concern and an attitude without love or feelings. Ultimately, this disregards people's fundamental humanity, because it is our emotions that make us human. Moreover, sincere dialogue constructs a language around caring in order to verbalize and express one's feelings. Unfortunately, for many African American males—and males in general, for that matter—there are very few clear pathways or opportunities for such sincere dialogue, where one can openly discuss one's fears, loves, hesitations, adulations, speculations, or even joys. Shields (2004) noted that we must first overcome "pathologies of silence" (p. 117) that cause men to assume care and concern but seldom seek to authenticate its existence through verbal confirmation.

Another aspect of caring is modeling. "From modeling, youth see caring in action, which makes it easier to imitate" (Beachum & McCray, 2011, p. 60). Positive role models are needed for African American males in general. With regard to caring, it is important to demonstrate caring in action rather than just verbalizing care (Noddings, 1992). In addition, modeling "helps deter skepticism and accusations of hypocrisy" (Beachum & McCray, 2011, p. 61). Finally, practice gives us the chance to apply what we have learned or witnessed, so African American males need the opportunity to practice caring. In this situation, caring becomes a two-way street. Once a person experiences caring, the likelihood is greater that he or she will be able to care for someone else. When we begin to practice caring ourselves, we can make greater connections to others and the world around us since, according to Grumet (1995), our "relationships to the world are rooted in our relationships to the people who care for us" (p. 19). Being cared for enables caring for others, and African American males need more experience with both.

CONCLUSION

The state of American education today is one that has resulted from our collective past, policies, and decisions. Seldom are the solutions to educational problems simple, and too many times there are various complexities that characterize different sides of educational issues. The trajectory of K–12 schooling is one of progression and regression, gains and losses, tremendous strides and difficult lapses. Much of this is centered on issues of diversity (McCray & Beachum, 2014, p. xvi). Similarly, the situation facing African American males is one that has resulted from many years of oppression, legislation, tradition, expectation, and discrimination (Beachum, 2011; Dyson, 2004; Kunjufu, 2001; McCray, 2008; Noguera, 2009; Wacquant, 2001). At the intersection of these issues and education is the notion of individual and collective efforts. Surely, African American males have a personal responsibility to face their problems, strive for success, push past barriers, and pursue excellence. At the same time, African American males overwhelmingly come from disadvantaged backgrounds, have to deal with more stereotypes, are over-disciplined and under-taught, and are more negatively impacted by policies than their White peers. Utilizing aspects of Starratt's (1991) claims, critique, justice, and caring become ways to construct the kind of multifaceted approach that is needed. Beachum et al. (2007) advocated Community Uplift Theory (CUT), which also promotes an individual and a collective approach:

> CUT combines both individual and collective concerns to guide urban school leaders. It fuses scholarly insight and ethical decision making with principles that are common sense, if not common knowledge. CUT's value becomes apparent when considering the African American experience and educational context. (p. 277)

Many of the suggestions and insights provided in this chapter have been informed by academic knowledge combined with concepts of ethics, along with a critical consideration of the African American contextual experience, especially with regard to the K–16 schooling experience. But, for ultimate success, strong collaboration between families and schools, insightful leadership from school administrators, professional and personal commitment from educators, the reexamination of college/university organizational culture, and the collective will of all to make more successful situations for African American males are needed. In suggesting a new discourse on African American males, we agree with Beachum (2010), who wrote:

> This discourse is one that is well-anchored in the history of the African American experience. A downfall for far too many African-American males is that we do not know where we came from or where we are going. This discourse also emphasizes the importance of attitude in all that we do. Whether you are an educator working with African-American male students or an African-American male in a school, your attitude impacts your work, interactions with others, and reality. This discourse also pushes for counternarratives that correct years of mis-education, overt discrimination, and historical alienation. In essence, this discourse embraces the best, and sometimes worst, of the African-American experience and uses it as a torch to illuminate contemporary and future practices. (p. 68)

In order to inform the future success of African American males, then, we must use our collective past and current experiences and knowledge, as well as reexamine cultural attitudes and behaviors, to facilitate an evolution of identity.

REFERENCES

Alexander, M. (2012). *The new Jim Crow: Mass incarceration in the age of colorblindness.* New York, NY: The New Press.

Beachum, F. D. (2010). Fearless faith. *Journal of African-American Males in Education, 1*(2), 63–72. Retrieved from http://journalofafricanamericanmales.com/wp-content/uploads/downloads/2010/05/FINAL-BEACHUM.pdf

Beachum, F. D. (2011). Culturally relevant leadership for complex 21st century school contexts. In F. W. English (Ed.), *Sage encyclopedia of educational leadership and administration* (2nd ed., pp. 27–35). Thousand Oaks, CA: Sage.

Beachum, F. D. (2013). The reality of racism: Recounting memories of schooling as an African American student with gifts and talents. In R. Smith & F. E. Obiakor (Eds.), *Special education practices: Personal narratives of African American scholars, educators, and related professionals* (pp. 123–132). Hauppauge, NY: Nova Science.

Beachum, F. D., & McCray, C. R. (2008). Dealing with cultural collision in urban schools: What pre-service educators should know. In G. S. Goodman (Ed.), *Education psychology: An application of critical constructivism.* New York, NY: Peter Lang.

Beachum, F. D., & McCray, C. R. (2011). *Cultural collision and collusion: Reflections on hip-hop culture, values, and schools.* New York, NY: Peter Lang.

Beachum, F. D., McCray, C. R., Yawn, C. D., & Obiakor, F. E. (2012). Multidimensional leadership in urban schools. *The National Journal of Urban Education and Practice, 5*(3), 300–314.

Beachum, F. D., Obiakor, F. E., & McCray, C. R. (2007). Community uplift theory for positive change of African Americans in urban schools. In M. C. Brown & R. D. Bartee (Eds.), *Still not equal: Expanding educational opportunity in society* (pp. 269–278). New York, NY: Peter Lang.

Beck, L. G. (1994). *Reclaiming educational administration as a caring profession.* New York, NY: Teachers College Press.

Best, R. (1983). *We've all got scars: What boys and girls learn in elementary school.* Bloomington: Indiana University Press.

Carter, P. L. (2003). Black cultural capital, status positioning, and the conflict of schooling for low-income African American youth. *Social Problems, 50*(1), 136–155.

Cleveland, D. (Ed.). (2004). *A long way to go: Conversations about race by African American faculty and graduate students.* New York, NY: Peter Lang.

College Board Advocacy & Policy Center. (2010). *The educational crisis facing young men of color: Reflections on four days of dialogue on the educational challenges of minority males.* Retrieved from http://www.advocacy.collegeboard.org/sites/default/files/educational-crisis-facing-young-men-of-color.pdf

Connell, R. W. (1993). Disruptions: Improper masculinities and schooling. In L. Fine & M. Fine (Eds.), *Beyond silenced voices: Class, race and gender in United States schools* (pp. 191–208). Albany, NY: SUNY Press.

Cose, E. (2002). *The envy of the world: On being a Black man in America.* New York, NY: Washington Square Press.

Cruse, H. (1967). *The crisis of the Negro intellectual.* New York, NY: William Morrow.

Cunningham, W. G., & Cordeiro, P. A. (2003). *Educational leadership: A problem-based approach* (2nd ed.). Boston, MA: Allyn & Bacon.

Dantley, M., Beachum, F. D., & McCray, C. M. (2008). Exploring the intersectionality of multiple centers within notions of social justice. *Journal of School Leadership, 18*(2), 124–133.

Davis, J. E. (2003). Early schooling and academic achievement of African-American males. *Urban Education, 38*(5), 515–537.

Day-Vines, N. L., & Day-Hairston, B. O. (2005). Culturally congruent strategies for addressing the behavioral needs of urban, African-American male adolescents. *Professional School Counseling, 8*(3), 236–243.

Delgado Bernal, D., & Villalpando, O. (2002). An apartheid of knowledge in academia: The struggle over the "legitimate" knowledge of faculty of color. *Equity & Excellence in Education, 35*(2), 169–180.

Du Bois, W. E. B. (2003). *Souls of black folk.* New York, NY: Barnes & Noble Classics.

Dyson, M. E. (2004). *The Michael Eric Dyson reader.* New York, NY: Basic Civitas Books.

Dyson, M. E. (2005). *Is Bill Cosby right? Or has the Black middle class lost its mind?* New York, NY: Basic Civitas Books.

Dyson, M. E. (2007). *Know what I mean? Reflections on hip hop.* New York, NY: Basic Civitas Books.

Fenning, P., & Rose, J. (2007). Overrepresentation of African American students in exclusionary discipline: The role of school policy. *Urban Education, 42*(6), 536–559.

Ferguson, A. A. (2001). *Bad boys: Public school in the making of Black masculinity.* Ann Arbor: University of Michigan Press.

Franklin, C. W. (1984). Black male-Black female conflict individually caused and culturally nurtured. *Journal of Black Studies, 15*(2), 139–154.

Freire, P. (1973). *Pedagogy of the oppressed.* New York, NY: Seabury Press.

Gilligan, C. (1982). *In a different voice: Psychological theory and women's development.* Cambridge, MA: Harvard University Press.

Gordon, J. (2002). *The Black male in White America.* Hauppauge, NY: Nova Science.

Grumet, M. R. (1995). The curriculum: What are the basics and are we teaching them? In J. L. Kincheloe & S. R. Steinberg (Eds.), *Thirteen questions* (2nd ed., pp. 15–21). New York, NY: Peter Lang.

Harper, S. R. (2004). The measure of a man: Conceptualizations of masculinity among high-achieving African-American male college students. *Berkeley Journal of Sociology, 48*(1), 89–107.

Harris, S. M. (1995). Psychosocial development and Black male masculinity: Implications for counseling economically disadvantaged African-American male adolescents. *Journal of Counseling & Development, 73*(3), 279–287.

Harro, B. (2000). The cycle of socialization. In M. Adams, W. J. Blumenfield, R. Castaneda, H. W. Hackman, M. L. Peters, & X. Zuniga (Eds.), *Reading for diversity and social justice: An anthology on racism, anti-Semitism, sexism, heterosexism, ableism, classism* (pp. 16–21). New York, NY: Routledge.

hooks, b. (2004). *We real cool: Black men and masculinity.* New York, NY: Routledge.

Isom, D. A. (2007). Performance, resistance, caring: Radicalized gender identity in African American boys. *The Urban Review, 39*(4), 405–423.

Kitwana, B. (2002). *The hip-hop generation: Young Blacks and the crisis in African American culture.* New York, NY: Basic Civitas Books.

Kunjufu, J. (2001). *State of emergency: We must save African-American males.* Chicago, IL: African American Images.

Kunjufu, J. (2002). *Black students, middle class teachers.* Chicago, IL: African American Images.

Kunjufu, J. (2005). *Keeping Black boys out of special education.* Chicago, IL: African American Images.

Lewis, C. W., & Erskine, K. F. (2008). *The dilemmas of being an African-American male in the new millennium: Solutions for life transformation.* West Conshohocken, PA: Infinity.

Majors, R., & Billson, J. M. (1993). *Cool pose: The dilemma of Black manhood in America.* New York, NY: Touchstone.

Majors, R. G., Tyler, R., Peden, B., & Hall, R. E. (1994). Cool pose: A symbolic mechanism for masculine role enactment and copying by Black males. In R. G. Majors & J. U. Gordan (Eds.), *The American Black male: His present status and his future* (pp. 245–259). Chicago, IL: Nelson-Hall.

McCall, N. (1995). *Makes me wanna holler: A young Black man in America.* New York, NY: Vintage Books.

McCray, C. R. (2008). Constructing a positive intrasection of race and class for the 21st century. *Journal of School Leadership, 18*(2), 249–267.

McCray, C. R., & Beachum, F. D. (2006). A critique of zero tolerance policies: An issue of justice and caring. *Values and Ethics in Educational Administration, 5*(1), 1–8. Retrieved from http://www.ed.psu.edu/UCEACSLE/VEEA/VEEA_Vol5Num1.pdf

McCray, C. R., & Beachum, F. D. (2011). Capital matters: A pedagogy of self-development: Making room for alternative forms of capital. In R. Bartee (Ed.), *Contemporary perspectives on capital in educational context* (pp. 79–100). Charlotte, NC: Information Age.

McCray, C. R., & Beachum, F. D. (2014). *School leadership in a diverse society: Helping schools to prepare all students for success.* Charlotte, NC: Information Age.

Miller, J. G. (1996). *Search and destroy: African-American males in the criminal justice system.* New York, NY: Cambridge University Press.

Morris, J. E. (2009). *Troubling the waters: Fulfilling the promise of quality public schooling for Black children.* New York, NY: Teachers College Press.

Morrison, P., & Eardley, T. (1985). *About men.* Philadelphia, PA: Open University Press.

Nichols, J. D. (2004). An exploration of discipline and suspension data. *Journal of Negro Education, 73*(4), 408–423.

Noddings, N. (1992). *The challenge to care in schools: Alternative approaches to education.* New York, NY: Teachers College Press.

Noguera, P. A. (2009). *The trouble with black boys ... and other reflections on race, equity, and the future of public education.* Hoboken, NJ: John Wiley & Sons.

Obiakor, F. E. (2001). *It even happens in "good" schools: Responding to culturally diversity in today's classrooms.* Thousand Oaks, CA: Corwin Press.

Obiakor, F. E., Harris, M. K., & Beachum, F. D. (2009). The state of special education for African American learners in Milwaukee. In G. L. Williams & F. E. Obiakor (Eds.), *The state of education of urban learners and possible solutions: The Milwaukee experience* (pp. 31–48). Dubuque, IA: Kendall Hunt.

Oliver, W. (2006). "The streets": An alternative Black male socialization institution. *Journal of Black Studies, 36*(6), 918–937.

Powell, J. (1997). *Derrida for beginners.* Danbury, CT: Writers and Readers.

Prier, D., & Beachum, F. D. (2008). Conceptualizing a critical discourse around hip-hop culture and Black male youth in educational scholarship and research. *International Journal of Qualitative Studies in Education, 21*(5), 519–535.

Ryan, J. (2006). *Inclusive leadership.* San Francisco, CA: Jossey-Bass.

Schott Foundation for Public Education. (2010). *Yes we can: The Schott 50 state report on public education and Black males.* Retrieved from http://schottfoundation.org/publications/schott-2010-black-male-report.pdf

Shields, C. M. (2004). Dialogic leadership for social justice: Overcoming pathologies of silence. *Educational Administration Quarterly, 40*(1), 109–132.

Siddle Walker, V., & Snarey, J. R. (2004). Race matters in moral formation. In V. Siddle Walker & J. R. Snarey (Eds.), *Race-ing moral formation: African American perspectives on care and justice* (pp. 1–22). New York, NY: Teachers College Press.

Skiba, R. J., & Knesting, K. (2001). Zero tolerance, zero evidence: An analysis of school disciplinary practice. *New Directions for Youth Development, 92,* 17–43.

Skiba, R. J., & Peterson, R. L. (1999). Zap zero tolerance. *Education Digest, 64*(8), 24–30.

Slaughter-Defoe, D. T., & Richards, H. (1994). Literacy as empowerment: The case for African American males. In V. L. Gadsden & D. A. Wagner (Eds.), *Literacy among African American youth: Issues in learning, teaching, and schooling* (pp. 125–147). Cresskill, NJ: Hampton Press.

Smith, W. (2004). Black faculty coping with racial battle fatigue: The campus racial climate in a post-civil rights era. In D. Cleveland (Ed.), *A long way to go: Conversations about race by African American faculty and graduate students.* New York, NY: Peter Lang.

Starratt, R. J. (1991). Building an ethical school: A theory of practice in educational leadership. *Educational Administration Quarterly, 27*(2), 185–202.

Tatum, B. D. (1997). *"Why are all the Black kids sitting together in the cafeteria?" And other conversations about race.* New York, NY: Basic Books.

Thomas, D. E., & Stevenson, H. (2009). Gender risks and education: The particular classroom challenges for urban low-income African American boys. *Review of Research in Education, 33,* 160–180.

Villegas, A. M., & Lucas, T. (2002). *Educating culturally responsive teachers: A coherent approach.* Albany, NY: SUNY Press.

Wacquant, L. (2001). Deadly symbiosis: When ghetto and prison meet and mesh. *Punishment and Society, 3*(1), 95–134.

West, C. (1994). *Race matters*. New York, NY: Vintage Books.

West, C. (2004). *Democracy matters: Winning the fight against imperialism*. New York, NY: Penguin Press.

Yawn, C., & Obiakor, F. E. (Eds.). (2013). *Urban special education: The New York experience*. Dubuque, IA: Kendall Hunt.

CHAPTER FIVE

Masking Mentorship

Critical (Race) Care among Black Males in Special Education

VONZELL AGOSTO AND RODERICK JONES

INTRODUCTION

Throughout the annals of U.S. history, Black males have been portrayed as a violent, irrational, and dysfunctional subgroup deserving of societal animus (Hutchison, 1996). Hutchison (1996) offers a well-argued critique of media as a major force in the widespread misrepresentations of Black males. Though it is not uncommon to hear public declarations that the election of the first Black male president of the United States helped mollify harmful racial beliefs and tensions, hardly a day passes in which the image of Black men is not assailed. Even President Barack Obama's citizenship and therefore legitimacy as president has been challenged through commentary transmitted via television, radio, print, and the Internet. Notably, when his presidential opponent Mitt Romney (a White Republican) implied President Obama's citizenry was uncertain at best, he was not questioned or challenged by media correspondents (Haake, 2012).

While the media construct negative representations and narratives of Black males, they are not the only institutions to do so. To some degree, schooling acts in concert with institutions—such as those governing media, justice, and health. Schooling thus reproduces, reflects, and responds to harmful sociocultural narratives and practices assailing the image of Black men. Moreover, systems of formal education support the dehumanization of Black males through acts that marginalize, commodify, or reinforce sources contributing to their degradation or maltreatment. Giroux (2011) describes this assault on youth as the politics of disposability. In other words, disposability increases the probability that Black males will drop out of school, be pushed out, or become ensnared in the penal system (Togut, 2011), which presents unique structural challenges for the development and sustainability of positive, nurturing mentor relationships. The pervasiveness of damaging portrayals of Black males means that leaving school (by graduating, dropping out, or being pushed out) is not an escape from assault.

Researchers, educators, parent groups, and community organizations have made various attempts to understand and confront the obstacles that undermine the social and academic achievement of adolescent Black males in schools (Bailey & Paisley, 2004; Howard, 2008). For instance, disproportionality in the incarceration rates, out-of-school suspensions, and dropout rates among Black males have been identified as structural impediments that diminish their life experiences (Hall & Karanxha, 2012; Noguera, 1997). Additionally, the overrepresentation of Black males in special education (Harry & Anderson, 1994; Patton, 1998), as well as their absence from advanced courses and programs (Ford & Grantham, 2003; Patterson, 2005; Whiting, 2006), have been well documented. As Ladson-Billings (2011) observes, Black males are bound in a love-hate relationship with society, both nationally and globally. Society often embraces them as icons of youth culture even as it excommunicates them as problems in need of eradication or oddities trespassing in spaces typically reserved for those more admired and invested with care. Such spaces include classrooms reserved for students labeled as gifted and talented, programs offering Advanced Placement courses that facilitate college access, or higher education settings like doctoral programs.

Media portrayals of the current president and the situations described above continue to tell a narrative of the Black male in crisis. While this narrative can shed light on the plight of the Black male image as depicted through a broader public lens, it simultaneously reinscribes the problematic image of Black men as being beyond love (Duncan, 2002). As a master narrative, then, it projects the danger of a single story (Adichie, 2009). Whether told through the media or literature in education or in the broader span of the social sciences, this master narrative of Black males in crisis reproduces negative stereotypes about them (Brown, 2011; Brown & Donnor, 2011; Fultz & Brown, 2008). In contrast to the narrative of the Black male in crisis (Noguera, 1996, 1997) are narratives of care.

Mentoring can be viewed as a manifestation of an ethic of care (Noddings, 2005), which can help educators to envisage public schooling beyond the current orthodoxy of high-stakes testing policies, competitions, school-choice schemes (Ravitch, 2011). Mentoring in the spirit of care can entail confronting how education funding (unfunded, underfunded, defunded) primarily limits educational opportunities for students of color (Kozol, 1992). More recent research explores how Black males are caring for one another (Jackson, Sealey-Ruiz, & Watson,

2014). However, not enough is known about the ethic of care for Black males such as how they care for others or are cared for through mentoring.

Following Smith's (1997) description of the role of care in mentoring, we discuss mentoring as a form of leadership that can be invested with care. Given the scant research in this area, we turn to critical race theory and care theory to present a counter narrative of Black males in special education as giving and accepting care. This counter narrative provides educators in K–12 and postsecondary institutions a mentoring framework that recognizes the politics of care and values the act of masking. Framing critical (race) mentorship as a counternarrative and expression of leadership aligns with Tillman's (2004) position that "we must reverse the 'manufactured crisis' in the education of African-American children" (p. 301). We present the major tenets of critical race theory, and how they have informed the scholarship on the education of Black males in schools, before examining the extant literature on mentoring and ethical theory centering concepts such as care and risk. These theoretical perspectives provide a backdrop for our personal narratives of masking mentoring and a framework for critical (race) mentorship.

TENETS OF CRITICAL RACE THEORY

Scholarship on the education of Black males and other people of color has brought attention to the broader context and narrative of how formal institutions of education systematically construct an apartheid system of knowledge (Delgado Bernal & Villalpando, 2002). Such scholarship has relied on critical race theory (CRT) as in critical race ethnography (Duncan, 2002) or research from the social sciences (Brown, 2011; Brown & Donnor, 2011) focused on students from K–12 to graduate school (Gildersleeve, Croom, & Vasquez, 2011; Solórzano & Villalpando, 1998; Villalpando, 2004; Yosso, Smith, Ceja, & Solórzano, 2009), as well as adults working in schools.

CRT provides a framework for understanding how race, racism, and antiracism are constructed and perpetuated at the levels of individual experience, institutional constructs, and societal interactions like the social constructions of race and the normative everyday practices of people in relationships; all of these factors are reflected in CRT as a broader collection of individual and institutional forces that can coalesce in national and international trends. The tenets of CRT, now collated by critical race legal theorists and scholars in education (Ladson-Billings, 1998; Ladson-Billings & Tate, 1995), are summarized by Villalpando (2004) to include race and racism, contestation of dominant ideologies, social justice theory and practice, experiential knowledge, and historical context. The tenets of CRT bring theoretical focus and ethical grounding to inquiry into race-related phenomena involving exchanges of power and the intersectionality of race with other identities vulnerable to social oppression.

Analytical tools such as intersectionality (Crenshaw, 1995), counter-stories, and counter narratives (Bell, 1992; Delgado, 1989) are hallmarks within CRT's methodological and pedagogical repertoire. CRT has been further elaborated through the historical narratives on the conditions faced by multidimensional social groups in order to understand race, racism, and anti-racism alongside another defining features of social difference. Inquiry and interventions into race and racism (i.e., anti-racism) at the intersection with gender, sexual orientation, ethnicity, tribal affiliation, immigration status, and/or language are evident in expressions of CRT such as Latino/a Critical Theory; Critical Race Feminist Theory, Whiteness Studies, and TribalCrit. Through the various expressions of CRT, have arisen counter-stories and counter narratives, which have brought attention to how stories can be crafted into a destructive single tale (stereotypes) that operates as or serves a grand or master-narrative. A master-narrative can be countered with multiple stories to undercut it as an expression of anti-oppressive action (i.e., naming patterns of injustice or sharing experiences around which to collectivize).

The tenets of CRT have provided methods to raise attention to the marginalization of students from underrepresented racial and ethnic minority groups in higher education, and equip them to overcome related obstacles. These include creating an awareness of microaggressions, creating counter-stories, and creating counter spaces in which to share their counter-stories that challenge microaggressions (Howard-Hamilton, 1997). For the purpose of this chapter, we focus on mentoring that provides academic counter spaces (Solórzano et al., 2000; Solórzano & Villalpando, 1998). Counter spaces are also referred to as safe spaces and safe places (Ballard & Cintrón, 2010), venues that marginalized groups use to express their counter-stories (Delgado & Stefancic, 2001). Recalling Derrick Bell's counter narrative *Space Traders,* Howard (2008) interprets its subtext as posing the question: *Who would really care if African Americans no longer existed in this country?*

COLOR(FUL) CRITICAL RACE CARE THROUGH MENTORING

Pimentel (2011) describes critical approaches to caring in contrast to colorblind or aesthetic approaches to caring, noting that they are "grounded in a political, color-conscious, and culturally relevant perspective that is concerned about the well-being and education of the whole child—not just school-sanctioned criteria for academic achievement" (p. 3). Furthermore, Pimentel (2011) asserts that providing critical care to students in assimilationist and deficit-oriented school contexts is not necessarily a straightforward process. Instead, providing color(ful) critical care requires educators' understanding of the context (Rolón-Dow, 2005), such as how schooling structures emphasize some forms of caring and conditions over others to influence whether or not schools operate as sanctuaries (DeJesús & Antrop-González, 2006) or how they mediate tensions to coalesce into politics of caring that students perceive as authentic with the potential for mutuality.

Researchers have begun to explore the importance of fostering caring mentoring relationships for Black male adolescents in K–12 sites of education (Bailey & Paisley, 2004; Grant & Dieker, 2011), and young adults in higher education (Harper, 2006), to improve their life experiences. Grantham (2004) identifies mutual caring as part of a multicultural approach to mentoring that helped to increase the integration of Black males in gifted education. Several studies of mentoring for Black male students have shown it to be a deterrent to their risk of failure (Grant & Dieker, 2010; Smith, 1997). However, formal mentoring has also been found to further marginalize individuals when such programs are planned and operated from a sense of false empathy rather than love (Duncan, 2002).

For adults, multipurpose and multi-tiered support networks that extend into local educational communities and connect to scholars and practitioners of color at the national and international levels have been recommended (Young & Brooks, 2008; Young, Petersen, & Short, 2002). Such findings and recommendations point to the promise of research to provide a more robust understanding of the kinds of mentoring and related principles—such as critical care—that oppose the crisis narrative by undermining the structures from which it is constructed. However, in the literature on Black males, the "political and ideological dimensions of caring and loving are seldom addressed" (Bartolomé, 2008, p. 2).

PROFESSOR V. AGOSTO'S COUNTER NARRATIVE OF MASKING CRITICAL (RACE) MENTORING

My personal experience teaching at the K–12 level in special education was the precursor to my academic engagement with critical multicultural theory, political clarity, and critical race studies. These areas of study and experiences working with students in secondary and postsecondary settings have informed how I participate in mentoring relationships with Black males in particular. Additionally, working with primarily African American/Black and Latino/Hispanic males in secondary education and their families as we negotiated special education helped me develop political and ideological clarity about how relationships among youth, schools, and society differentially structure their successes and failures. In not so subtle ways, structures told me who (not) to love (Bartolomé, 1994). In other words, I gained political clarity as I became more conscious about the interaction between micro- and macro-level instances of systemic injustices and discrepancies between the dominant and counter narratives I embraced or resisted. Just as important to the development of political clarity was the realization that I could harness my sense of power and responsibility into an assault against stereotypes imposed on my students (Beauboeuf-Lafontant, 2002), some of which also plague me as a woman of African American and Mexican American descent. Stereotypes about limited cognitive ability, excessive rates of reproduction, and flawed character (the angry Black woman, the submissive Mexican) suggest that I, like many of my Black and Brown male colleagues or students, do not belong. Even while an assistant (now associate) professor, I have had White female students question whether or not I was married when they found out that I had a child and note that they did not see a wedding ring on my finger—all within earshot of a Black woman mentee. The racial overtones of such comments were not lost on the mentee, who later commented in our counter space outside of class that she perceived several students to be racist.

Narratives of women in educational leadership (Karanxha, Agosto, & Elam, 2011) and theories of care (Noddings, 2005) among teachers guided by political clarity (Bartolomé, 1994, 2008) have informed my thinking about leadership and its expression through mentorship. For instance, Beauboeuf-Lafontant's (2002) characterization of womanist caring among teachers as the embrace of the maternal, political clarity, and an ethic of risk resonates with my perception of what is involved in caring relationships with students who have been historically, consistently, and systematically marginalized in most major institutions. Although the maternal quality of womanist caring is not a quality that resonates with my own sense of care, I do recognize that gender—and, therefore the gendered way one knows and mentors—is an inescapable feature of academia and the United States more broadly. To break with the status quo and care for Black males working and studying in special education is to embrace risk. To provide critical (race) care at times requires me to mask my mentorship and the resulting academic counterspaces created (i.e., funding, presenting, publishing, networking). As a professor, I serve as a mentor for Roderick—who has called me mother hen on a few occasions.

Inviting Roderick to explore the possibility of entering a doctoral program is where our lived experience first intertwined. We met while I was conducting a study of inclusion in a school where he worked in a semi-administrative position as a behavior specialist. I was immediately impressed with his thoughtfulness and intellectual acuity. Roderick, as well as a few other male students of color I met who were in similar professional positions while studying at the graduate level, appeared to have greater aspirations but little encouragement to leave the position in special education to pursue higher positions of authority and decision making. My perception of their situations helped me to recall literature on how Black men are often placed in schools and programs to control Black male youth: arguably, that may be part of the impetus for dissuading men like them from moving on to higher-level positions.

I became curious as to whether Black men entering the principalship were being tracked, namely, into assistant principal positions focused on discipline rather than curriculum. Encounters with men like Roderick have made me suspicious that eugenics discourse (i.e., limitations of Black men attributed to genetics affecting their body, character, or cognition) remain deeply ingrained in society and evidenced in education leadership decisions about which people should be primed for leadership roles. Notably, the literature on educational leadership confirms the underrepresentation of African Americans in particular, for they represent only 10.8% of all principals nationally (Tillman, 2004).

To provide another angle into critical (race) care mentoring, I am recalling our attendance at a conference where we presented on a paper we were beginning to write. I noticed how several Black men (who had not previously approached me at earlier events) approached Roderick. I did not perceive them as unfriendly or unwilling to interact with me—when I initiated the interaction. Yet while observing how they interacted with Roderick I became more aware of the gendered dynamics of mentoring. As a woman, I had to initiate interaction in order to open the lines of communication with potential male mentors, whereas Roderick was approached, offered business cards, and urged by many to "keep in touch." In other words, when seeking mentorship from Black males in particular, I had to work for what they graciously offered my Black male student.

By the same token, Black women at the conference approached me, or I engaged with them, more fluidly and promptly; they offered advice, invitations, and opportunities as the men did with Roderick. Such clear gender dynamics and behavior disparities suggest the need to pay more attention to how mixed-gender mentoring relationships, as in males of color mentoring or sponsoring women of color or vice versa, come with the risk of gossip, jealousy, and sexual attraction or tension (Noe, 1988).

Such risks, relations, and tensions can deter cross-gendered professional supports, yet illuminate the need to mask mentoring as indifference in order to avoid giving the appearance of caring too much, or at all. In an example of masking mentoring, to support Roderick's travel to other conference I sought funding from multiple sources on his behalf, largely due to my concern about funding equity for students of color and the differential amount of effort required of them to attain funding such as travel grants. After several failed attempts to obtain the funding support that a colleague promised to provide, I paid Rod's travel expenses but did not inform that colleague or any other. Soon after, while he was enrolled in my class, I paid less attention to him than other students in class to mask the fact that our relationship was more developed. Moreover, I did not want other students to accuse me of favoritism or assume I was less available or open to working with them because of my sponsoring relationship with Roderick.

As Roderick continued in the program and proceeded to develop his identity as a scholar (Whiting, 2006), he began communicating an interest in pursuing an academic career. As a driven individual seeking an academic position, Roderick was a gem for professors chairing doctoral committees. In other words, talented students who are likely to do well and plan to continue in academia generally require less work and worry from their advisors. Additionally, their success helps to build their advisor's reputation as a successful mentor. As they advance in their careers, for example, in research-intensive universities, they may also be inclined to promote or at least cite their advisor's scholarship. While I want to mentor Roderick and serve in whatever professional capacity makes sense for his studies, socialization, and career trajectory, I am opposed to the commodification of students in this way.

I am troubled by professors who track students into and out of the stream of advisees. My suspicion is that such tracking across race, gender, and academic ability happens subtly and is rationalized away under the pretense of caring for the student. Commodification of doctoral students is part of the process of dehumanization or un-selfing. Un-selfing, as described by a Black teacher (Iola Taylor) in a study conducted by Wilson and Seagall (2001), "means that you either overtly or covertly take a person's dignity. It can be done very, very subtly, but it can be done" (p. 41). I have attempted to mask my suspicions about these mentoring/advising dynamics from Roderick and, instead, I emphasize the need for all doctoral students to make informed and thoughtful decisions about the composition of their dissertation committee.

Critical (race) care mentoring reminds me to pay attention to the racial and gendered power dynamics in the institution, namely, how relationships with advisors and mentors serve students pursuing degrees and careers in educational leadership and special education, where race and gender still matter. Even as I reflect on leaving my role as a high school teacher to pursue a doctorate, I recall being convinced that I could help instigate change to reduce the oppression of students. Around that time, I was asked by a young adult Black male, "Why do you care so much about other people?" To which I responded, "How do you not [care]?" The young man's question still baffles me, but I think it is a question that needs to be asked directly of those entering educational leadership.

I imagine a critical (race) care framework built on political clarity, ethics of risk and care, and the tenets of critical race theory will contribute to the conversation on mentoring Black men through constructions of race, gender, and dis/ability. As I mentor Black men as doctoral students who plan to work or study in special education settings or, more generally, with dis/ability, I work through them and with them to model a moral activist stance (Ladson-Billings & Donner, 2005) that aims to reduce those oppressive forces that impede the opportunities and conditions that enable youth to flourish as they travel in and out of counterspaces and sanctuaries.

Roderick's Counter narrative of Masking Critical (Race) Mentoring

The concept of *in loco parentis*, a Latin phrase meaning "in the place of the parent," vouchsafes my ability as a Black male, K–12 special educator to develop caring mentoring relationships with Black male adolescents. I use the term *in loco parentis* to illuminate my teaching and mentoring experiences over the years as embodiments of genuine acts of care—and even a sense of love—in the lives of many Black male adolescents who affected me as much I did them. I have since come to understand the myriad ways in which my ability to act as a parental figure has led me to negotiate the politics of race, disability, and gender, including my relational space to female students.

One political overture, shared by other educators and family members (usually Black women), demanded that I (as a young Black man teaching in secondary schools) remain cautious of close affiliations with adolescent girls. Consequently, as an act of professional self-preservation and desire to avoid perceptions of impropriety, I sustained few mentor-mentee relationships with young females. Even the few times when I chose to resist this narrative, I still kept my mentoring relationship with female students, namely from racial minority groups, professional and very public. However, as deficit-oriented discourses (Duncan, 2002) and racial microaggressions (Solórzano et al., 2000) surrounding Black male students permeated my teaching experiences, I often felt obliged to conceal or mask rather than outright spurn my efforts to care for and to receive care from them. It was not uncommon to hear, and disrupt with my unexpected arrival, colleagues' conversations about Black males who exhibited learning or behavioral challenges. Some teachers would call for the students' permanent removal from class, while others did not go as far. Yet, notably, the assumptions that informed these teachers' actions were often undergirded by a narrative that blamed Black males' underachievement on their home life and/or a lack of good parenting skills.

Official displays of mentoring appropriated much of my time. However, more authentic acts of caring (Bartolomé, 2008), that took place between me and my Black male mentees, often transpired in the privacy of my office. This physical counter space allowed me to engage Black males in a sort of "unseen and unspoken" pedagogical rite of passage as they encountered personal and familial/peer situations, or institutional mores like policies and rules that were either unsettling or too complex for them to mediate alone. Over the years, many students told me that I acted as if I were their "father." Whether they simply wanted a place to visit or receive advice about their day-to-day academic and behavioral experiences, this counter space served as a safe harbor for us—one Black male to another—to articulate our mutual concerns about institutional discrepancies that appeared institutionally neutral yet were disproportionately adverse for Black males on a wider scale. At times, these concerns resulted in my expression of personal views that blatantly challenged the rationale of my mentees' perceptions of the concept of fairness. Conversely, our masked conversations allowed me to internalize their collective frustrations and formulate counter narratives that they could later use to reject stereotypes that transgressed their sense of self-efficacy and self-worth. It also served as a means to establish a relational metric of trust and refresh our sense of purpose and hope in the wake of institutional encroachments that stymied our ability to evince positive Black male imagery.

As I delve into more personalized and nuanced acts of care and masking I invoke two of several assumptions regarding the nurturing of African American males in relation to academic achievement put forth by Bailey and Paisley (2004), specifically the belief that "all [Black males] are worthy of love, nurturing, guidance, support, and meaningful relationships; and stereotypes of male African Americans can only be changed by providing positive views of male African Americans" (p. 12). Taking into account these considerations, especially when asked by Black male mentees to provide financial assistance to help pay for their school lunch, school supplies, or admission to a much-anticipated school event like the prom, I always seek to mitigate my ambivalence toward helping them financially by encouraging or helping them pursue alternative school-based financial assistance.

For the most part, it is considered unethical for public school educators to provide students with financial assistance. Careful discernment is paramount here because public perception regarding the provision of monetary aid by teachers to students can easily transform an intended act of altruism into an unprofessional and, even worse, criminal act. In such situations, I directly provided assistance to Black male mentees within the privacy of my office, knowing that it would be otherwise untenable for me to do so in plain sight of other students or colleagues. Yet many of them were too prideful to ask for financial aid or educational assistance (Bailey & Paisley, 2004; Duncan, 2002) from those they did not trust. I initially identified with this sentiment because I often believed that my White colleagues' distrust of my skills hampered my own professional experiences. Additionally, my mentees solicited other types of educational resources from me, including my computer to complete assignments; my office or personal cellular phone to contact parents in emergency situations; and my intervention in matters involving disciplinary referrals they had received.

Over the past three years, my position as a behavior specialist, a semi-administrative position funded through the district's Special Education Department, has allowed me to work extensively with special education and general education students with serious disciplinary issues and histories. In addition, my role involved assisting teachers of both special education and general education with behavioral interventions to modify and extinguish undesirable student behavior. Most of my work in this regard has dealt with males from racial minority groups. Rather than doling out formulaic punitive prescriptions, there were many instances in which I actually lessened the disciplinary consequences I could have administered per the school's policies. Moreover, I also routinely encouraged Black males and their parents to appeal disciplinary consequences assigned by administrators and their assistants that we considered too harsh compared with the treatment of other students with comparable discipline histories who had committed similar infractions.

Again, such discussions not only involved serious professional risk, but were also a cornerstone to the perpetuity of the masking project. On one hand, I worked against colleagues by helping Black males and their parents interrogate the inequities of our school's discipline policy, fully aware that these students and their parents could have implicated me at any time during the disciplinary process. On the other hand, my sense of care and love for Black males, especially my mentees, prevented me from encouraging them to dismiss actions as merely part of a neutral policy agenda. I was unable to view the policy as carrying no serious educational, social, or lifelong implications, particularly insofar as the deleterious effects of out-of-school suspensions on Black males' lives is concerned (Hall & Karanxha, 2012). Ultimately, our success or failure in the masking project could only be realized as a consequence of care and support and, therefore, the maximization or deprivation of trust that we were willing to extend to each other.

CONCLUSION

The low prevalence of Black males thriving in K–12 and postsecondary education, coupled with the destruction of the Black males' image in society, provides ample ground for further academic inquiry. We have attempted to provide a preliminary framework that situates the care of Black males as a response to Howard's (2008) question, "Who really cares ... about the disenfranchisement of African American males?" (p. 954). While our personal narratives highlight our experiences mentoring individuals, our critique of schooling systems and institutions working in combination to construct the experience of Black males in special education is much broader. The tenets of critical race theory help us point to both the systematic patterns of intersectional oppression and the lived experiences that are felt individually, collectively, and relationally.

Critical (race) care as a framework for mentoring addresses the need for recognitive justice without ignoring other facets or paradigms of social justice such as distributive, procedural, and restorative justice. Critical (race) care offers a response for leadership that includes mentoring as an action-oriented response that often requires masking because it challenges injustice, White supremacy, liberal forms of equality, analyses along a single axis of oppression or form of identity, and race neutrality. In other words, critical (race) care mentoring reflects the moral activist role for critical race leadership.

REFERENCES

Adichie, C. (2009, July). Chimamanda Adichie: The danger of a single story [Video file]. Retrieved from http://www.ted.com/talks/chimamanda_adichie_the_danger_of_a_single_story.html

Bailey, D. F., & Paisley, P. O. (2004). Developing and nurturing excellence in African American male adolescents. *Journal of Counseling and Development, 82*(1), 10–17.

Ballard, H. E., & Cintrón, R. (2010). Critical race theory as an analytical tool: African American male success in doctoral education. *Journal of College Teaching and Learning, 7*(10), 11–24.

Bartolomé, L. I. (1994). Beyond the methods fetish: Toward a humanizing pedagogy. *Harvard Educational Review, 64*(2), 173–194.

Bartolomé, L. I. (2008). Authentic cariño and respect in minority education: The political and ideological dimensions of love. *International Journal of Critical Pedagogy, 1*(1), 1–17.

Beauboeuf-Lafontant, T. (2002). A womanist experience of caring: Understanding the pedagogy of exemplary Black women teachers. *The Urban Review, 34*(1), 71–86.

Bell, D. (1992). *Faces at the bottom of the well: The permanence of racism*. New York, NY: Basic Books.

Brown, A. L. (2011). "Same old stories": The Black male in social science and educational literature, 1930s to the present. *Teachers College Record, 113*(9), 2047–2079.

Brown, A. L., & Donnor, J. K. (2011). Toward a new narrative on Black males, education, and public policy. *Race Ethnicity and Education, 14*(1), 17–32.

Crenshaw, K. (1995). Mapping the margins: Intersectionality, identity politics and violence against women of color. In K. Crenshaw, N. Gotanda, G. Peller, & K. Thomas (Eds.), *Critical race theory: The key writings that formed the movement* (pp. 357–383). New York, NY: New Press.

De Jesús, A., & Antrop-González, R. (2006). Instrumental relationships and high expectations: Exploring critical care in two Latino community-based schools. *Intercultural Education, 17*(3), 281–299.

Delgado, R. (1989). Storytelling for oppositionists and others: A plea for narrative. *Michigan Law Review, 87*, 2411–2441.

Delgado, R., & Stefancic, J. (2001). *Critical race theory: An introduction*. New York: New York University Press.

Delgado Bernal, D., & Villalpando, O. (2002). The apartheid of knowledge in the academy: The struggle over "legitimate" knowledge of faculty of color. *Equity & Excellence in Education* [Special issue on Critical Race Theory in Education], *35*(2), 169–180.

Duncan, G. (2002). Beyond love: A critical race ethnography of the schooling of adolescent Black males. *Equity & Excellence in Education, 35*(2), 131–143.

Ford, D. Y., & Grantham, T. C. (2003). Providing access for culturally diverse gifted students: From deficit to dynamic thinking. *Theory into Practice, 42*(3), 217–225.

Fultz, M., & Brown, A. L. (2008). Historical perspectives of African American males as subjects of education policy. *American Behavioral Scientist, 51*(7), 854–871.

Gildersleeve, R. E., Croom, N. N., & Vasquez, P. L. (2011). "Am I going crazy?!": A critical race analysis of doctoral education. *Equity & Excellence in Education, 44*(1), 93–114.

Giroux, H. (2011). Youth in the suspect society and the politics of disposability. *Power Play, 3*(1), 3–20.

Grant, D. G., & Dieker, L. A. (2011). Listening to Black male student voices using web-based mentoring. *Remedial and Special Education, 32*(4), 322–333.

Grantham, T. C. (2004). Multicultural mentoring to increase Black male representation in gifted programs. *Gifted Child Quarterly, 48*(3), 232–245.

Haake, G. (2012, August 24). Romney in Michigan: No one ever asked to see my birth certificate. *NBC News*. Retrieved from http://firstread.nbcnews.com/_news/2012/08/24/13458214-romney-in-michigan-no-one-has-ever-asked-to-see-my-birth-certificate

Hall, E. S., & Karanxha, Z. (2012). School today, jail tomorrow: The impact of zero tolerance on the over-representation of minority youth in the juvenile system. *Power Play, 4*(1), 111–144.

Harper, S. R. (2006). *Black male students at public flagship universities in the U.S.: Status, trends, and implications for policy and practice*. Washington, DC: Joint Center for Political and Economic Studies.

Harry, B., & Anderson, M. G. (1994). The disproportionate placement of African American males in special education programs: A critique of the process. *The Journal of Negro Education, 63*(4), 602–619.

Howard, T. (2008). Who really cares? The disenfranchisement of African American males in preK–12 schools: A critical race theory perspective. *Teachers College Record, 110*(5), 954–985.

Howard-Hamilton, M. F. (1997). Theory to practice: Applying developmental theories relevant to African American men. *New Directions for Student Services, 80*, 17–30.

Hutchison, E. O. (1996). *The assassination of the Black male image* (2nd ed.). New York, NY: Simon & Schuster.

Jackson, I., Sealey-Ruiz, Y., & Watson, W. (2014). Reciprocal love mentoring Black and Latino males through an ethos of care. *Urban Education, 49*(4), 394–417.

Karanxha, Z., Agosto, V., & Elam, D. (2011). Journey of Elam: Her servant-leadership pedagogy as a public intellectual. *Vitae Scholasticae, 28*(2), 65–82.

Kozol, J. (1992). *Savage inequalities: Children in America's schools*. New York, NY: Harper Perennial.

Ladson-Billings, G. (1998). Just what is critical race theory and what's it doing in a nice field like education? *International Journal of Qualitative Studies in Education, 11*(1), 7–24.

Ladson-Billings, G. (2011). Boyz to men? Teaching to restore Black boys' childhood. *Race Ethnicity and Education, 14*(1), 7–15.

Ladson-Billings, G., & Donner, J. (2005). The moral activist role of critical race theory scholarship. In N. K. Denzin & Y. S. Lincoln (Eds.), *The Sage handbook of qualitative research* (3rd ed., pp. 279–301). Thousand Oaks, CA: Sage.

Ladson-Billings, G., & Tate, W. F., IV. (1995). Toward a critical race theory of education. *Teachers College Record, 97*(1), 47–68.

Noddings, N. (2005). *The challenge to care in schools: An alternative approach to education* (2nd ed.). New York, NY: Teachers College Press.

Noe, R. A. (1988). An investigation of the determinants of successful assigned mentoring relationships. *Personnel Psychology, 41*(3), 457–479.

Noguera, P. (1996). Responding to the crisis confronting California's Black male youth: Providing support without furthering marginalization. *The Journal of Negro Education, 65*(2), 219–236.

Noguera, P. A. (1997). Reconsidering the "crisis" of the Black male in America. *Social Justice, 24*(2), 147–164.

Patterson, K. B. (2005). Increasing positive outcomes for African American males in special education with the use of guided notes. *The Journal of Negro Education, 74*(4), 311–320.

Patton, J. M. (1998). The disproportionate representation of African Americans in special education: Looking behind the curtain for understanding and solutions. *Journal of Special Education, 32*(1), 25–31.

Pimentel, C. (2011). The politics of caring in a bilingual classroom: A case study on the (im)possibilities of critical care in an assimilationist school context. *Journal of Praxis in Multicultural Education, 6*(1), 49–60.

Ravitch, D. (2011). *The death and life of the great American school system: How testing and choice are undermining education.* New York, NY: Basic Books.

Rolón-Dow, R. (2005). Critical care: A color(full) analysis of care narratives in the schooling experiences of Puerto Rican girls. *American Educational Research Journal, 4*(1), 77–111.

Smith, V. G. (1997). The effects of caring on the achievement of African American males: Case studies. *Challenge: A Journal of Research on African American Men, 8*(1), 1–15.

Solórzano, D., Ceja, M., & Yosso, T. J. (2000). Critical race theory, racial microaggressions, and campus racial climate: The experiences of African American college students. *The Journal of Negro Education, 69*(1/2), 60–73.

Solórzano, D., & Villalpando, O. (1998). Critical race theory, marginality, and the experience of minority students in higher education. In C. Torres & T. Mitchell (Eds.), *Emerging issues in the sociology of education: Comparative perspectives* (pp. 211–224). Albany, NY: SUNY Press.

Tillman, L. (2004). (Un)intended consequences? The impact of the *Brown v. Board of Education* decision on the employment status of Black educators. *Education and Urban Society, 36*(3), 280–303.

Togut, T. D. (2011). The gestalt of the school-to-prison pipeline: The duality of overrepresentation of minorities in special education and racial disparity in school discipline on minorities. *American University Journal of Gender Social Policy and Law, 20*(1), 163–181.

Villalpando, O. (2002). The impact of diversity and multiculturalism on all students: Findings from a national study. *Journal of Student Affairs, Research, and Practice, 40*(1), 124–144.

Villalpando, O. (2004). Practical considerations of critical race theory and Latino critical theory for Latino college students. *New Directions for Student Services, 2004*(105), 41–50.

Whiting, G. W. (2006). From at risk to at promise: Developing scholar identities among Black males. *Journal of Advanced Academics, 17*(4), 222–229.

Wilson, A. V., & Seagall, W. E. (2001). *Oh, do I remember! Experiences of teachers during the desegregation of Austin's schools.* Albany, NY: SUNY Press.

Yosso, T. J., Smith, W. A., Ceja, M., & Solórzano, D. G. (2009). Critical race theory, racial microaggressions, and campus racial climate for Latina/o undergraduates. *Harvard Educational Review, 79*(4), 659–691.

Young, M. D., & Brooks, J. (2011). Supporting graduate students of color in educational administration preparation programs: Faculty perspectives on best practices, possibilities, and problems. *Educational Administration Quarterly, 44*(3), 391–423.

Young, M. D., Petersen, G. J., & Short, P. M. (2002). The complexity of substantive reform: A call for interdependence among key stakeholders. *Educational Administration Quarterly, 38*(2), 137–175.

PART TWO

Black Masculine Caring

In Fatherhood, and Spirituality, and Historical Traditions

CHAPTER SIX

Black Fathers AS Curriculum

Adopting Sons and Advancing Progressive-Regressive Black Masculinity

TY-RON M. O. DOUGLAS

INTRODUCTION

This chapter presents an adoption model for Black males that is historically and culturally sensitive to the unique dynamics of Black masculinity. To inform the theoretical framework of this curriculum plan, elements of Henderson and Hawthorne's (2000) "Eclectic Problem Solving" approach; Dantley's (2005) theoretical proposal for a more hopeful, spiritually grounded curriculum for African American children; and Kincheloe and Steinberg's (1993) discussion of post-formal thinking are incorporated. Moreover, these paradigms are undergirded by a historical contextualization that includes Watkin's (1993) analysis of "Black Curriculum Orientations," as well as a critique of Mutua's (2006) notions regarding progressive Black masculinities.

Together, these dynamics serve as the springboard for the specific "snapshots" that will allow the reader to peer into the essential roles that Black men play as both fathers and educators. In this light, the term *educator* is broadly defined to include and overlap with fathering. As such, the curriculum plan proposed herein transcends the boundaries of traditional schooling, even as it simultaneously provides a historically and culturally grounded call for more Black male educators to adopt "our sons" both inside and outside of the schoolhouse. It should be noted, however, that this work does not mean to suggest generalizability, since every family and father is different. In fact, as Eisner (2002) suggested, the ideas and plans offered should be seen as tools rather than as a blueprint; still, curricular lessons certainly can be gleaned from the intersections between theory and my own experiences as an educator and adoptive father.

Walker and Soltis's (1997) discussion of knowledge is particularly relevant to this project:

> Knowledge can … be used applicatively, that is, called to mind for use in solving a problem and not just as an answer to a question (replication) or in connection with other things (association). The applicative use of knowledge is aptly demonstrated in the work of the engineer. The engineer uses special knowledge and skills in solving novel problems. (p. 41)

In a very real sense, then, I serve as a sort of curriculum—not because my experiences allow me to essentialize the boundless parameters of Black masculinity or fathering, but because critical reflection on my own epistemological underpinnings, coupled with a consideration of the implications of post-formalist thinking, revealed "patterns" that have striking implications for other Black males (Douglas, 2012a; Kincheloe & Steinberg, 1993). Walker and Soltis (1997) note:

> Applying knowledge requires seeing the connection between what one knows and what one wants to achieve. It is far easier to replicate and associate knowledge than it is to apply it. Application requires a degree of creativity and flexibility, as well as considerable intelligence. (p. 41)

While the focus herein is on masculinity and the specific roles of Black fathers as educators, the purpose is not to ostracize other positional identities. Still, the constraints of time and space were not the only factors in my decision to use the lens of Black masculinity for this analysis and curriculum plan. Certainly, my own identity and the well-documented, systematic challenges that many Black males face have had their influence on the trajectory of this work (Douglas, 2012a, 2012b; Douglas & Gause, 2009; Douglas & Peck, 2013; Ferguson, 2001). To see and understand the connection between what I know and what I want to achieve as a Black male academician has been a difficult process that continues to demand introspection, honesty, and the dismantling of my insatiable desire to be "normal" (Britzman, 1998; Walker & Soltis, 1997). Thus, this curriculum plan is not an end in itself, but merely the beginning of a larger project that will articulate a holistic approach to the adoption of our sons—both inside and outside of the schoolhouse. Not only do I challenge the very notion of normality itself, but I also officially reject efforts to be "normal" by sharing elements of my "abnormal" and wonderful experiences as a Black male educator and adoptive father of a teenage son.

To further assist in navigating this curriculum plan, there are a few other underlying tenets that should be expressed explicitly. First, there is a need to extend the narrow parameters of what many define as Black families, Black culture, Black history, and Black masculinity. For example, any classroom or schoolhouse that contains Black people (teachers and/or students) should be considered an extension of the Black family, and the implications of this claim are elucidated through a discussion of (1) how Black students have been positioned as systematic orphans, and (2) the roles of Black male educators as surrogate and adoptive fathers. Furthermore, there is transformational power in using a historically grounded, hopeful approach to Black masculinity partnered with the affirmation, inclusion, and retooling of Black men in various pedagogical spaces.

HISTORICAL AND THEORETICAL FRAMEWORK

Arguably, many Black families need a new vision of what it means to be both Black and educated in America. Beyond the "Black scholars [who] tend to be mere academicians, narrowly confined to specialized disciplines with little sense of the broader life of the mind and hardly any engagement with battles in the streets" (West, 1993, p. 40), there is a pervasive spirit of anti-intellectualism and educational apathy among many Black youth, and particularly Black males, that extinguishes academic dreams and drains Black communities of the next generation of critical agents (Douglas, 2012b). Far too many Black students are marginalized by schools that continue to ignore Black culture and history, while inequitably funded educational systems continue to offer little promise of future fiscal advancement for Black students (Delpit, 2006; Gause, 2008; Howard, 2000, 2010). Similarly, many Black male students find themselves victimized by a shortsighted understanding of Blackness and masculinity, which has been shaped, in no small part, by the media's poisonous and parasitic messages regarding Black masculinity (Douglas, 2012b; Howard, 2013). Gause (2008) asserts:

> Masculinities are not expressed in isolation, but are influenced, informed, and shaped by school culture. The continued assault of popular culture on school culture and family culture is increasingly affecting how Black males mediate their gendered identities. ... Schools sort children along racial, social class, and gender lines, and this contributes to inequalities in educational and occupational outcomes. (p. 9)

Dantley (2005) echoes these sentiments by noting that "what happens in any schoolhouse is inextricably linked to what is going on in the local and wider community" (p. 653). Hence, Black educators must redefine the culture of education for Black youth through a self-determined reevaluation and reintroduction of what it means to be both African and American. Similarly, in order to combat the debilitating effects of media consumption, Black educators, including Black parents and fathers, must lead the charge in arming Black students with the shield of media literacy and the sword of a healthy self-image (Howard, 2000). Notably, a healthy self-image should include an understanding of the joy of being Black and the necessity of spirituality, which "is the core of who we are ... [and] connects our lives to meaning and purpose" (Dantley, 2005, p. 654). Ultimately, this ideological renaissance will require some retooling of Black male educators in the contexts of home, school, and community.

KEY IDEAS

There are a number of key ideas that require further explanation before continuing with the rest of this chapter. One such term is *culture*, which can be defined as "the totality of thought and practice by which a people creates itself, celebrates, sustains, and develops itself, and introduces itself to history and humanity" (Karenga & Karenga, 2007, p. 11). Defining culture in this way provides a vital context for this analysis because it elucidates the interconnectedness between culture and agency for Black families in general, and Black males in particular. Karenga and Karenga (2007) further posit:

> the key crisis and challenge in Black life is the cultural one, and thus it is imperative that we recover, reconstruct, and bring forth the best of our culture and use it to free ourselves from internal and external constraints and oppression and to enrich and expand our lives in the most meaningful and effective of ways. (p. 10)

Such a definition of culture is apropos because it encompasses more than traits, customs, and activities, and places vital emphasis on the establishment of identity and the agency to communicate that identity to others. Historically, it should be noted that Black people were not given the opportunity to "introduce" themselves to America since they were introduced to the country under the oppressive regime of slavery (Watkins, 1993). Concomitantly, because the master script on the history of African Americans rarely transcends the borders of the United States to appreciate our Africa-ness, many people wrongly assume that Black culture is limited to the vile system that brought us here. Watkins (1993) asserts that the "culture of poverty hypothesis ... suggests that Blacks are culturally deficient. The notion of Black pathology prescribes the construction of a culture to which Blacks adapt. ... Black education has evolved as a function of the sub-culture status of its people" (p. 323). Sadly, many Black people have embraced such a jaded perspective because they do not understand that we introduced ourselves to "history and humanity" (Karenga & Karenga, 2007, p. 11) in Africa. Additionally, Black children in America have been treated like systematic orphans in public schools, due in no small part to the fact that public schools were created to educate middle- and upper-class White boys exclusively, with little regard for people of color or for girls. Undoubtedly, then, "Black curriculum development is inextricably tied to Black America's experience of slavery and oppression in the United States"

(Watkins, 1993, p. 321). Like Black people's introduction to America, Black students were introduced to the public school as unwanted and unwelcomed intruders. Sadly, Black youth continue to be harmed by the idea that their culture and history began in subjugation.

REFRAMING THE PAST AND REAFFIRMING PURPOSE THROUGH CURRICULAR EMBODIMENT

To address these historical and cultural biases, there is a clear need for broader conceptualizations of curriculum and what we consider as *texts*. Curricula and texts are everywhere: for example, commercials, culture, and fathers all have curricular and textual identities (Douglas & Peck, 2013). Joseph (2000) connects these various texts in a manner that reframes the presentation of history and demands a reevaluation of the dominant discourses on Black masculinity. He opines:

> Conceiving curriculum as text or discourse compels us to listen to and make sense of the words, phrases, and patterns of language that characterize curriculum and to be aware of how this language itself shapes curriculum. We are encouraged to consider not only the ways that people talk about curriculum, but to seek understanding of its inherent themes and structures. (Joseph, 2000, p. 5)

There is a reciprocity, then, in the curriculum-forming process wherein personal embodiment and concocted or contrived identities, personal and community, encroach upon each other. In a very real sense, curriculum systematizes models that individuals emulate and institutions frame and promote for others. The potency of this reality becomes even more apparent when we consider how Black males have been historically framed.

The masterscript on Black men has been crafted and reinforced since our arrival in chains on the shores of America. Documents and deficit doctrines like Daniel Moynihan's (1965) report on the Black family, *The Negro Family: The Case for National Action*, have served as vehicles for establishing and maintaining Black male stereotypes of abortment, apathy, and abuse (Dodson, 2007)—a very dangerous curriculum. The pathologizing and systematic regulation of Black men and women have exacerbated the transition of Black people from chattel to citizens. Yet, it is the dominant views about Black men that prove particularly problematic and persistent. Unlike the Black woman who, in spite of her horrific experiences at the hands of systematic oppression, is believed to have maintained her parental instincts, the Black man's instinctual capacities have been misappropriated and his intentions misunderstood; he must not only overcome the dominant ideology that the paternal instincts of men are void of the capacity to nurture, but he must also prove that his instincts as a Black man are not animalistic, anarchic, and anti-intellectual, as is often portrayed. The paradox becomes embarrassingly explicit when we compare Black male stereotypes of abortment, apathy, and abuse with Brown and Davis's (2000) description of the verb *mother*, which they define as "to give life to, to nurture and protect, and/or assist in the development of a person" (p. 4). In schools, these dominant ideologies about Black people and, in particular, Black men, go largely unchallenged (Howard, 2000).

One explanation for the mistaken representations of Blacks is in faulty education. Students are taught about the institution and legacy of slavery in America from a deficit-based lens that detaches the lived realities of Black people today from the generational residue of systematic oppression. African American students are often forced to piece together personal and national identities through historical lessons that begin with their people in chains and bonds (Watkins, 1993). Students are rarely challenged to consider what it means to be both African and American—for if they did, the rich history of a resilient people would provide a counternarrative to the discourses of textbooks and instructors that usually reflect the identity or ideology of the dominant White power structure. Sudarkasa's (2007) discussion of the intersections between the diverse history of Black families, the understanding of culture, and the implications for today is especially telling. She states:

> Just as surely as Black American family patterns are in part an outgrowth of the descent into slavery, so too are they partly a reflection of the archetypical African institutions and values that informed and influenced the behavior of those Africans who were enslaved in America. With respect to "class" and "culture," it is indeed the case that the variations in historical and contemporary Black family patterns cannot be explained without reference to the socioeconomic contexts in which they developed. But neither can they be explained without reference to the cultural contexts from which they derived. (Sudarkasa, 2007, pp. 29–30)

Notably, the absence of educators who challenge a defeatist reading of slavery is one way that the system of slavery continues to function, since "many if not most scholars working on African American families have argued or assumed that African family heritage was all but obliterated by the institution of slavery" (Sudarkasa, 2007, p. 31). For Black students, then, self-definition becomes highly problematic without the tangible intervention of thoughtful educators who recognize and challenge existing deficit doctrines (Howard, 2000). However, Black educators and fathers can provide alternative perspectives through their words, deeds, and actions.

The danger of Moynihan's (1965) report and similar deficit-based literature is not just the role it has played in maintaining institutionalized inferiority for Black people and privilege for White people. It also skews the perceptions and realities of gender roles while creating wedges between Black men and Black women and feminists. Angela Davis (1981) addresses the damaging legacy of Moynihan's text:

The root of oppression was described [in the report] as a "tangle of pathology" created by the absence of male authority among Black people! The controversial finale of the Moynihan report was to introduce male authority (meaning male supremacy of course!) into the Black family and the community at large. (p. 13)

Davis goes on to note the fact that more progressive thinkers than Moynihan held equally deleterious views of Black people, pointing specifically to sociologist Lee Rainwater's 1966 article, "Crucible of Identity: The Negro Lower-Class Family." In it, Rainwater expressed disagreement with many of Moynihan's ideas and even encouraged civil rights activism, yet he still presented a wholly injurious view of the social importance and familial roles of Black men in suggesting that slavery had destroyed the Black family unit and left a "mother-centered family with its emphasis on the primacy of the mother-child relation and only tenuous ties to a man" (as cited in Davis, 1981, p. 13).

Notably, the debilitating and debatable conclusions put forth by Moynihan and Rainwater articulate a breach between Black men and Black families. Still, it is Moynihan's supposition that is most relevant to the current discussion because it demonstrates how the intentions and actions of Black men can be inaccurately framed by others based on a White supremacist paradigm (Watkins, 1993). Davis's (1981) sarcastically toned statement that male authority is equivalent to male supremacy reveals how the oppression of Blacks by White male patriarchy created distrust in not only White men, but indeed in all men. Dynamics like these have further complicated Black male identity formation and necessitate an intentional, holistic curricular approach to better equipping Black fathers and sons. Moreover, we must ask, as Connelly and Clandinin (1988) asked about learners, "what assumptions are held about [Black males/fathers]—how they learn and what they need to learn? What expectations are made about the role of [Black males/fathers]? Who should have power over curriculum making?" (as cited in Joseph, 2000, p. 7). In the next section, I address Mutua's (2006) notion of "progressive Black masculinities" in order to further exhibit how even well-intentioned allies have framed Black masculinities problematically.

CRITIQUING PROGRESSIVE BLACK MASCULINITIES

In many ways, Mutua's (2006) vision for "progressive Black masculinities" is rooted in a similar distrust and a deficit-based analysis of Black masculinity. Her discussions of "ideal masculinity as domination" (Mutua, 2006, p. 16) position African American men exclusively within an American context. Like most school lessons on Black history, her analysis only goes back as far as Africans in America (Watkins, 1993) and provides no acknowledgment of what ideal Black masculinity might have actually looked like before these men were subjected to American slavery and capitalism. In fact, Mutua (2006) states, "Domination over others is one of the central understandings and practices of masculinity. Stated differently, normative masculinity is predicated on the domination of others" (p. 17). By couching masculinity within the capitalistic trappings of the American economy and American history, she presents Black masculinity through the same deficit lens that has been used since the early days of slavery. If Black men are to define ourselves for ourselves, any discussions of what makes up "ideal masculinity" must, at the very least, acknowledge that masculinity may have been quite different when we were in a more self-defined space. Moreover, it is important to note that the history of Black men in Africa suggests that egalitarian family relationships and fluid gender roles were common (Sudarkasa, 2007). Similarly, communal responsibility, respect, and love for wives, mothers, and children characterized African family interactions. Sudarkasa (2007) explains:

> Separate rather than joint decision making was common [in Africa]. In fact, husbands and wives normally had distinct purviews and responsibilities within the conjugal family. … Even though husbands typically had "ultimate" authority over wives in various matters, authority did not extend to control over their wives' properties. Moreover, even though women were subordinate in their roles as wife, as mother, and sister, they wielded considerable authority, power, and influence. This distinction in the power attached to female roles is symbolized by the fact that in the same society where a wife knelt before her husband, sons prostrated before their mothers, and seniority was determined by age rather than gender-governed relationships among siblings. (p. 35)

In the context of African culture, then, a powerful counternarrative is revealed. Domination and distrust did not appear to be underlying ideals for African society, even as notions of authority and decision making played a role in family interactions. Acknowledging this reality is just as important as the recognition that Black history did not begin with slavery in America. Arguably, Black culture would benefit from Black men and boys being taught that there is something worth retrieving and holding on to from their history, particularly as it relates to family dynamics. Black male educators as fathers can play an important role in that process.

THE VISION

Henderson and Hawthorne's (2000) model for practicing what they term "eclectic problem solving" reveals that accountability on an individual level is merely the starting point of systematic reformation and the retooling of Black fathers. They suggest:

> Would-be transformative curriculum leaders understand the systemic nature of successful reform. They know that even though reform movements can begin with isolated pockets

of interested individuals, they cannot spread or have a positive impact without penetrating into the multiple layers and departments of the organization. (Henderson & Hawthorne, 2000, p. 187)

Based on this assertion, it seems that considering *progressive-regressive* Black masculinities rather than merely *progressive* Black masculinities would be appropriate; this would mean equipping Black males to look to their African roots for a model of Black masculinity that has not been defined and dictated by the American masculine ideal. In essence, such an approach would provide a new-old vision of what it means to be and become a Black man based on a cultural legacy beyond that of slavery (Watkins, 1993). While many Black men already embrace and embody such an ideological approach, systemic reformation demands that we acknowledge and address the fact that a number of Black fathers do not (Henderson & Hawthorne, 2000). Thus, *progressive-regressive Black masculinities* should encourage Black fathers to reevaluate their curricular embodiments and invite Black men to become surrogate and adoptive fathers through their work as educators in the families of the home, the schoolhouse, and beyond.

THE CURRICULAR DESIGN

Theoretical Foundations

Kincheloe and Steinberg's (1993) discussion of post-formal thinking is the hub of the curricular design proposed herein, particularly their emphasis on "the importance of producing one's own knowledge [and] patterns—understanding the connections and systems that construct perception, alienation, privilege, success, and life-meaning" (Villaverde, 2010). These two tenets—evaluating knowledge production and exploring patterns—dovetail with Joseph's (2000) conceptualization of "curriculum as text" (p. 5) and Henderson and Hawthorne's (2000) vision for "systemic reformers" (pp. 187–188). Thus, the following section includes elements of my story as the adoptive father of my oldest son, Jalen, or "Jay" as I call him, because, as Henderson and Hawthorne (2000) maintain, systemic reformers must be honest and straightforward. Admittedly, though, doing so is not easy.

Daddy-O as Curriculum

To this point, I have kept details of my family and its dynamics separate from my academic relationships and work. Believing that my family is who and what I determine, and frankly no one else's concern, I have ignored the comments of nosy and seemingly dumbfounded individuals who have tried to calculate how I could have a twenty-two-year-old son, and I have challenged those who had the gumption to ask if he was my "real" son. In fact, some of the most disturbing and ridiculous comments have come from people in the academy. Often, these individuals have been scholars who espouse notions of social justice and advocacy in their rhetoric and writing, but see no problem questioning my age and parental circumstances with comments like "How is that possible?" or "You will be a grandfather soon." While many of these comments have come from new scholarly acquaintances I met at academic conferences, some have also come from more familiar colleagues at various institutions. Even more disturbing is the fact that too few of these commenters have ventured past their puzzlement over the nature of our relationship to find out that my son is a healthy, happy college student studying communications. I was particularly appalled by one senior scholar who, after giving a keynote on Black males and engaging in discourse about the troubling case of Trayvon Martin, quipped, "How do you have a son that old?" Although my son and I had stayed behind to thank him for and discuss his lecture, I was disheartened by the scholar's focus on my son's age and failure to acknowledge Jalen's interest in hearing his presentation.

That said, and our differing last names aside, Jalen is my *real* son and I am his *real* dad, or "Daddy-O" as he affectionately calls me. Jalen tragically lost his father to cancer at the tender age of nine, so I am the only dad he has; my wife was previously married to Jalen's father and cared for him until his untimely passing. I never desired to have Jalen's last name changed because I have always respected his identity and history. I had also cared for his father and wanted Jalen's life and legacy to remain forever connected to him, something a good dad can do when he is secure and views the child as his regardless of particulars.

Tangentially, the (re)naming process in which Jalen did engage as part of my role in his life was significant. While his surname remained the same, we welcomed the idea of giving me a new name—he chose "Daddy-O"—that pointed to the evolution of our relationship and showed respect for my newfound role in his life. The self-determination he demonstrated in articulating my new title once his mother and I married parallels Joseph's (2000) discussion of language, culture, and norms:

> Each discourse contains particular language, patterns of thoughts, and norms about what is appropriate and valuable. Curriculum as text illustrates the continual dialogue of culture—the conversations and themes that are important to people who "live" in the culture or who portray it. (p. 5)

By embracing a title he deemed appropriate for my *curricular* role in his life, then, Jalen determined his own norm. Harkening back to Kincheloe and Steinberg (1993), my relationship with Jalen has helped me to explore deep structures like Black masculinity, tacit forces like societal norms, and hidden assumptions regarding the supposed ingredients of a "real" family. Not surprisingly, I have often felt the tension created by my family's unnamed and unconventional embodiment of difference (Davis, Sumara, & Luce-Kapler, 2008), and observed the perplexity of people we meet as they try to figure us out. I do not try to understand others' confusion, nor do I offer footnotes explaining my wife and sons, because to do so would be to perpetuate the belief that our family does not fit the societal norm, regardless of how government and culture try to hierarchize parental relationships to fit a standard. Even more, I am intentional about challenging stereotypical assumptions about if and how Black fathers care for their children. Ultimately, I have determined that I will not allow my relationship with my oldest son to be described with an asterisk, as if I am not his "real" dad or he is not my "real" son. I acknowledge that, in some regards, putting these feelings in writing may be a bit of a compromise, but the process is necessary; naming our reality is an integral part of self-determination and self-advocacy, and not an abdication of legitimacy to dominant ideologies of normalcy (Davis et al., 2008). Plus, my personal experiences as an adoptive father serve as the backdrop for much of my research, as well as the impetus for my teaching and capacity to *radically love* students (Douglas & Nganga, 2015) and the inspiration for lessons that other Black males can utilize. Thus, I hereby name it and, in so doing, push past one of my own limits (Britzman, 1998)—not because it is anyone's business or for purgative effect, but because my mission as an educational engineer requires it. Through my honesty and authenticity, I believe that a necessary brand of Black masculine caring can be articulated and trust can be established as other men connect to my experiences and the lesson plans I offer in the next section.

THE PLAN

Preparing for the Relationship

Jalen and I both agree that we have a unique and special relationship. The adoption of male teenagers, according to the social worker who conducted the adoption observation, is about as rare as the relationship we enjoy. So, in preparing for this project, I asked Jalen to share the factors that he felt accounted for my smooth transition into his life. His list included the development of trust, our common interests, such as in sports, and the fact that he feels I am a "cool" person; he also cited my wedding to his mother as a fun, memorable, and special occasion. While my list was a lot longer than my son's, I chose to focus on the overlap between them as four key moments or experiences.

Overarching Principles and Requirements

As mentioned previously, every father-son relationship is different. Still, these general principles and resources are integral parts of my adoption model, and other Black fathers may find it useful as they embrace their role as a kind of parental curriculum. Following are elements that help define a Black man or father as curriculum:

Needed resources

Commitment to the young man and the family is critical for a successful adoption. For us, prayer and personal faith and spirituality have been integral and essential at every stage of the adoptive experience and our lives.

Duration or time

It is important to realize that a man never stops being a father; it is a twenty-four-hours-a-day, seven-days-a-week responsibility. While the father's role may change, as will the needs of the son, fathering is a lifelong commitment.

Learning experiences and events

Respecting the child's history is critical to the development of a future relationship as the adoptive dad. At the same time, creating and capturing new memories is as essential as allowing the adopted son to reflect on old memories. Celebrate occasions together, but also be flexible to the need to amalgamate traditions based on personal histories. More details will be given on this in the specific snapshot that follows, but as Eisner (2002) noted, "All educational programs [including building trust in an adoptive father-son relationship] occur over time" (p. 141).

Sequence

Adopting and fathering are fluid processes. Establishing trust, making connections, building a relationship, establishing new responsibilities, and determining joint expectations, as well as consistency, routines, and goal-setting are all key elements during the transition to becoming a family.

Space

Fathers must play a role in establishing a son's space, making sure he is secure, safe, and as comfortable as possible, and communicating in words and actions that the child's best interest is the priority.

Support

In addition to support within the immediate family, a supportive extended family—"the village"—that embraces the young man and lets him know that he is part of the family is very helpful. Generally, extended families that are not confined by societal definitions of "normalcy" will be better at this than others.

Reflections

Taking time to reflect on your experiences and role as a father is helpful in identifying and improving weaknesses and building on strengths. Moreover, admitting mistakes is one of the most powerful pedagogical acts in which a father or parent can engage.

References

The following list contains selected authors and titles that can serve as resources for Black fathers. However, it is not intended to be exhaustive and does not include research texts formally cited throughout the chapter.

- *Along the Road to Manhood*, by Stu Weber
- *Bad Boys: Public Schools in the Making of Black Masculinity*, by Ann A. Ferguson
- *Bringing Up Boys*, by James Dobson
- *Building Character in a Mentoring Relationship*, by Howard & William Hendricks
- *Child Guidance*, by E. G. White
- *Dreams of My Father*, by Barack Obama
- *From the Hood to the Hill: A Story of Overcoming*, by Barry C. Black
- *Gifted Hands*, by Ben Carson
- *Healing the Masculine Soul*, by Gordon Dalbey
- *He-Motions*, by T. D. Jakes
- *Loose That Man and Let Him Go*, by T. D. Jakes
- *The Resolution for Men*, by Stephen Kendrick, Randy Alcorn, & Alex Kendrick
- *Think Big*, by Ben Carson
- *Twelve Shades of Man: Testimonies and Transitions to Manhood*, edited by Eric Thomas & Jeremy Anderson

SOME SNAPSHOTS OF SPECIAL MOMENTS

Snapshot One—The Wedding Day

Purpose

In order to become one family; on the wedding day, an adoptive father also *marries* the son.

Preparation

Unlike a nine-month pregnancy, adoptive fathers often become *official* parents overnight. To facilitate a successful father-son relationship, dialogue between the adoptive father and son is critical prior to this day. Additionally, the son must be assured that he is important and special; he should not be made to feel like an appendage.

Process/Procedure

Maintain open and honest communication. Include your son in the wedding plans and, if possible, in the actual ceremony.

Pointers/Pitfalls

Be flexible and sensitive to the nuances of your specific situation. For example, consider the potential influences of the child's biological father and family. Is his biological father alive, active in his life, or absent for another reason? Based on these dynamics, determine appropriate ways to help your new son process the fact that he is gaining another dad/father figure.

It is also critical to communicate that you cannot and will not try to replace his father; instead, communicate that he is gaining family rather than being required to relinquish the family he already has.

Ponderings

Adoptive fathers are educators who embody progressive-regressive masculinity and consciously accept and advocate for the inclusion of the totality of the child's identity, culture, and history. For help, utilize other resources in your community, such as school counselors, community leaders, and faith groups.

Practical example

Our wedding day happened to fall on Father's Day. On the morning of the wedding, Jalen and I took flowers to his father's grave. Together, we decided to pick three flowers as we journeyed to the graveyard: one flower for his father, one flower for Jalen, and one flower for me. This gesture symbolized that I was embracing him and his mother, who was to be my new wife, as individuals and as a family unit. Jalen also participated in walking his mom down the aisle, along with my wife's father, my father-in-law.

Snapshot Two—Establishing Our New Home Together

Purpose

As a new family, it is important to create a space that respects the communal and personal needs of each family member.

Preparation

Within your means and resources, try to ensure that your adopted son has a safe, secure, and (if possible) comfortable place to live/sleep.

Process/Procedure

Try to make appropriate living arrangements prior to the wedding, and collaboratively determine expectations. Communicate clearly and openly, and show patience as everyone adjusts to the new environment. Make adjustments as necessary to ensure everyone is happy.

Pointers/Pitfalls

Your son should not be made to feel like an afterthought by the lack of preparation given to his living environment. Demonstrate that he is important by the care you give to his space, his needs, and his perspective on the transition.

Ponderings

Adoptive fathers/educators who embody progressive-regressive masculinity try to ensure that their sons occupy comfortable living and learning environments. Contrary to deficit literature, Black men have historically taken care of their families. Thus, as curriculum, today's adoptive fathers should do the same.

Practical example

Upon our return from our honeymoon, I had to repair Jalen's futon bed. Although there were three of us living in a small one-bedroom apartment at the time, Jalen was made to feel important by the care given to his space, which was the living room. That night, I could see the admiration in his eyes as I secured nails and a concrete block to support the broken wood frame. We eventually replaced the futon and later moved so that he could have his own room, but the powerful effect of the care he saw me give to ensure the comfort of his initial sleeping quarters cannot be understated. That night, I solidified my position as Daddy-O.

Snapshot Three—The Birth of a Sibling

Purpose

When a new member is added to the family, it is crucial for the family to welcome that new person without destabilizing the security of your adopted son.

Preparation

Your adopted son must be assured that he will not be replaced by the new child or loved any less because of the new addition to the family. Hence, allow your adopted son to participate in the preparation process, such as selecting a name, picking out of furniture, and setting up the baby's room or space.

Process/Procedure

Communication is vital. Share relevant and new information with him as early as possible. For example, if the adopted child is old enough, let him attend a doctor's appointment or ultrasound session prior to the birth, and encourage him to participate on the day of the baby's birth as much as possible.

Pointers/Pitfalls

Avoid harmful comparisons between the new child and the adopted son.

Ponderings

Adoptive fathers/educators who embody progressive-regressive masculinity recognize the potential for and value of mentorship for the adopted son and the new baby. Thus, the adoptive fathers/educators nurture these relationships and capitalize on teachable moments that will arise through their lived experiences.

Practical example

Jalen participated in every stage of the preparation process for his little brother. We painted the baby's room, set up the crib together, and discussed possible baby names. Although my wife and I concealed the gender of our new baby from everyone, we promised Jalen that he would be the first person to know. Soon after my wife and I celebrated the arrival of our youngest son, I whispered "it's a boy" in Jalen's ear before even telling my mother, who was in the waiting room, thus fulfilling our promise to him. Jalen was hoping for a brother, and he was even more excited when we told him his baby brother's name would be Essien, because Essien is the name of one of the star players of Jalen's favorite soccer team, Chelsea.

Jalen and Essien have enjoyed an extremely close relationship. Even more, Jalen consistently demonstrates care for his brother, as he exhibited recently by holding hands with him as they walked together on Essien's fifth birthday. Jalen also nurtures and educates Essien by sharing elements of his college experience with him.

Snapshot Four—The First Black President

Purpose

It is important for a new family to experience history together, especially events that highlight Black history and the accomplishments of people of color.

Preparation

Stay abreast of current events and encourage your son daily to do the same. Discuss significant events during family meals and secure a regular and safe space for family dialogue; work to minimize distractions during family discussions, such as by turning off the television during dinner.

Process/Procedure

Use media, news broadcasts, the Internet, and other resources to encourage and tap into shared interests. Find ways to connect your son's interests to larger lessons and learning opportunities. Make arrangements for father-son field trips whenever possible.

Pointers/Pitfalls

Do not focus on the size or significance of the event or shared moment. For the benefit of family bonding, it does not have to be a big event. In fact, simple events suffice, such as Black History Month lectures or activities on university campuses, or even just a visit to the library together.

Ponderings

An adoptive father/educator who embodies progressive-regressive masculinity recognizes that in order to reshape and retool the next generation of Black males, he must be the curriculum he wants his son to emulate. Adding to that curriculum, it is wise to utilize other resources and examples to integrate Black history, Black culture, and current events.

Practical example

Although Jalen and I didn't make it to Washington, D.C., for the inauguration of President Barack Obama, we were able to watch it together and share the experience. Though a school snow day made it easier, in fact, my wife, Bobbie, and I planned to keep him home to watch it in any case, since his school had not made provisions for the students to see the historic event. Jalen and I have attended lectures together given by speakers like Senate Chaplain Barry Black, Reverend

Al Sharpton, and journalist Roland Martin. At each of these events, we purchased books to commemorate the experience and had the authors sign our copies.

CONCLUSION

Contrary to some misguided views and negative portrayals in media, Black men do, in fact, care for their families and their children. It is not my intention to suggest that I am an exception. On the contrary, I come from a line of men who have consistently and without fanfare adopted and educated "other people's children," whether officially or informally. Today, I stand and serve as a *border crossing brotha-scholar* (Douglas, 2013) because my "dad" adopted me as his own and, along with my mother, loved me as I developed a healthy masculine identity. He has been the only dad I have ever really known, and his adopted "dad" did the same thing for him. Caring is what we do as Black men. We fight on, love much, and work hard, and being misunderstood is an unfortunate part of that reality.

Speaking to such contradictions and misunderstandings, the Black family unit has been a resilient and relevant construct for Black people before, during, and after slavery (Billingsley, 1992; Franklin, 2007; Sudarkasa, 2007). If more Black males are taught about the rich reservoir of hope in their history, they can be equipped not only to tap into that hope, but also to consider how they might more actively participate in the adoption process in the family and as educators "adopting" students. Lorde (1984) claims, "if you don't define yourself for yourself, then you will be crushed into other's fantasies of you and eaten alive" (p. 6), and her words are a stark reminder of the power embedded in self-determination and self-actualization. Moreover, as Black men are encouraged to consider the value of progressive-regressive masculinity, they will acquire a more grounded sense of self both within and beyond the context of American education. Black men must retool themselves and reintroduce their culture to education as well as to "history and humanity" (Karenga & Karenga, 2007, p. 11). Thus, biological and adoptive fathers inside and outside the schoolhouse must play a significant role in this process for the sake of our sons, ourselves, and our culture as a whole.

REFERENCES

Billingsley, A. (1992). *Climbing Jacob's ladder: The enduring legacy of African-American families.* New York, NY: Touchstone Books.

Britzman, D. (1998). Is there a queer pedagogy? Or, stop reading straight. In W. F. Pinar (Ed.), *Curriculum: Toward new identities* (pp. 211–231). New York, NY: Garland.

Brown, M. C., & Davis, J. E. (2000). *Black sons to mothers: Compliments, critiques, and challenges for cultural workers in education.* New York, NY: Peter Lang.

Connelly, F. M., & Clandinin, D. J. (1988). *Teachers as curriculum planners: Narratives of experience.* New York, NY: Teachers College Press.

Dantley, M. E. (2005). African American spirituality and Cornell West's notions of prophetic pragmatism: Restructuring educational leadership in American urban schools. *Educational Administration Quarterly, 41*(4), 651–674.

Davis, A. Y. (1981). *Women, race, and class.* New York, NY: Vintage Books.

Davis, B., Sumara, D., & Luce-Kapler, R. (2008). *Engaging minds: Changing teaching in complex times.* Mahwah, NJ: Lawrence Erlbaum.

Delpit, L. (2006). *Other people's children.* New York, NY: The New Press.

Dodson, J. E. (2007). Conceptualizations and research of African American family life in the United States. In H. P. McAdoo (Ed.), *Black families* (4th ed., pp. 51–68). Thousand Oaks, CA: Sage.

Douglas, T. M. O. (2012a). *Border crossing brothas': A study of Black Bermudian masculinity, success, and the role of community-based pedagogical spaces* (Unpublished doctoral dissertation). University of North Carolina at Greensboro.

Douglas, T. M. O. (2012b). Resisting idol worship at HBCUs: The malignity of materialism, Western masculinity, and spiritual malefaction. *The Urban Review, 44*(3), 378–400.

Douglas, T. M. O. (2013). Confessions of a border crossing *brotha-scholar:* Teaching race with all of me. In D. J. Davis & P. Boyer (Eds.), *Social Justice and Racism in the College Classroom: Perspectives from Different Voices* (pp. 55–67). Bingley, England: Emerald Publishing Group Ltd.

Douglas, T. M. O., & Gause, C. P. (2009). Beacons of light in oceans of darkness: Exploring Black Bermudian masculinity. *Learning for Democracy, 3*(2), 85–102.

Douglas, T. M. O., & Nganga, C. (2015). What's radical love got to do with it? Navigating identity, pedagogy, and positionality in pre-service education. *International Journal of Critical Pedagogy, 6*(1), 58–82.

Douglas, T. M. O., & Peck, C. M. (2013). Education by any means necessary: An historical exploration of community-based pedagogical spaces for peoples of African descent. *Educational Studies, 49*(1), 67–91.

Eisner, E. (2002). *The educational imagination: On the design and evaluation of school programs* (3rd ed.). Upper Saddle River, NJ: Merrill/Prentice Hall.

Ferguson, A. A. (2001). *Bad boys: Public schools in the making of Black masculinity.* Ann Arbor: University of Michigan Press.

Franklin, J. H. (2007). African American families: A historical note. In H. P. McAdoo (Ed.), *Black families* (4th ed., pp. 3–6). Thousand Oaks, CA: Sage.

Gause, C. P. (2008). *Integration matters: Navigating identity, culture, and resistance.* New York, NY: Peter Lang.

Henderson, J. G., & Hawthorne, R. D. (2000). *Transformative curriculum leadership* (2nd ed.). Upper Saddle River, NJ: Merrill/Prentice Hall.

Howard, T. C. (2000). Reconceptualizing multicultural education: Design principles for educating African American males. In M. C. Brown II & J. E. Davis (Eds.), *Black sons to mothers: Compliments, critiques, and challenges for cultural workers in education* (pp. 155–172). New York. NY: Peter Lang.

Howard, T. C. (2010). *Why race and culture matters in schools: Closing the achievement gap in America's classrooms.* New York, NY: Teachers College Press.

Howard, T. C. (2013). *Black male(d): Peril and promise in the education of African American males.* New York, NY: Teachers College Press.

Joseph, P. B. (2000). *Culture of curriculum.* Mahwah, NJ: Lawrence Erlbaum.

Karenga, M., & Karenga, T. (2007). The Nguzo Saba and the Black family: Principles and practices of well-being and flourishing. In H. P. McAdoo (Ed.), *Black families* (4th ed., pp. 7–28). Thousand Oaks, CA. Sage.

Kincheloe, J. L., & Steinberg, S. R. (1993). A tentative description of post-formal thinking: The critical confrontation with cognitive theory. *Harvard Educational Review, 63*(3), 296–321.

Lorde, A. G. (1984). *Sister outsider: Essays and speeches.* Freedom, CA: Crossing Press.

Moynihan, D. P. (1965). *The Negro family: The case for national action.* Washington, DC: U.S. Department of Labor.

Mutua, A. D. (Ed.). (2006). *Theorizing progressive Black masculinities.* New York, NY: Routledge.

Sudarkasa, N. (2007). Interpreting the African heritage in African American family organization. In H. P. McAdoo (Ed.), *Black families* (4th ed., pp. 29–48). Thousand Oaks, CA: Sage.

Villaverde, L. E. (2010). *Notes from a lecture on curriculum development.* Archives of the Department of Educational Leadership and Cultural Foundations, University of North Carolina at Greensboro, Greensboro, NC.

Walker, D. F., & Soltis, J. F. (1997). *Curriculum and Aims.* New York, NY: Teachers College Press.

Watkins, W. H. (1993). Black curriculum orientations: A preliminary inquiry. *Harvard Educational Review, 63*(3), 321–338.

West, C. (1993). *Race matters.* Boston, MA: Beacon Press.

CHAPTER SEVEN

African American Men OF Faith Care

The Intersection of Religion, Gender, and the Ethic of Care

PAUL F. BITTING

INTRODUCTION

This chapter addresses an ethical theory regarding how those who care about morality can most sensitively know and evaluate their sense of the ethic of caring. This ethical theory developed out of feminist literature and has challenged the dominant and traditional approaches to ethical thought (Gilligan, 1982). Since our ethical values make up each of our personal constitutions, the work I address here is of considerable importance. Ethical thought is arguably too important to be left to the professional ethicists alone and, since everyone is an ethicist in his or her own fashion, it is critical that all people consider the topic of ethics as it relates to their own lives, behaviors, and perceptions. Still, the ethicist should provide a service to all those whom they can reach, and that service is theory. Without theory, the alternative is fiat and caprice at the level of individuality and the absence of harmony at the cultural level. Life is a series of ethical choices that we must each make on a continual basis—there is no area of deliberate human behavior that lacks an ethical dimension. This is especially true for those who would be leaders in an educational environment, because education is inherently a moral endeavor, as Fenstermacher (1990) noted:

> What makes education a moral endeavor is that it is, quite centrally, human action undertaken in regard to human beings. Thus, matters of what is fair, right, just, and virtuous are

always present. Whenever a teacher asks a student to share something with another student, or decides between combatants in a schoolyard dispute, or sets procedures for who will go first, second, or third and so on, or discusses the welfare of a student with another teacher, moral considerations are present ... education is a profoundly moral activity. (p. 133)

Thus, that decisions in education should give rise to ethical questions is not a matter of contingency but of necessity.

The rationale underlying the ideas in this chapter is the view that no one can genuinely prepare to be a leader in the realm of education without becoming aware of and gaining some mastery in the techniques surrounding the ethical questions embedded in our relationships, decisions, culture, and the human condition overall. Such questions become inescapable beyond a certain level of awareness and reflectiveness in policy studies, administrative theory, curriculum development, learning theory, school law, educational research, or, simply, lived experience. Without exposure to these concepts, our preparation as professionals is incomplete. Ethical values are more basic than the values embedded in these studies, because they address not just what we do or experience as professionals, but also touch on the kind of persons we *are*. Admittedly, it is unfortunate if an educational leader is not gifted and well versed in policy, organizational theory, curriculum development, or school law. But, it is a qualitative leap beyond the merely "unfortunate" if an educational leader is an unjust or unkind person, or if they are a liar, racist, or thief. Here, the failure is at the level of what one is and has to be as a *person*. Confusion at this level is intolerable and often lethal, and thoughtful evaluation is the only alternative to such confusion. Moreover, the absence of evaluation and reflection may generate perplexities in the minds of leaders about matters fundamental for the functioning of people and institutions without providing exposure to responsible ways of addressing them. Animals and beasts operating from instinct are better off, even without reflection, because their instinct imbues them with the wisdom of survival. We as humans have no such advantage. We will neither survive nor flourish by instinct, but only by the activation of our ethical consciousness. Like an animal thrust back into the wild with its instincts disturbed by domestication, we are left neither guidelines nor a responsible way of proceeding. In some ways, those blindly secure in the grips of ethical tradition, the cultural counterpart of instinct, may be more fortunate that those liberated from tradition but with no rational substitute.

Most people who address ethics formally in the discipline of philosophy or theology or who touch upon it in the social sciences underestimate its complexity, so there is a compelling need to address it in full depth and breadth. For too many professional moralists, ethics has been seen as a matter of principle, language, and reason; while it is all of that, it is also much more. Moral understanding can also unfold by way of the exquisite power of creative imagination; through feeling, affectivity, and caring; in mind-forming relationships with various constituencies;

in the special perspectives of comedic or tragic experience; in ways that are unique to the individual; and in ways that bear the mark of the group. Additionally, all of us moral "knowers" have a history and a social matrix, with all of its myths and moods, out of which our thinking grows with more organic continuity and dependency than we are disposed to concede. Anyone attempting to aptly discuss the art or science of moral choice must address all of these areas.

Herein, then, I have attempted to give full vent to the theoretical needs of my subject while attempting not to join those moralists whom Schopenhauer (1915) indicted for rendering unintelligible the simplest relationships of life. I have also attempted to thoroughly address the theoretical challenges of ethics without falling under the shadow of philosopher H. A. Prichard's 1912 lament about the "the comparative remoteness of the discussions of Moral Philosophy from the facts of life" (as cited in Lauritzen, 1992, p. 21). Thus, my discussion of moral theory as care is interlaced with copious examples and applications. There is an obvious mercy in this, since unrelieved theory is, at the least, unkind; but, aside from motives of gentleness, unrelieved theory might easily also be called dishonest. If one is unwilling to illustrate the applicability of a theory to the facts of life, it may be that the theory is itself irrelevant to life. In other words, ethics is about life, and so should be visible when one addresses it. Be advised, however, that my examples may not do justice to the theory, and may reflect my bias more than my method, as human thinking is inherently and fatally fraught with such failures.

In examining ethics, I begin with the theory, the task being first to fix my terms when addressing the intersection among ethics, faith, and gender. I then go on to clarify a possible relationship between the theory and community of faith. Here, I address the question of the extent to which a commitment to religious faith presupposes the theory. As I continue in my pursuit of the relationship of ideas, I then move to a discussion of what it means to be an African American male in a position of leadership in an educational environment with a deep commitment to a faith-based community, and examine how this links to the theory. I conclude by identifying examples of such leaders and allowing their voices to be heard.

THE ETHIC OF CARE

For those of us who have not visited our own fundamental ethical questions—such as how one ought to behave or what kind of person one should be—with careful reflection, the chances are that our approach to such questions will be biased and imperfect. In our zeal to get right to the questions, we often underestimate their complexity. The ethic of care is often viewed as a moral theory to be addressed as an alternative to the dominant moral theories (Held, 2006). Philosophers who acknowledge a basic master plan for human life presupposed in moral criticism of our lives have divided, for the most part, into two broad categories: those who think that the master plan pertains to the constitution of one's self and to worthy life for a human being, and those who think that it provides principles of decision making in terms of what is to be achieved through action. Our focus is on the first group, those who emphasize virtue. For instance, Plato (1992) talked about ethics as concerned with the proper organization and functioning of the soul.

Aristotle spoke of the activity of the soul in accordance with virtue; and the classical Stoics thought of the "good" person as one who understands and accepts reality with tranquility, for they believed that reality, except in the case of human subjectivity, is always the way it ought to be. Similarly, Christians think of the good person as loving and caring, one who is moved and guided by devotion to what is of highest worth, and Kant (1969) thought of the good person as one with good will determined by respect for the moral law. We may call the second group *utilitarians*—those who think that moral appraisals presuppose the imperative to maximize values through the effects of action. Bentham (1948), for example, held that the principle of utility is the principle presupposed by the meaning of our moral terms and by our moral appraisals of our actions. However, the emphasis here is on the first group, on what a person ought to be and the kind of life one ought to live.

An oft-repeated adage among those who work with children in school environments is that, "children don't care what you know, they only want to know that you care." Among the virtue ethicists mentioned above are those with a primary focus on care. The ethic of care, as it relates to education, has been described by Noddings (1992) as the first job of the schools, and other ethicists likewise view the virtue of care as the centerpiece of ethics (Beck, 1994; Gilligan, 1982; Gilligan, Ward, & Taylor, 1988; Held, 2006). Care ethicists hold that ethical decisions arise through caring in a way that is not equal to or better than the way they arise when questions of justice, rules, and principles decide things; in other words, care is not merely another virtue, but it is basic to ethical reflection itself (Shapiro & Stefkovich, 2005).

There are some conceptions of the ethic of care that view it as contrasting with an ethic of justice. Such conceptions require that one must choose between them. According to Held (2006), the ethic of justice focuses on questions of fairness, equality, individual rights, abstract principles, and consistent application of each. Conversely, she maintains that an ethic of care "focuses on attentiveness, trust, responsiveness to need, narrative nuance, and cultivating caring relations" (Held, 2006, p. 15). In the sense that justice protects equality and freedom, care fosters social bonds and aids cooperation. Though Held (2006) makes clear the distinction between justice and care, she also reminds us of the moral importance of both and leads us to explore how they might be combined in a satisfactory morality. We are left, then, with the implication that justice and care should not be separated into different "ethics," but instead should be seen always in tandem with each other (Ruddick, 1995). In addition, the tradition has been to connect justice with reason and care with affection, thereby contrasting reason and affection in ways similar to the contrast between justice and care. Ethical reason is in pursuit of moral values. Values, however, are appreciated affectively as well as intellectually. Thus, ethical reasoning is especially bound up with affectivity as justice is bound up with care. One is not, though, to take from this that ethics is reducible to affectivity or even care. It is, however, infused with the affective response that makes moral inquiry meaningful. A value is a perceived good, and the primary response to value is in its connection to caring. According to Perry (1926), "Value is any object of any interest" (p. 250). If we are interested, it means that we are not just cold, detached, and purely intellectual in our approach—it means we care. All morality, then, is grounded in care, in the foundational moral experience of personal value.

It should be made clear that I am not speaking of the grounding of ethics in care. I am speaking more specifically of how a recognition of the cognitive nature of care can afford a higher level of moral awareness. It is my contention that a systematic account must be taken of the value of awareness that comes to us through that expression of our subjectivity that we call feeling, affection, or care. Educational leaders as ethicists should take this into account as they address particular cases that might arise in their work.

Much influential thinking has been impaled on the horns of the fallacious dilemma, which divorces care from justice, feeling from intelligence, and affectivity from knowledge. It is my contention here that feeling and care form a knowing experience and that extreme mischief has been wrought, especially in ethics, by the failure to recognize this. An example might illustrate the natural appearance of care in its connection to affectivity, reason, and justice. Baggini and Fosl (2007) remind us of Jean Valjean, Victor Hugo's hero in *Les Miserables*, being sent to prison for stealing a loaf of bread to feed his starving sister and her seven children. We are told that Valjean was not a bad man, but believed that the need to care for his poverty-stricken family was more pressing and more valuable than his duty to obey certain fixed moral laws concerning the rightful purchase of commodities. Valjean's decision was not made in the absence of reason or a consideration of justice, but in anticipation of those more recent theorists who have advocated what has come to be called the "ethic of care."

FAITH AND CARE

Ethicists have come to see their discipline as bruised and misunderstood, for it has come to mean everything from etiquette, religion, and law to customs. Pojman (2002) makes the distinction by offering etiquette as a cultural invention while presenting ethics as a discovery. In order to avoid oversimplification, in our distinction we view our study as neither pure art nor pure science. As a way of addressing both the sensitivity embedded in the ethic of care and the methods required of those who seek justice, we view the work of ethics as an art/science that seeks to bring sensitivity and method to the discernment of values within the moral realm. Its artistic dimension is expressed through the recognition that it is in the heart that ethics has its birth. Its science is discerned through demonstrations of coherence, logical consistency, and truthfulness of one's positions, but it is through feelings that we are moved to act. The value of persons can be demonstrated, I argue, through an elaborate proof growing out of a relationship between organic unity as a value theory (Nozick, 1981) and what it means to be a person (Adams, 1975). The foundational moral experience, however, is an affective reaction to such value. Action upon such rationally agreed upon value grows out of its being affectively appreciated. In locating the ethical experience within the realm of affect and care, I must quickly add that I am not among those who offer an emotive theory of value language, which in its purest form maintains that value utterances say nothing but are used to evince or show the feelings or attitudes of the speaker or writer, and to elicit or to incite like feelings or attitudes in one's audience (Hume, 1911). What is born in the heart, then, is to some degree expressible in the language of the mind. Though ethics starts with care, it proceeds to reason. Thus, there is no attempt here to suggest that morality and ethics are just a matter of feeling.

Gilligan's (1982) *In a Different Voice* provided impetus for the development of the ethic of care and for viewing the affective as a way of knowing. To what extent, now, might faith be linked to the affective and, thus, also be seen as a way of knowing? Might the foundational moral experience also be a faith experience? Like much that pertains to the moral realm of general discourse, faith has achieved a bad reputation among many intellectuals. Its status is suspect because it reeks of association with superstition and with anti-scientific and anti-intellectual bias.

To know is to believe. It would serve as a real challenge to one's sense of reason to hear, "I know that 2 + 2 = 4, but I don't believe it." Thus, epistemologists have come to accept belief as a necessary condition of knowing. Audi (1998) considers its connection to perceiving or seeing by asking, "How, then, should we answer the question whether seeing entails believing?" (p. 21). One response offered by Audi (1998) is that, contrary to the common wisdom, seeing is not believing. Believing is knowing what you cannot see or prove, but is still accepted and held with firmness; such knowledge, in ordinary language, is accepted as faith, and has its source in affectivity. The lover accepts such knowledge, even when the insights of the heart cannot be explained nor justified with reasons, and yet calmly believes that these make consummate sense. The faithful are as certain of their beliefs as they are of things that can be seen or proved.

Thomas Aquinas says that faith lends a kind of certitude that is "in the genre of affection" (as cited in Magill, 1961, p. 325). It is knowledge, but it is knowledge that comes from the will and is best described in terms of affectivity. This kind of knowing characterizes the foundational moral experience and fits into a fuller understanding of moral knowledge. The mind seeks meaning. In some areas where meaning is not evident to us intellectually, or when we are not able to grasp it through the use of reason alone, the mind is equipped to find meaning in care and affect. In a sense, our affections can be a divining power that goes further into reality than our reasoning minds can take us. We feel, sense, and care more than we see or explain, and such feeling can be a way of knowing. Knowledge, then, becomes a form of sensitive awareness, and faith is a type of this kind of knowing.

Thus, care and morality are works of faith. Never has there been genuine care and love that was not an adventure in faith. Care, as we have now come to understand it, is a fulfillment of morality. The moral experience discussed here admits the weakness of reason alone. It reflects Hume's (1911) notion of reason always being a slave to the passions. This does not mean that knowledge fails, but that moral knowledge sometimes unfolds in a mystical and contemplative form. At its core, ethics is believing and engaging in what Aristotle calls the contemplative life. It is at the depths of contemplation that we are opened to the mystery embedded within the value of persons. It is here that the impact of persons is felt, and caring begins.

MYTHS OF GENDER AND CARE

The act of knowing is interpretive. The mind is not to be thought of as a camera that records reality or a mirror that reflects things back to us as they are. The mind cannot stand a vacuum of meaning; it must make sense of things. As such, when we are confronted with knowable reality, it is not just simply ingested. To be accepted within our store of knowledge, that which is to be known must be connected to that which is already known. Knowledge, in this sense, is relational; we know truth by relating new knowledge to what we already hold as true. When an object or situation becomes known, it is brought into a community of other knowns (Alston, 1989). What this implies is that the mind values meaning above knowledge. We would rather not know that which appears meaningless, and our hunger for meaning is such that we may project more than is actually there in our search for it. In such cases, the knowledge that results may not as much be an image of what is real as it is an image that we have imposed. Hence, in these cases, we do not discover meaning—we fabricate meaning, and the fabrication is often derived from our history and social setting. These elements act as filters, socially and intrapersonally derived, which stand between us and the nature of things.

Part of the task of ethics in its attempt at knowing the ways of moral understanding is to expose such fabrications.

Defining Myth

Myth is a silent but busy filter. Immediately, then, it is necessary to fix our terms for discussing gender myths in relation to the ethic of care. Words, like people, have many relatives. Ludwig Wittgenstein (1968), one of the leaders of the twentieth-century philosophical revolution, reminded us of this as he argued that philosophers from Socrates to Moore had been mistaken in thinking that a formula could be found that would encompass the different uses of words like *justice* or *knowledge*. Rather, the uses of a word are often related, as Wittgenstein (1968) noted, by forming a kind of "family" united by a complicated network of overlapping and crisscrossing similarities—sometimes overall similarities, sometimes similarities in detail. This is particularly true of the sorts of terms in which ethicists are interested, for they are usually very general terms which have developed a life of their own in a variety of contexts. As we have decided to focus upon *myth* for our particular purpose here, we should clarify in advance its meaning to avoid confusion with the whole family of associations. *Myth*, as used herein, involves "a complex of feelings, attitudes, symbols, memories, and experienced relationships through which reality is filtered and interpreted" (Maguire, 1970, pp. 15–17). The myth springs first from our horror of a vacuum of meaning because, as mentioned earlier, some sense must be made of things, and the myth fulfills that requirement. In addition, the myth is social and historical in its roots. Though we may speak of a private myth developed in the history of one person, this is not part of its common usage. Instead, we normally speak of myth as a phenomenon that is present in the culture and waiting for us to fall under its spell.

The Myth of Gender

Because a man does not get pregnant and cannot nurse a child, men were the more natural candidates to leave the cave and go forth to meet the challenges of the hunt and secure provisions for survival. Growing out of this history, there emerged the cultural myth that a woman is essentially a creature of the home and the child. Cooking, childbearing, and caring for matters of the home became the realities that characterized women. Hence, when a woman is engaged in such contexts, her true being as defined by myth is accurately reflected. Domesticity, then, became women's identifying essence according to this deep-rooted myth.

One of the most significant developments in the attitude of the Western mind toward gender occurred in the first part of the fifth century AD and was related to religious teachings. Contrary to more than four centuries of previous Christian doctrine, Augustine, Bishop of Hippo, held that the Bible's story of Adam and Eve's fall from grace meant that their sins, as the first parents, were transmitted through sexual reproduction to all future humans; because of such "original sin," subsequent humanity was believed to be incapable of exercising free will (Pagels, 1988). Such an interpretation placed a distinct burden on Eve and on women in general. Pagels (1988) succinctly points to the gender ramifications of Augustine's interpretation:

> Although originally created equal with man in regard to her rational soul, woman's formation from Adam's rib established her as the "weaker part of the human couple." Being closely connected with bodily passion, woman, although created to be man's helper, became his temptress and led him into disaster. The Genesis account describes the result: God himself reinforced the husband's authority over his wife, placing divine sanction upon the social, legal, and economic machinery of male domination. (p. 114)

Thus, by dividing humankind into two inherently different kinds of beings, Bishop Augustine encouraged the notion of women being seen as complementary to, but yet different from, men. Women were seen as passionate, nurturing, and caring, suited for the domicile, while men were seen as rational, reserved, and fit for work and public life. Men were to govern, whereas women were to obey. Because of their supposed deficiency in rational capacity and their purportedly unstable emotional nature, women were also subject to the more rational nature of their fathers and then their husbands.

Even centuries later, the gender myth of the Augustinian legacy would influence belief and guide public behavior during the formation of America as a nation. Sons were educated and trained to become productive workers, effective political agents, and independent thinkers, but daughters were prepared for a future as wives and mothers and not as independent, rational beings. As long as the home remained the primary economic unit in society, a girl prepared for her adult roles there, where she was encouraged to emulate her mother and obey her father (Fine & Weis, 1993).

The Myth of Care

The psychology of ethics would be tidier if we could draw a sharp dividing line between care and reason, between the affective and the cognitive. However, such tidiness is suspect and seems clearly wrong. Before there was feminist philosophy, there was the avoidance of the concept of affective knowledge, as evidenced by Kant (trans. 1969), who spoke with little patience of this "alleged special sense, the moral feeling" (section 2). The appeal to moral feeling is "superficial, since those who cannot think expect help from feeling" (Kant, trans. 1969, section 2). Basing morality solely on reason and sharing the view that women were deficient in reason, Kant therefore concluded that women were incapable of being true moral agents (Held, 2006). Thus, with the myth that women operate from the heart and men from the head, ethics has gone forward with a kind of "heartless head" in command.

There would, of course, be the possibility of havoc if, instead, headless hearts were in charge of human affairs, leading with emotion but without reason. Yet, there is also an equivalent capacity for chaos in the potential for cruelty in the heartless head. To solve this dilemma, ethics seeks to align the head and the heart. Using social criticism and ethical theory, the myths embedded within our historical and social understanding of gender disparity are finally being brought to light. Such cultural criticism is the practical side of pure philosophy. Cultural criticism is to philosophy as technology is to science; it is what philosophy, apart from its intrinsic intellectual value, is good for (Adams, 1975). Thus, feminist philosophy has assisted the field greatly by fulfilling an important therapeutic function. Feminist philosophy as a component of a culture with major philosophical issues in its myths and assumptions suffers from a derangement that thwarts the people's efforts to know and understand each other and their proper role in the world.

One of the very practical reasons modern ethics has not sufficiently addressed evaluations of care and affect is that it is difficult to say, in a systematic ethical treatment, just how one goes about applying an ethic of care. However, to speak of moral principles, imperatives, or rules, as Kant does, for instance, is a more manageable task and provides tangible knowledge that one can use in discussing concepts including the relationship of the general will to the particular and the meaning of universalizability. By doing this, one can gain a good understanding of what one might hope to accomplish. But, how, in attempting to analyze the moral import of a situation, can the ethic of care be summoned? Should one escape to a meditation room to assess feelings about the cases at hand, and then bring back a report to contribute to the ongoing hard ethical analyses? Are there men serving as leaders in schools who have themselves defied the myth of headiness in decision making and problem solving by calling on their faith and appealing to an ethic of care? If such men exist, they have come to recognize that sensitivity to the moral dimension of decision making is not achieved only through reasoning or the application of principle; an ethics that only stresses one or some of these is erroneous by partiality. To address the practical side of our inquiry, I was tasked to identify male practitioners and describe their attempts at seeking to develop an awareness of all the ways in which consciousness awakens to the reality of the moral. Specifically, how has feminist philosophy spoken to men? How does care operate in the ethical analysis of a situation? To fully understand the therapeutic contribution offered by feminist philosophy, it is necessary to show its applicability and appropriateness for men as well as for women.

FAITH AND CARE AMONG AFRICAN AMERICAN MEN IN LEADERSHIP POSITIONS IN EDUCATION

There is a story about a philosopher who rose up from his deathbed to announce to his assembled friends, "I have it! I have found the answer!" only to sink back into a coma before sharing it with anyone. Hours later he rose again, this time to ask, "What was the question?" The story is akin to the pressures placed on educational leaders to generate academic results in their schools, often forcing them to solve their problems without asking the appropriate questions. In some ways, such an approach has been the genius of our civilization, but also our pathology. Now, the pathology has begun to overtake the genius, and educators are beginning to sense this everywhere. The way questions are framed and discussed by those who would lead in our schools reflects and helps shape how issues are approached in the world beyond schooling, no matter how otherworldly academic debate may sometimes seem. Bennis (1989), in his insightful and often humorous book, *Why Leaders Can't Lead*, states:

> There are too many predicaments, too many grievances, too many ironies, polarities, dichotomies, dualities, ambivalences, paradoxes, contradictions, confusions, complexities, and messes, and so we naturally incline toward people with answers—without even bothering to wonder what the questions, the real questions are. (p. 112)

Hence, academicians and practitioners addressing the issues and problems of education have often lost touch with the questions, and end up expending enormous resources to generate the right—or at least partially right—answers for what we consider to be the wrong questions. In particular, the organizing moral questions for educational leaders have generally centered on issues of power, duty, and justice. Questions of duty have taken their lead from Kant, holding that a good means of carrying out educational leadership is to act from those principles that the person wishes everyone would hold (Rebore, 2001). However, proponents of an ethic of care, with its emphasis on a sympathetic bond among persons, would ask a different kind of question. For example, they would wonder how schools could put an end to intimidation and bullying among students, faculty, and staff. Can gender, racial, religious, or cultural differences create an insurmountable divide between colleagues? How might an administrator circumvent such a potential divide (Wagner & Simpson, 2009)? The traditional moral questions arose from the specific global and local interests of particular populations, which are primarily Western and male. Thus, the seemingly universal view from nowhere may well be a particular view from somewhere; the magisterial voice from the heavens turns out to be broadcast from earth. Moreover, it is often through the emergence of alternative views and voices that one begins to appreciate how much of that which had seemed genuinely universalistic was in fact particular. The clearest example of this phenomenon, as we have discussed, can be seen in new work being done on gender. One of the most exciting developments in moral philosophy during the latter part of the last century has been the growth of a feminist theory stimulated by women's entry into the moral conversation. New questions have been asked, new theoretical horizons have been opened, revealing realities that were always there in a sense, but were either not seen or deemed unworthy of real consideration. The "maleness" of orthodox moral philosophy is now visible in a way that it had not been previously. This, however, is not to assume the absence of males in its practice. Thus, our efforts in linking the worlds of faith and the affective among male educational leaders shall culminate in identifying the experiences of such leaders and the role that faith and care might have played in their decision making and problem solving.

For the current study, four African American males who hold or have held positions of leadership in institutions of learning agreed to participate in a focus group addressing questions about the role that faith and an ethic of care might have played in their decision making. The administrators' ages ranged from forty-one to sixty-eight. Two of the administrators were K–12 public school principals, one was an art and mathematics teacher and assistant headmaster for an independent school, and the fourth was a higher education administrator. Notably, two of the participants served as ministers in African Methodist Episcopal (AME) and Baptist churches, and the other two as church deacons. Thus, all of the focus group participants described themselves as men of faith.

Thoughtful Reflection and Educational Leadership

For many, the claim that educational leadership is a highly moral undertaking seems unquestionable. Price (2006), though, asserted that leaders believe that they are special, that they feel ordinary rules do not apply to them, and that followers should be expected to do as the leader says and not as the leader does. Such a claim clearly shows that the moral dimensions of leadership are often ignored or forgotten. What makes educational leadership a moral endeavor is perfectly in line with Fenstermacher's (1990) statement that it is "quite centrally human action undertaken in regard to other human action" (p. 133). Supporting this, in the current study, AME minister and former New York City middle school principal Reverend Ron recognized that a leader's conduct, at all times and in all ways, is a moral matter. As such, decisions require what he called "thoughtful reflection," which he maintained is grounded in faith. Reverend Ron explained:

> In my years as an administrator in the schools I found myself often having to simply react or deciding on the basis of thoughtful reflection. Thoughtful reflection requires time. Thus, one must find the time for such reflection. Here I refer to Jesus' model of theological reflection. Jesus took time out to go to the mountaintop to carefully reflect upon what the next

stage of his mission should be. He then went back to share the results of that reflection with his disciples. The question of such thoughtful reflection becomes that of "how can I operate with integrity without damaging my Christian values?" Jesus' model of taking that time-out is my starting point in decision-making. (personal communication, August 16, 2013)

Reverend Ron appears to describe "thoughtful reflection" as both a spiritual and cognitive concept. It appeals to a kind of "faith knowledge" with its source in affectivity. The experience being described here admits the weakness of reason alone. This is not to lead us to a form of moral relativism or nihilism, but to an understanding that primal moral knowledge unfolds in a contemplative form. Its bases lie in what Thomas Carlyle (1860) called those "quiet mysterious depths" (p. 9) that exist in the center of personality "underneath the region of argument and conscious discourse" (p. 9). It is here, Reverend Ron believed, that the impact of his position as leader is felt, and the ethic of care begins.

Trust and Service in Leadership

With a faith in thoughtful reflection as the basis for decision making and problem solving, Deacon Len, another middle school principal, recognized that such reflection might occur either at the macro level, where one is making long-term general decisions, or at the micro, day-to-day, level where decisions have to be made as they relate to specific situations. Reverend Ron responded to Deacon Len's observation:

> There are two routes to be taken here. These can be divided into long-range and short-range planning. As I am asked to link my personal world of faith with my professional world of decision making, I do so by considering several groups in my planning process. In my planning, I must consider the needs of students, parents, guardians, teachers, support staff, school boards, community CEOs, et cetera. In considering the needs of these various constituents, I do so from a servanthood perspective. In considering my role as servant, the question arises: "What is it that they need?" As I attempt to address the immediate problems and needs of individuals, in the micro sense of your question, then the importance of my having established caring relationships comes to the fore. My ability to adequately address such immediate problems requires trust. That is, trust in my ability to reach an appropriate conclusion and make good decisions based on my experience. (personal communication, August 16, 2013)

The notion of the leader as servant goes back at least to Plato (trans. 1992), who argues that "every kind of rule, insofar as it rules, doesn't seek anything other than what is best for the things it rules and cares for, and this is true both of public and private kinds of rule" (p. 21, 345d–e). Thus, the task of the leader is to serve those who are to follow. Such service, Reverend Ron told us, requires a knowledge of the needs of those being served. Such knowledge also requires, then, a relationship with those to be served. Even more, serving well through an environment of trust requires trust, which should be exhibited both by the servant and those being served.

Additionally, it is possible to speak of leadership in two distinct but related senses. One pertains to beliefs or knowledge, which we may call "epistemic" leadership, and the other relates to the form that concerns us here regarding decisions and actions which may be appropriately called "moral leadership." With regard to "epistemic" leadership, we speak of one as a leader in a particular field of study; this means being in a position to know about the subject or, in a somewhat stronger sense, to be one whose business it is to know about such things and to have credentials such that others less learned are justified in accepting the leader's views on the subject. Conversely, leadership in the area of decision and action is different in that such leadership concerns knowledge of what to do rather than knowledge of facts or what to believe. The kind of leadership specific to the area of decision and action concerns the responsibility or the right to decide or to act in such a way that commits others or obligates others to commit themselves accordingly. Such leadership is grounded in trust. Bok (1978) reminds us that "whatever matters to human beings, trust in the atmosphere in which it thrives" (p. 31). Baier (1986) goes on to support Bok's claim by offering that "without trust, what matters to me would be unsafe, unless like the Stoic I attach myself only to what can thrive, or be safe from harm, *however* others act" (p. 231, emphasis added). In our earlier reference to Plato (trans. 1992) and his supreme work on leadership, it seems that he presumes that the majority of citizens will trust the philosopher king to rule wisely, and expects that the elite will trust their underlings not to poison their wine nor set fire to their libraries. But Plato's presumption may not hold. Thus, Baier (1986) reminds us of the need to add to Bok's statement concerning the value of trust. She says that "not all the things that thrive when there is trust between people, and which matter, are things that should be encouraged to thrive. Exploitation and conspiracy, as much as justice and fellowship, thrive better in an atmosphere of trust" (pp. 11–12). Excessive reliance on leadership is a singular approach to ethics that ultimately represents a distrust in our capacity to know. There is, however, a healthy a reliance on leadership that is part of an integral approach to understanding the right thing to do. Proper reliance on leadership is both a practical necessity and a community-building form of trust. Baier's (1986) admonition reminds us, however, that reliance on leadership must be critical and not naïve.

Care and After-Care

Held (2006) reminds us that it is "characteristic of the ethics of care to view persons as relational and as interdependent" (p. 46). Reverend Shaw, the Baptist minister and university administrator, addressed Reverend Ron's notion of the importance of leaders establishing relationships when serving the needs of constituents and recognized that the ethic of care requires what he called "after-care." He says:

We are able to speak of care in a number of ways. One might "care for," "care to," "care about," "care with," et cetera. The common element of all these forms of caring is the relationship established between ourselves and the object of care. The relationship is a caring one. Showing that we care requires that we engage in a concept that you taught us in your ethics class. I think you called it the "supererogatory." If I remember correctly, this entails going beyond that which is obligatory, beyond that which is required of us. The best way I know to express this sense of care is to call it a form of "after-care." That is, the stronger part of my faith requires that I ask, "What do you do after you've done what you are required to do?" What I mean to suggest is that there are my professional obligations as an administrator that are dictated by policy. Those are the things I am required to do. But if I am understanding us as we talk about an ethic of care and how it is to impact our relationship with those we lead, I am led to believe that a true sense of this ethics requires that we go beyond the call of duty and into the supererogatory—into "after-care." (Reverend Shaw, personal communication, August 16, 2013)

Upon hearing Reverend Shaw explain his sense of the nature of the relationship required in demonstrating an ethic of care, Reverend Ron was reminded of his own form of "after-care" and commented on it:

As I listen, I am reminded of situations where parents or students were in need of services beyond those provided by the school. Using your language, Reverend Shaw, I found it necessary to "extend care" beyond that required by my role as principal. I did so by referring parents to programs I was aware of in the community, counseling, scouts, church groups, tutoring, et cetera. This speaks again to my understanding of leadership involving a sense of service. To serve in this extended way is to care. (personal communication, August 16, 2013)

In response to Reverend Ron's statement, Reverend Shaw asked:

Do you find yourself offering this sense of "after-care" more often to those who share your cultural background? Would you care more for African American students because you could relate to them better or identify with their needs? Do you feel a particular affinity towards those like yourself? (personal communication, August 16, 2013)

After brief consideration, Reverend Ron answered:

My faith demands that I love my neighbor as myself. My neighbor as described in Scripture was to be specifically identified as others not like me. My faith requires that they be treated as if they were me. Thus, I am to care for others as I care for myself, or care for those not like me as I would care for those like me. (personal communication, August 16, 2013)

With these claims in mind, how might this sense of "after-care for the other" be understood? Is it to be treated as a rule, as in "love thy neighbor as thyself" as the Bible states? An ethic of care, as has been suggested, is best seen as art and science. Like art, it cannot be entered into simply by following the rules. However well instructed we are by principles, there is a certain point at which one's care for the personal and contextual factors of a situation become crucially important.

The rules cannot tell you how to approach another who needs help in such a way as to avoid their suspicion of an ulterior motive. The final judgment of the fitting way to proceed will be based on an immediate sense of caring and a sympathetic sense of what this concrete situation requires.

To an extent, we move beyond rules and into the realm of caring perception and intuition when it comes to the basic ethical necessities such as contextual sensitivity, delicacy, tact, and a sense of timing and compassion. So, the myth of such attributes being limited to women has been exposed. As suggested earlier, it has finally been brought under the searing light of criticism and allowed a conclusion to be reached: African American men of faith care. Still, the task for ethics here has not ended, since even if we manage to critique and dislodge one deleterious myth, there is always another underlying myth to substitute for it. As we demythologize, we possibly re-mythologize. But since all myth is marked by stereotypical thinking and, therefore, the failure to make distinctions where there are relevant differences, all myths call for criticism.

SUMMARY

Permit me to summarize by offering a caution against a possible misreading of this chapter. It is not anti-science, anti-male, anti-justice, or anti-reason. The historical pursuit of scientific discovery, justice, and procedures of right reason have generated some of the great achievements of the human mind, and have been highly fruitful in so many constructive ways. What I have argued against here is the overextension and domination of science, justice, and reason as primary approaches to moral discernment. Science, reason, and the continued pursuit of justice and its positive fruits must be preserved and furthered. The problem is how to assure this while putting them in their rightful place in our intellectual life and culture, so that all aspects of ourselves and all sectors of the culture can flourish in a healthy manner—that is, so that we can view them alongside faith in its epistemological sense and care in its affective sense as contributors to our attempt to see the world from a moral point of view. To accomplish this, we need a new moral philosophy, one which is congruent with and indeed integrated into a comprehensive philosophy of culture based on an epistemology and psychology that recognizes and does justice to the full range of our epistemic abilities and social powers.

REFERENCES

Adams, E. M. (1975). *Philosophy and the modern mind: A philosophical critique of modern Western civilization*. Chapel Hill: University of North Carolina Press.

Alston, W. P. (1989). *Epistemic justification: Essays in the theory of knowledge*. Ithaca, NY: Cornell University Press.

Audi, R. (1998). *Epistemology: A contemporary introduction to the theory of knowledge*. New York, NY: Harper & Row.

Baggini, J., & Fosl, P. S. (2007). *The ethics tool kit: A compendium of ethical concepts and methods*. Malden, MA: Blackwell.

Baier, A. (1986). Trust and antitrust. *Ethics, 95*(2), 231–260.

Beck, L. G. (1994). *Reclaiming educational administration as a caring profession: Critical issues in educational leadership series*. New York, NY: Teachers College Press.

Bennis, W. (1989). *On becoming a leader*. Reading, MA: Addison-Wesley.

Bentham, J. (1948). *An introduction to the principles of morals and legislation*. New York, NY: Hafner.

Bok, S. (1978). *Lying*. New York, NY: Pantheon Books.

Carlyle, T. (1860). Characteristics. In *Critical and miscellaneous essays* (Vol. 3). Boston, MA: Brown and Taggard.

Fenstermacher, G. D. (1990). Some moral considerations on teaching as a profession. In J. I. Goodlad, R. Soder, & K. A. Sirotnik (Eds.), *The moral dimensions of teaching* (pp. 130–151). San Francisco, CA: Jossey-Bass.

Fine, M., & Weis, L. (1993). *Beyond silenced voices: Class, race, and gender in U.S. schools*. Albany, NY: SUNY Press.

Gilligan, C. (1982). *In a different voice: Psychological theory and women's development*. Cambridge, MA: Harvard University Press.

Gilligan, C., Ward, J. V., & Taylor, J. M. (Eds.). (1988). *Mapping the moral domain*. Cambridge, MA: Harvard University Press.

Goodlad, J. I., Soder, R., & Sirotnik, K. A. (Eds.). (1990). *The moral dimensions of teaching*. San Francisco, CA: Jossey-Bass.

Held, V. (Ed.). (1995). *Justice and care: Essential readings in feminist ethics*. Boulder, CO: Westview Press.

Held, V. (2006). *The ethics of care*. New York, NY: Oxford University Press.

Hume, D. (1911). *A treatise of human nature*. New York, NY: E. P. Dutton & Co.

Jones, W. T., Sontag, F., Beckner, M. D., & Fogelin, R. J. (1969). *Approaches to ethics* (2nd ed.). New York, NY: McGraw-Hill.

Kant, I. (trans. 1969). *Foundations of the metaphysics of morals*. L. W. Beck (Trans.). Indianapolis, IN: Bobbs-Merrill.

Lauritzen, P. (1992). *Religious belief and emotional transformation: A Light in the Heart, Inc*. Cranberry, NY: Associated University Presses.

Magill, F. (Ed.). (1961). *Masterpieces of world philosophy*. New York, NY: Harper & Row.

Maguire, D. C. (1970). Myths in politics. *Worldview, 13*(10), 15–17.

Noddings, N. (1992). *The challenge to care in schools: An alternative approach to education*. New York, NY: Teachers College Press.

Nozick, R. (1981). *Philosophic explanations*. Cambridge, MA: Harvard University Press.

Pagels, E. (1988). *Adam, Eve, and the serpent*. New York, NY: Random House.

Perry, R. B. (1926). *General theory of value*. New York, NY: Longmans, Green & Co.

Plato. (1992). *The republic*. G. M. A. Grude (Trans.). Indianapolis, IN: Hackett.

Pojman, L. P. (2002). *Ethics: Discovering right & wrong* (4th ed.). Belmont, CA: Wadsworth/Thomson Learning.

Price, T. L. (2006). *Understanding ethical failures in leadership*. New York, NY: Cambridge University Press.

Prichard, H. A. (1969). Does moral philosophy rest on a mistake? In W. T. Jones, F. Sontag, M. D. Beckner, & R. J. Fogelin, *Approaches to ethics* (2nd ed.). New York, NY: McGraw-Hill. (Reprinted from *Mind, 21*, 1912.)

Rebore, R. W. (2001). *The ethics of educational leadership*. Upper Saddle River, NJ: Prentice Hall.

Ruddick, S. (1995). Injustice in families: Assault and domination. In V. Held (Ed.), *Justice and care: Essential readings in feminist ethics* (pp. 203–223). Boulder, CO: Westview Press.

Schopenhauer, A. (1915). *The basis of morality* (2nd ed.). London, England: George Allen & Unwin.

Shapiro, J. P., & Stefkovich, J. A. (2005). *Ethical leadership and decision-making in education: Applying theoretical perspectives to complex dilemmas* (2nd ed.). Mahwah, NJ: Lawrence Erlbaum.

Wagner, P. A., & Simpson, D. J. (2009). *Ethical decision-making in school administration*. Thousand Oaks, CA: Sage.

Wittgenstein, L. (1968). *Philosophical investigation* (3rd ed.). G. E. M. Anscombe (Trans.). New York, NY: Macmillan.

CHAPTER EIGHT

Spirituality AND Religion

The Foundation for Caring African American Males' Identity

ROBERT A. HORNE

Spirituality and religion are guiding forces in the lives of caring African American males. However, most previous research regarding African American males has focused on pathology or maladaptive behaviors associated with illegal drugs, violence, or the criminal justice system. While African American males are, in fact, disproportionately represented in the mental health and criminal justice systems, the preponderance of current literature depicts only a small element of the African American male population. A broader exploration of African American males, their behaviors, and their psyches reveals that African American males are not a homogeneous population. Moreover, a more extensive investigation into African American male culture would reveal them to be inordinately spiritual, religious, family oriented, and caring (Cone, 1975; Letiecq, 2007; Mbiti, 1990; Perry, 2013).

African American male spirituality and religiosity are reflective of the greater spiritual and religious culture of the African American community. Among ethnic groups in the United States, African Americans generally present the highest rates of absolute belief in God or a higher power (88%); religious affiliation (85%); participation in daily prayer (76%); belief in supernatural forces such as angels and demons (68%); and religious service attendance (53%) (Pew Research Center, 2008). Likewise, among African Americans who claim no religious affiliation, 70% indicate spirituality and religion are a "somewhat" or "very important" factor in their lives (Pew Research Center, 2008). Still, African Americans who claim no religious affiliation tend to engage in daily prayer nearly as often as do European

Americans who profess affiliation with mainstream Protestant religions, 48% and 53%, respectively (Pew Research Center, 2008). Such statistical data provide some quantifiable understanding of religion in African Americans' lives; however, little research literature actually focuses on the role of spirituality and religion in shaping African American males' identities, self- and world schemas, behavioral patterns, or value systems. Even less research literature exists that investigates African American males' spirituality and religiosity as they relate to concepts of caring, caring behaviors, or interpersonal relationships. Thus, the dearth of research and literature aptly investigating African American males' spiritual and religious beliefs and practices as they relate to their behaviors and relationships demands further inquiry.

CHALLENGES WITH DISTINGUISHING AFRICAN AMERICAN MALES' CARING BEHAVIORS

Understanding the role of spirituality and religiosity in shaping African American males' identities, caring attitudes, and interpersonal relationships requires navigating a complex dynamic. First, the true measure of these relationships can be viewed and comprehended only within the context of the greater role of spirituality and religion in African American culture and the African American male experience. However, a challenge in comprehending these phenomena originates from the distinctly subjective nature of spirituality and religion, resulting in their lack of clear definitions in research literature. Customarily, the terms *spirituality* and *religion* have been used interchangeably to represent faith-based activities, establishments, and belief systems (Cashwell, Bentley, & Bigbee, 2007; Dancy, 2010; Pargament, 1999). However, the recent move away from participation in organized religion has led to a greater distinction between spirituality and religion (Myers & Willard, 2003; Pargament, 1999). For the purpose of this chapter, then, *spirituality* describes the individual or collective experiential and/or existential search for the sacred or transformative meaning in life, which may or may not include a higher power or ritualistic approach; by comparison, *religion* is conceptualized as the individual or collective experiential and/or existential search for the sacred or transformative meaning in life, which may or may not include a higher power but typically utilizes a ritualistic or structured approach (Myers & Willard, 2003; Pargament, 1999). Such a distinction is necessary to facilitate a complete examination of African American males' behaviors and care practices.

In addition to differentiating spirituality from religion, African American males' use of *masking* is a phenomenon that makes it difficult to assess their emotions, caring behaviors, and intricacies of their interpersonal relationships. Masking, or *cool pose*, as it is called in the African American community, refers to physically posturing to convey strength, pride, and control (Majors & Mancini, 1993; Phillips, 2006), largely viewed as a method of emotionally surviving in what may be considered an unreceptive or hostile environment. Masking allows African American males to outwardly adapt to situations by role-playing that they are emotionally unaffected by or in control of their surroundings. However, the constant role-playing may create psychological hindrances that negatively impact African American males' identity, caring attitude, and self- and world schemas (Phillips, 2006). The consistent use of masking or the cool pose persona may also obstruct African American males' ability to demonstrate what are typically considered acceptable normative behaviors associated with compassion and caring (Majors & Mancini, 1993; Phillips, 2006). However, almost every African American male has used the cool pose at some point. Majors and Mancini (1993) suggest African American males' enculturation into the cool pose phenomenon is based on their African heritage as well as their maltreatment during slavery and segregation in America. In African culture, coolness is the state of being able to control one's emotions while under pressure or persecution (Majors & Mancini, 1993; Phillips, 2006), and such an ability was considered to be a sign of maturity in African tradition and folklore. Similarly, during the periods of slavery and segregation, African American males were trained either to control or not to show their emotions in order to protect themselves against retaliation when they were disrespected, dehumanized, or made to watch their family members endure similar maltreatment (Leary, 2005; Majors & Mancini, 1993). In order to fully understand African American males' behaviors, it is therefore necessary to recognize and take into account the challenge presented by the practice of masking among African American men.

SPIRITUALITY, RELIGION, AND THE AFRICAN AMERICAN MALE IDENTITY

Since African American males' caring attitude is rooted in their spiritual and religious legacy, the significance of the Black Church in forming such attitudes is paramount. During the periods of slavery and segregation, in particular, the Black Church gained momentum and prominence as an institutional safe haven in African American culture. The Black Church (BC) refers to the aggregate African American Christian community, rather than a specific denomination or physical structure. More important, the term *Black Church* also represents the intangible and subjective ethos that connects African Americans to each other in a safe and caring way, a kind of web that validates the humanity and inherent worth of each individual while intricately connecting each individual to the compassionate, collectivistic community. Likewise, the Black Church ethos provides mutual spiritual and emotional support that facilitates communication and caring behaviors among African Americans (Cone, 1975; Dancy, 2010; Lincoln & Mamiya, 1998; Moore, 1991; Moore-Thomas & Day-Vitts, 2008). Therefore, the Black Church ethos permeates African American culture and establishes a spiritual and religious context that has long promoted and facilitated a sense of well-being, community, and caring among African American males.

The fact that spirituality and religion greatly impact African Americans' culture, practices, and beliefs is well known and firmly established. Less discussed in current literature, though, is the role and influence of spirituality and religion on the African American male identity and psyche. In the modern era of multiculturalism, it is easy to forget that many African American males still face social and economic oppression, isolation, and discrimination. For example, African American males have the lowest college graduation rates of all ethnic groups, and those with a college degree are 3% less likely to be called back for a follow-up job interview than their European American counterparts with high school diplomas and felony convictions (Harper, 2012; Kethineni & Falcone, 2007). Also, African American males are six times more likely to be arrested than European American males, so they must live each day with the knowledge and fear that they are more likely to be detained by law enforcement officers. In fact, it is estimated one out of three African American males will go to prison during their lifetime (Bonzcar, 2003; Mauer & King, 2007). All of these discriminating factors serve as stressors that negatively impact African American males' identity and sense of self-worth.

In many ways, these modern stressors reinforce the feelings of hostility and disenfranchisement that African American males felt during slavery and segregation (Leary, 2005). Many African American males, living with the legacy of slavery, still feel they exist in a hostile and prejudiced environment, and so continue to use masking behaviors to hide their fear of being physically or emotionally hurt. As a result, the African American male masking process appears to have led many non–African Americans to misinterpret such behavior as a lack of compassion or concern; in fact, however, it serves as not only a self-protective coping mechanism, but also as a method of establishing one's masculine identity in the community (Jackson & Moore, 2008; Leary, 2005; Majors & Mancini, 1993; Phillips, 2006). These same measures of coping and identity formation have likewise been credited to the role of spirituality and religion in African American males' lives.

THE ROLE OF SLAVERY IN SPIRITUALITY, RELIGION, AND THE AFRICAN AMERICAN MALE IDENTITY

Traditionally, the African American male identity has been tied to spiritual and religious identity as well as collectivistic experience. To fully comprehend this connection, it is necessary to understand that most African and African American spiritual and religious cultures make no distinction between individual identity and religious identity (Lincoln & Mamiya, 1998; Mbiti, 1990; Raboteau, 1978; Snowden, 1983); this concept is based on a traditional belief of the interconnectedness of God with all people and things, held in most parts of the world prior to the beginning of slavery (Mbiti, 1990; Raboteau, 1978). Religious rites in traditional African cultures defined an individual's existence and concept of self as well as one's role and behavior in the community. Therefore, the African American male's concept of self or personal identity is drawn from an ethnic heritage wherein identity has always been inescapably tied to and influenced by spirituality and religion.

Such a pairing of spiritual and personal identity is perhaps best illustrated by the Bantu African tribe, who believed themselves to be *muntu*, sentient beings that possess volition, or free will. In Bantu tradition, muntu include deities, the living, the dead, the living dead, and the uninitiated, or those who have not completed the spiritually based rites of passage into the tribe. However, the dehumanization encountered during slavery took African American males from the category of muntu and placed them into the lesser category of kintu that includes objects lacking volition, such as animals and rocks (Mbiti, 1990). The move from muntu to kintu further debased African American males and shattered their identity and concept of self, working to diminish their self-worth or valuable emotional attachments in order to make them more compliant slaves (Lincoln & Mamiya, 1998; Raboteau, 1978). In effect, the dehumanization of African American male slaves served as a means of restructuring their former identity and natural tendency toward positive communal associations.

Spirituality and religion served as a means for restoring normative African American males' identity, positive communal associations, and caring behaviors. Several reasons exist for how and why spirituality and religion positively affected African American males' identity and communal associations during slavery. First, it is well documented that African Americans have traditionally gravitated toward spirituality and religion during periods of distress (Lincoln & Mamiya, 1998; Moore-Thomas & Day-Vitts, 2008; Roberts, 1994), supporting the likelihood that many disenfranchised African American males would have sought out spiritual and religious guidance and/or relief during slavery. Second, it is also well documented that African American slaves sought out opportunities to celebrate their spiritual and religious beliefs communally, even under penalty of persecution (Moore-Thomas & Day-Vitts, 2008; Raboteau, 1978; Wilmore, 1989). It can be thus concluded that some African American male slaves valued spiritual and communal associations above their personal safety, and it has even been suggested that the Black Church has maintained its relevance in part because of its role in developing and fostering the new African identity in America (Raboteau,

1978; Wilmore, 1989). Third, spirituality and religion are transformative constructs that seek to positively change an individual's basic beliefs about oneself and one's environment, as well one's behavioral patterns (Roberts, 1994; Stansbury, Harley, King, Nelson, & Speight, 2012; Wimberly, 1991). Furthermore, the Judeo-based Christian religion presented to America's slaves represented an ideology similar to many traditional African religions (Mbiti, 1990; Raboteau, 1978). The shared African and Christian ideologies included concepts of a supreme deity, a divine mediator who actively demonstrates compassion and concern for people, an antagonistic entity, stories of creation, and stories of humanity's downfall and redemption (Mbiti, 1990). Fourth, spiritual and religious practices expressed and transmitted information to each generation of slaves about men's roles and responsibilities to their deity, families, and neighbors, and these ideals became embedded in African American culture. Finally, African American spiritual and religious entities provided a safe place where African American male slaves felt empowered and respected, thereby assisting in sustaining their sense of self-worth and identity.

SPIRITUALITY, RELIGION, AND AFRICAN AMERICAN MALES' CARING BELIEFS AND BEHAVIORS

Male African American slaves eventually developed a personal and collective identity tied to the Christian religion. They associated their new identity with the prophetic texts of the Bible, which spoke of liberation and equality (Raboteau, 1978; Roberts, 1994), illuminating the caring aspects of God's nature and exemplifying God's compassion for oppressed people like them. Specifically, many parts of the Bible detail God's promise to liberate his spiritual and religious followers from captivity and subjugation, and such depictions of God serve as the basis for Black Liberation Theology. Dr. James Cone, a founding leader of the concept, indicated that Black Liberation Theology was established in order to liberate subjugated people of color as well as to reframe the interpretation of theology in light of the experiences of oppressed people (Cone, 1975). Such concepts of liberation and aiding the oppressed remain major constructs in the Black Church's identity and theological perspective today.

Assisting the oppressed and others in need is a major identity component for African American males who adhere to spiritual and religious precepts. African American males were encouraged to recognize their own worth and dignity in light of their spiritual and religious constructs (Hood, 1990; Raboteau, 1978; Roberts, 1994), realizing that they were created by and in the image of a benevolent God who proclaimed justice and equality. Such a belief provided a theological and psychological foundation for African American males to consider themselves equal in society (Hood, 1990; Roberts, 1994), and it was reinforced by the Bible's claims that indicated God equally valued the inherent worth of all people. Moreover, African Americans directly correlated their subjugation and challenges with those endured by the Hebrews in Judeo-Christian theology, so the biblical narrative of the Hebrews' exodus served as a key component in African Americans' new spiritual and psychological identity (Hood, 1990; Roberts, 1994). Moses, the spiritual leader of the Hebrews, thus became an African American symbol for liberation, leadership, and spirituality, and he remains a recognizable image within the African American culture. Even today, the title of "Black Moses" is bestowed upon African American males who reflect compassionate service to the community while exhibiting extraordinary leadership and spiritual qualities.

AFRICAN AMERICAN MALES' MANIFESTATIONS OF CARING

As spirituality and religion continue to be vital components of African American males' personal and social identity, spiritual and religious beliefs markedly influence their caring behaviors. Based on data drawn from the Pew Research Center (2008), it seems that most African American males acknowledge the principal precepts of spirituality and religion in their everyday life. Primary among these is family association and responsibility (Daniels, 2012; Morris, 2012; Perry, 2013). It is important to note that African American culture reflects a spiritual and religious view of family, meaning that the term *family* can be applied to blood relatives as well as friends or persons who share a communal bond. Among African American males in particular, the term *family* also implies safety and protection, spiritual bond and loyalty, as well as responsibility and work. In fact, many African American males consider the family to be the most important and positive aspect of African American culture.

Despite the importance placed on family, African American males' involvement with drugs and gang violence may seem to contradict their beliefs about familial caring and communal association. For better or for worse, though, even these seemingly negative portrayals of caring and affection relate directly to African American males' interpretation of spiritual and religious principles. That is, since basic familial associations and responsibilities are such important elements of the African American male identity, selling drugs in order to support a family can be viewed as a moral decision; this is especially true among adolescent African American males from single-parent homes or low-income communities, and those with little education who feel obligated to assist in caring for their families. Daniels (2012) indicated that former adolescent African American male drug dealers identified family association and earning economic support for their families as key factors in the decision to traffic drugs. Although these activities may present a negative image of African American males, they also illustrate the dangerous extremes to which African American males will go in order to care for their families (Morris, 2012). Similarly, the social institution of gangs reveals the inherent need of African American males to feel connected to what they perceive to be caring, family-like institutions, and it is also important to note the presence of spiritual and religious attributes like faith, respect, love, nurturing, and safety as constructs in many African American gangs (Morris, 2012).

Spiritual and religious attributes continually influence and impact African American males' thoughts and actions. Faith provides a context for viewing oneself and the world and fuels hope. From faith, then, African American males draw the inner strength needed to face the struggles of the world. In many cases, hope energizes African American males' desire to achieve something better for themselves, their families, and their community. Interestingly, President Barack Obama, the first African American leader of the United States, used the theme of hope as the platform for his 2008 presidential campaign, exhibiting a caring concern for the needs of others that is also demonstrated by African American males in many spiritual and religious institutions. Likewise, there is a positive correlation between African American males' volunteerism and community service and their spirituality and religiosity, as Mattis et al. (2000) indicate—the higher the level of an African American male's spirituality or religiosity, the more he feels an obligation to assist in caring for, liberating, and educating others.

CONCLUSION

Spirituality and religion have influenced African and African American males' identity, thoughts, and behaviors at least since African pygmies embraced monotheism in 750,000 BCE (Jochannan, 1991). The abiding influence of spirituality and religion in shaping African and African American males' identity, and African American culture as a whole, is well documented. However, there exists a tremendous gap in literature addressing the salience of spirituality and religion on shaping African American males' caring behaviors. Using an anthropological approach to point out the deep interconnectedness between African American males' spiritual and religious experience and their caring identities and behaviors, there are three important facts for contextualizing spirituality and religion as the foundation for caring African American males. First, it is well acknowledged most Africans and African Americans have viewed personal identity within the context of spiritual and religious identity. Second, African and African American spirituality and religions clearly include core principles that promote collectivistic communalism and caring for others. Third, African and African Americans males' interconnectedness with spiritual and religious precepts fundamentally shapes their personal and social identity, as well as integrally influencing their caring behaviors and conceptions.

There are several challenges to understanding African American males' caring behaviors. First, persons not familiar with the role of spirituality and religion in African American culture lack the appropriate context for interpreting or understanding African American males' conceptions of care or caring behaviors. Second, African American males' caring behaviors are mitigated by psychosocial factors including the legacy of slavery and segregation, systemic social injustice reinforced by negative media imaging, and economic and judicial disparities. Third, *masking* and *cool pose*, which often serve vital roles among African American males, can hinder their authentic expression of caring behaviors, the interpretation and understanding of what constitutes African American males' caring behaviors, and assessments of what are normal and maladaptive representations of African American male caring.

Finally, it is critical to understand spiritual- and religious-based manifestations of caring behaviors in African American males' daily lives. African American males express caring behaviors and attributes in many ways, but the foci of their expressions of caring center on their view of family and community and their role in meeting these familial and communal obligations. Furthermore, African American males' caring behavior manifestations are mitigated by psychosocial and contextual factors that must be taken into account. Hence, spiritual- and religious-based caring attributes such as faith, respect, love, family, and loyalty may manifest in some sociably unacceptable behaviors. Altogether, African American males' manifestations or expressions of caring behavior cannot be separated from their personal and spiritual identity as Africans, Americans, Christians, and men.

REFERENCES

Bonzcar, T. P. (2003). *Prevalence of imprisonment in the U.S. population, 1974–2001*. Bureau of Justice Statistics Special Report. Retrieved from http://www.policyalmanac.org/crime/archive/prisoners_in_US_pop.pdf

Cashwell, C. S., Bentley, D. P., & Bigbee, A. (2007). Spirituality and counselor wellness. *The Journal of Humanistic Counseling, Education and Development, 46*(1), 66–81. doi:10.1002/j.2161-1939.2007.tb00026.x

Cone, J. H. (1975). *God of the oppressed*. San Francisco, CA: Harper & Row.

Dancy, T. E. (2010). Faith in the unseen: The intersection(s) of spirituality and identity among African-American males in college. *The Journal of Negro Education, 79*(3), 416–432. Retrieved from http://www.jstor.org/stable/20798359

Daniels, T. S. (2012). What influences some Black males to sell drugs during their adolescence? *McNair Scholars Journal, 13*, 21–39. Retrieved from http://www.csus.edu/McNair/_ALL-Scholars-Articles-Photos-Webpage/13_2011_2012/journal_2011-12/Tatiana_Starr_Daniels.pdf

Harper, S. R. (2012). *Black male student success in higher education: A report from the National Black Male College Achievement Study*. Philadelphia: University of Pennsylvania, Center for the Study of Race and Equity in Education.

Hood, R. E. (1990). *Must God remain Greek? Afro cultures and God-talk.* Minneapolis, MN: Fortress Press.

Jackson, J. F. L., & Moore, J. L., III. (2008). The African-American male crisis in education: A popular media infatuation or needed public policy response? *American Behavioral Scientist, 51*(7), 847–853. doi:10.1177/0002764207311992

Jochannan, Y. B. (1991). *African origins of the major "western religions."* Baltimore, MD: Black Classic Press.

Kethineni, S., & Falcone, D. N. (2007). Employment and ex-offenders in the United States: Effects of legal and extra legal factors. *The Journal of Community and Criminal Justice, 54*(1), 36–51. doi:10.1177/0264550507073325

Leary, J. D. (2005). *Post traumatic slave syndrome: America's legacy of enduring injury and healing.* Portland, OR: Uptone Press.

Letiecq, B. L. (2007). African-American fathering in violent neighborhoods: What role does spirituality play? *Fathering: A Journal of Theory, Research, & Practice about Men as Fathers, 5*(2), 111–128. doi:10.3149/fth.0502.111

Lincoln, C. E., & Mamiya, L. H. (1998). *The Black Church in African-American experience.* Durham, NC: Duke University Press.

Majors, R., & Mancini, J. (1993). *Cool pose.* New York, NY: Touchstone Books.

Mattis, J. S., Jagers, R. J., Hatcher, C. A., Lawhon, G. D., Murphy, E. J., & Murray, Y. F. (2000). Religiosity, volunteerism, and community involvement among African-American men: An exploratory analysis. *Journal of Community Psychology, 28*(4): 391–406. doi:10.1002/1520-6629(200007)28:4<391::AID-JCOP2>3.0.CO;2-A

Mauer, M., & King, R. S. (2007). *A 25-year quagmire: The war on drugs and its impact on American society.* The Sentencing Project: Research and Advocacy for Reform. Retrieved from http://www.sentencingproject.org/doc/publications/dp_25yearquagmire.pdf

Mbiti, J. S. (1990). *African religion and philosophy.* Portsmouth, NH: Heinemann Education.

Moore, T. (1991). The African-American church: A source of empowerment, mutual help, and social change. *Prevention in Human Services, 10*(1), 147–167. doi:10.1300/j293v10n01_09

Moore-Thomas, C., & Day-Vitts, N. L. (2008). Culturally competent counseling for religious and spiritual African-American adolescents. *Professional School Counseling, 11*(3), 159–165. doi:10.5330/PSC.n.2010-11.159

Morris, E. J. (2012). Respect, protection, faith, and love major care: Constructs identified within the subculture of selected urban African-American adolescent gang members. *Journal of Transcultural Nursing, 23*(3), 262–269. doi:10.1177/1043659612441014

Myers, J. E., & Willard, K. (2003). Integrating spirituality into counselor preparation: A developmental, wellness approach. *Counseling and Values, 47*(2), 142–155. doi:10.1002/j.2161-007X.2003.tb00231.x

Pargament, K. I. (1999). The psychology of religion and spirituality? Yes and no. *International Journal for the Psychology of Religion, 9*(1), 3–16. doi:10.1207/s15327582ijpr0901_2

Perry, A. R. (2013). African-American men's attitude toward marriage. *Journal of Black Studies, 44*(2), 182–202. doi:10.1177/0021934712472506

Pew Research Center. (2008). U.S. Religious Landscape Survey, Religion & Public Life Project. Retrieved from http://religions.pewforum.org/reports

Phillips, D. (2006). Masculinity, male development, gender, and identity: Modern and postmodern meanings. *Issues in Mental Health Nursing, 27*(4), 403–423. doi:10.1080/01612840600569666

Raboteau, A. (1978). *Slave religion: The invisible institution in the antebellum south.* New York, NY: Oxford University Press.
Roberts, J. D. (1994). *The prophethood of Black believers.* Louisville, KY: Westminster/John Knox Press.
Snowden, F. J. (1983). *Before color prejudice: The ancient view of Blacks.* Cambridge, MA: Harvard University Press.
Stansbury, K. L., Harley, D. A., King, L., Nelson, N., & Speight, G. (2012). African-American clergy: What are their perceptions of pastoral care and pastoral counseling? *Journal of Religion and Health, 51*(3), 961–969. doi:10.1007/s10943-010-9413-0
Wilmore, G. S. (Ed.). (1989). *African-American religious studies: An interdisciplinary anthology.* Durham, NC: Duke University Press.
Wimberly, E. P. (1991). *African-American pastoral care.* Nashville, TN: Abingdon Press.

CHAPTER NINE

Manhood Development AND Sustainable Institutional Care

John Hope at Morehouse College

AMBER JONES

The culturally responsive traditions and pedagogies of early twentieth-century African American educators have long been a resource for the discussion of African American care ethics (Foster, 1997; Irvine, 1990; Jones, 1981; Morris & Morris, 2000; Siddle Walker, 1996, 2000; Siddle Walker & Tompkins, 2004). These works argue that in spite of the strictures placed on education within a racist system, African American educators developed a working definition of professionalism that incorporated culturally based ideas of caring. Siddle Walker and Tompkins (2004), for example, examined a cross section of literature and histories pertaining to teachers and administrators in segregated schools. From this they theorized that African American educators of the past practiced care for their students both interpersonally and institutionally. Interpersonal care is "a state in which a person who is caring is concerned about, and willing to attempt to meet, the physical, psychological, and academic needs of the individual for whom that person is caring" (Siddle Walker & Tompkins, 2004, p. 79). Concurrently, institutional care involves the efforts of individuals to create and promote institutional structures that facilitate such interpersonal care. Institutional care, then, is paramount, as interpersonal care cannot reach its goals without institutional support. It is apparent that the system of interpersonal and institutional care for African American students involved many individuals, both men and women, in different capacities. Less is known about how African American men, as part of this system, created and expressed their masculine identities in ways that expose their ethic of care. This chapter explores the educational leadership of John Hope, a notable early twentieth-century educator and activist, within the traditions of interpersonal and institutional care in order to inform a discussion of African American men's ethic of care.

INTERNAL INTERPERSONAL CARE

From the beginning of his career as an educator, John Hope was noted for his interpersonal caring skills. John Hope, a native of Augusta, Georgia, first came to Atlanta Baptist College (ABC, formerly Augusta Institute, later Morehouse College) in 1898 as a professor of classics. Davis (1998, p. 108) describes the young Hope as having a straightforward southern temperament that made him appealing to both Whites and Blacks in Georgia and quickly won over his students to make him one of the most popular professors at the college. In the years leading up to his presidency of the college, Hope displayed many characteristics of what Siddle Walker and Tompkins (2004, pp. 80–84) describe as popular themes of interpersonal care: counselor, benefactor, race cheerleader, and encourager. As one of the earliest African American faculty members "students sought his advice on everything from finances to health and family. Even those assigned to other advisors frequently sought Hope's opinion first" (Davis, 1998, p. 108). Thus, Hope quickly established a reputation among his students for being stern, reliable, and readily available. Davis (1998) further notes, "One student remarked that 'If a boy needed a dose of medicine, castor oil, or a reprimand, [Hope] gave it to him. He had no hours'" (p. 109). No matter the request, Hope worked hard to meet the needs of his students, thereby infusing his educational practices with interpersonal care. When Hope became president of ABC in 1906, he was then able to further expand his efforts toward providing students with even better interpersonal care as a benefactor.

Beginning in 1906, Hope, as a college president striving to manage a number of new duties, still "worked hard to keep students in school, at times even borrowing money from friends to help students meet their financial obligations" (Davis, 1998, p. 198). Moreover, when scholarships and grants did not suffice to make all ends meet, Hope helped secure work for his students. For example, Davis notes that, by Hope's efforts, "Morehouse students worked on tobacco farms in Connecticut, in restaurants in Chicago, and in insurance companies in Durham and Atlanta" (p. 198). Though unable to help every student, Hope attempted to meet even the most difficult needs of his students and delivered the best interpersonal care that he could. Hope's efforts were matched by his attention to building and sustaining an institution that could continue his work.

EXTERNAL INSTITUTIONAL CARE

When John Hope was chosen to lead Atlanta Baptist College in 1906, there existed no established tradition for activism among American Baptist Home Mission Society[1] (ABHMS) Black college presidents. These presidents were tasked with furthering the mission of the ABHMS, but nothing in their job descriptions or duties obligated them to be involved in their students' civil rights. However, Hope broke this tradition in his first year as president; he was the only college president, Black or White, among more than one hundred participants to be a member of the radical Niagara Movement.[2] At the 1906 meeting, participants outlined and rededicated themselves to the principles of full civil rights for African Americans as well as quality education for all that equips future generations with the knowledge and skills to break the cycle of service and subordination to others ("Niagara Movement," n.d.). The activist group was important to Hope, and in a letter to W. E. B. Du Bois in 1910 he reflects on the significance of his attendance:

> I was the only president, colored or white, of our colleges that took part in the deliberations of that meeting. I cite this to show that I have dared to live up to my views even when they threw me in the midst of the most radical. Furthermore, every man on our faculty does the same and will as long as I am head of the institution. (Hope, 1910, n.p.)

Hope truly understood the meaning of his participation, and he also saw it as an important point that would define his leadership and the future of his institution, setting a precedent for radicalism that he encouraged in his staff. Davis (1998) notes, "It was only after Hope became the school's president in the first decade of the 20th century that community activism among faculty and administrators became an important part of the Atlanta Baptist College (and later Morehouse's) tradition" (p. 117). By way of his dynamic leadership, Hope was able to initiate a tradition of activism at ABC that would go on to guide and produce several generations of advocates for civil rights at the college. Along with his leadership to help sustain Morehouse College externally, Hope also advocated to his students ideas about manhood that would contribute to the future of the college.

SUSTAINABLE INSTITUTIONAL CARE

In 1917, the year the United States entered World War I, John Hope provides a glimpse into his thinking about manhood at Morehouse College. The year is significant, as with the U.S. involvement in World War I more Black men would have the opportunity to serve in the military and from that service demand their equal rights. Additionally, as the Great Migration is under way, the South is losing scores of Black men who would be potential Morehouse students and leaders of the Black community in Atlanta. Perhaps Hope sensed the importance of seizing the current political climate to emphasize his vision for manhood development at Morehouse College.

In the speech "Morehouse and Negro Education after Fifty Years," John Hope addressed his students on the fiftieth anniversary of the founding of their institution in March 1917. In this speech, Hope presented a narrative of how education for the Negro had generally progressed since the Civil War, purposely drawing a connection between manhood and acquiring an education. This speech spans not only history but also how Hope chooses to contextualize and learn from history. Early in the speech, Hope (1917) remarks that education, formal and informal, was the means in which "the emancipated slave was to build his manhood and get his substance." As Hope continues to discuss how education has been a means of adding substance to and building manhood, he brings his audience back to their own time period and asserts that when it comes to the connection between their education and their identities as men, "I wish it clearly understood that we have a liberal attitude toward truth and men." Within these parameters, this speech goes on to outline many of John Hope's foundational ideas about manhood development and its place in Negro education and Morehouse College.

Citing the biblical story of the young boy who helped to feed thousands with only five loaves of bread and two fish, Hope emphasized how much has been and can be accomplished with limited but fruitful resources. Resources for Negro education, like the few loaves and fish, seemed much less than what was needed to intellectually feed the masses of people. However, just as enslaved men took the scraps of lessons they could acquire from White children to build the substance of their manhood, they, too, had taken their meager resources to build a school that would, in turn, build men. Hope begins his narrative by citing an example much like his own early educational experiences. Hope says that in the days after the Civil War northern teachers who came to southern towns saw to it that "the Negro student while learning books learned to have a care for economy and today in town and country you find the stamp of the Negro school in the life of the home." Hope himself had been taught in primary school by graduates from Atlanta University who instilled in him the same ideals. One of his educators, Georgia Swift, Hope recalls, "'had a peculiar facility for making pupils efficient in arithmetic and instilling the principles of a true gentleman'" (Hope, 1917, p. 22). Hope took caring practices he learned from his female teachers and applied them to his own caring at Morehouse College. Care for economy and Victorian values of "cleanliness and utility" are recurring themes when John Hope is discussing the individual traits of ideal manhood. However, as the first Black president of Morehouse College and among the few successful Black college presidents of the time, it is clear and necessary to John Hope that manhood in connection to greater educational possibility needs to grow as well. Thus, as this narrative continues, Hope breaks down what it means to make an institution, and a manhood, that serves the needs of the time.

Continuing with his connection between manhood, education, and the institution, Hope explains, "the college, like men, is not simply what it does, but also what it is, and it is exceedingly difficult to sum up what a great institution *is*" (emphasis his). Hope is laying out the essential problem of how to measure a man and an institution. Where does the man end and the institution begin? To answer these questions he has set out for himself, Hope posits:

> Curriculum, books, laboratories are the necessary machinery of a college, but after all it is good men, men powerful and good, veritably smashing through the citadel of the youth and penetrating their very souls that make the school for the development of real leaders. (Hope, 1917, pp. 4–5)

The men of the college are to use the machinery of the college to shape the lives of youth. In this way, the fortitude of the men at the college is the most important aspect. As Hope looks to the future of Negro education, and his place in advancing that future, he lays out several ways that his school will build men along with proposed goals and products.

One strategy that John Hope lays out for manhood development is the unique role the Negro college plays in its larger community. Hope emphasizes that just as the Negro college should be concerned with evaluating the needs of the Negro community, this process also lends itself to building men to meet those needs. Hope (1917, p. 6) contends "the college will open new fields of study and research and always seek in the future to prepare men for the work of their generation." It is not enough to explore and expand academia; the Negro college, and specifically Morehouse, must aim to connect those academic advancements to the preparation of men to do the work of their generation. The pursuit of knowledge without practical application is not the brand of education John Hope is interested in. Hope further illustrates his point:

> Just as any people makes a study of its welfare and ideals and fashions its youth for their accomplishment, so the Negro college, through its gifted and consecrated professors, will decide what Negro boys and men must learn and do, and will work upon these youths until they accomplish it. (Hope, 1917, p. 6)

Not only will the Negro college have an active role in turning Black boys into men, but the leadership and faculty are also tasked with being connected with the needs of the community and dedicated to building men in that tradition. Hope puts the responsibility of knowing and building on the shoulders of his faculty, the strong and good men who teach at his institution. Hope also discusses what he envisions as the intended products and goals of this orientation for his institution.

In between laying out how the Negro institution will build men to serve the community, Hope includes various examples of what these products will look like. To help illustrate his points, Hope uses the example of theological seminaries that serve to discourage the vision of young Black men instead of build them up to utilize their talents and potential. Hope posits, "men must be broadened and deepened, and the devitalization of aggressive young men in theological seminaries must cease" (Hope, 1917, p. 5). Hope values the aggressiveness of youth and feels that instead of being discouraged, aggressiveness needs to be shaped and guided toward the necessary work of a generation. In a more generalized statement, Hope asserts another proposed product of his brand of manhood: "We must develop men who can move among men in all walks of life, know their difficulties and minister to their necessities" (p. 5). John Hope aims to build his students not only to have the fortitude to go to the places they will need to go, but also to be able to affect change.

In the closing of his speech, John Hope reveals the overarching goal of his brand of manhood development. Inspired and shaped by his example, and the example of his faculty, the Morehouse man will "bring to pass the full fruits of Christian manhood that will challenge and defy anything less at its country's hands than perfect fairness and real brotherhood" (Hope, 1917, p. 7). The ultimate goal, then, for shaping men is for those men to dismantle the system of discrimination that defines them as less than other men. The goal is to support true brotherhood in the United States, and through that brotherhood create and advocate for equality for the Black community.

John Hope's Morehouse commencement speech in 1931 continues his argument that good economy and thrift are principles that improve the life of an individual, the sustainability of an institution, and are essential to the work that needs to be done to uplift the Black community:

> Are you willing to live life and have it more abundantly as a college man knows life to be? If not, why talk about endowment for Morehouse College? Why talk about bigger salaries for teachers? Why talk about throwing around you every opportunity to develop ... if after getting that development you are apostic to it? ... And in thinking about that, I want to speak about just one thing; that is, the collegian's obligation to the public weal. (1931, n.p.)

John Hope connects the duties of a graduate, a Morehouse man, directly with various efforts, both pre- and post-secondary, to serve education in the Black community. The gendered identity of the Morehouse man is tied to his service to his community and support of the institution for future generations. All of these ideals combine to show how Hope envisioned the Negro college providing care for the development of men, and those men providing care for their communities.

This assertion is akin to the modern campaign at Morehouse College that Morehouse Men should be "Renaissance" Men who are Well read, Well spoken,

Well traveled, Well dressed, and Well balanced.[3] This campaign, coined by the tenth president of Morehouse College, Dr. Robert Franklin, emphasizes the goal of shaping the Morehouse Man into one who can fulfill the goals laid out here by John Hope. This represents a continuity of leadership of Morehouse College. Though the duties may change from generation to generation, the need to shape men who can meet those needs, whatever they may be, is crucial. However, though responsibility to community is key in both of these time periods, the definition of those communities has changed greatly over the years. In the contemporary iteration of this ideal, it is also important to emphasize that the Morehouse Man must be "well traveled" as the community he serves is not only local, but global. The difference between these two ideologies emphasizes the difficulty to pin down all that a Morehouse Man should do and be. From John Hope's educational philosophy, this identity needs to be tied to the work of its generation. In a contemporary perspective, this identity can be more broadly defined and applied. Both perspectives have at the core an interest in caring for the proper development of the "Morehouse Man" so that he too can care for his community however he defines it.

THRIVING MANHOOD, THRIVING COMMUNITY

During his years as a faculty member and president of Morehouse College John Hope posited many ideas on how to develop and care for Black men. Hope advocated that the highest goal of Black manhood ought to be the public good. The Negro college, as an extension of the Negro college president on down, should be institutions that cultivated knowledge that would aid in the mission of college educated men to serve their communities. Thus, the highest goal of Black manhood is tied to the Negro college and to education. Without the institution, with its racially minded college president and other Black male leaders advocating and modeling masculinity, the men produced would not be as effective in their goals. This thriving manhood model is situated in three conditions. The first condition is to possess leadership and a community of men that advocate for full racial equality.

To support a thriving manhood model, leadership and a community of men are needed to model the life, ideals, and behavior of race men to future generations. In his speech in 1917 Hope argues that the Negro college and "its gifted and consecrated professors, will decide what negro boys and men must learn and do, and will work upon these youths until they accomplish it."[4] Hope believes that the minutia of manhood development will and should be in the hands of the Negro college faculty. College men should be strong, value activism, and not shrink from their generational duties to care for their students. Through modeling and teaching Hope and these men provide examples for future generations of race leaders. The modeling and teachings of the college faculty also help to solidify the connection between manhood and working to understand how to best serve the community.

The second condition is that through that commitment and advocacy, and the common operations of an institute of higher learning, obtain knowledge that will be needed to address the needs of the Black community. Hope also emphasizes that the Negro college will study the Negro community in order to best serve its needs and contribute to racial equality. This idea was likely influenced by what many other educators, and Hope's wife, had been doing in Black communities. African American educators through their professional organizations often conducted studies to better understand the needs of their students and provide an education tied to their needs. The Neighborhood Union, founded by Lugenia Burns Hope and growing during this time also used studies of the Negro communities to advocate for better school conditions for Black students and equal pay for Negro teachers. Like Hope had likely seen from these organizations, it was not enough to be dedicated to solving a problem, one has to also know how to best address the foundational causes of the problem. The workings of Morehouse College, through its scholarship and cultivation of advocacy, should also be a center for knowledge on what needs to be done, what kind of people need to do it, how, and when. This third condition follows logically, with dedicated individuals, armed with the knowledge of the Negro community, must then possess the characteristics that make their work sustainable.

The third condition is to cultivate individuals that will fulfill their duty. Hope emphasizes Victorian ideals of thrift and economy, outside of the logic of the politics of respectability, as important practices that affirm the manhood of an individual and liberate him to better serve his community. In speeches from his later years as president when discussing how college men should carry themselves and the characteristics he wished to pass along to his students, Hope often referenced economy and thrift as major goals for men. According to Derrick Aldridge, in his intellectual histories of W. E. B. Du Bois and Anna Julia Cooper, Victorian ideals such as these, in mainstream United States culture, were steeped in "white supremacy and black inferiority" (Aldridge, 2007, p. 416). However, African American intellectuals, like Cooper, Du Bois, and I argue, Hope, "embraced aspects of Victorianism ... but reconciled the ideas and language of these ideologies to construct educational ideas that emphasized black equality and social advancement" (Aldridge, 2007, p. 417). Hope ties his emphasis of Victorian values to manhood and racial uplift. By utilizing the language and philosophy of the time, Hope is able to teach important values without sacrificing what he believed his students needed. Hope appeals thriving manhood to his students on an individual and collective level.

SUSTAINING INSTITUTIONAL CARE

In a brief biographical sketch written soon after John Hope's sudden passing in 1936, sociologist and educator Charles S. Johnson (1936) wrote of Hope, "He was never lured from his one dominant concern of building men to advertise his opinions on education." Johnson was only one of many who chose to honor the memory of John Hope with an emphasis on his career as an educator and his success at shaping young African American boys into men. Famous Black historian Carter G. Woodson also referred to John Hope as a "Maker of Men," as a disproportional number of men who would become college presidents were taught and shaped by John Hope during his tenure at Morehouse College and Atlanta University (Torrence, 1948). The legacy of John Hope, both in African American education and manhood development, is steeped in a care ethic that emphasizes internal and external institutional caring.

Hope, a prolific twentieth-century educator, displayed values of interpersonal and institutional care throughout his career. Hope's interpersonal skills made him a natural leader for African American Georgians and mentor to countless young men. Through his presidency, Hope established a legacy of civil rights activism that he modeled in himself and recreated within his faculty. This tradition of advocacy has fortified Morehouse College by creating an atmosphere that has nurtured several African American leaders and activists. Additionally, Hope's marrying of manhood and institutional sustainability ensured that his students would go on to serve their communities and see to it that the institution survives to provide care for future generations.

NOTES

1. The American Baptist Home Mission Society was organized to support Baptist churches and Christian education in the United States. The ABHMS established several schools across the South in the years after the Civil War to address the need for more schools to educate newly freed African Americans.
2. The Niagara Movement was one of the earliest organizations committed to civil rights and directing work for racial equality. The first meetings, held in 1905 and 1906, spearheaded a generation of civil rights activism and led to the founding of the National Association for the Advancement of Colored People. One of the founding principles of the Niagara Movement was to demand "full manhood rights" and that among them "the right to vote goes everything: freedom, manhood, the honor of our wives, the chastity of our daughters, the right to work and the chance to rise."
3. Robert M. Franklin. "Renaissance Men with a Social Conscience." The Five-Wells. www.morehouse.edu/pdf/Five-Wells.pdf (accessed January 10, 2013).
4. John Hope. (1917). "Morehouse and Negro Education."

REFERENCES

Aldridge, D. P. (2007). Of Victorianism, civilizationism, and progressivism: The educational ideas of Anna Julia Cooper and W. E. B. Du Bois, 1892–1940. *History of Education Quarterly, 47*(4), 416–446.

Davis, L. (1998). *A clashing of the soul: John Hope and the dilemma of African American leadership and Black higher education in the early twentieth century*. Athens: University of Georgia Press.

Foster, M. (1998). *Black teachers on teaching*. New York, NY: New Press.

Hope, J. (1910). *Letter to W. E. B. Du Bois*. In John Hope Presidential Papers. Woodruff Library, Atlanta University Center Archives Collection, Atlanta, GA.

Hope, J. (1917). *Morehouse and Negro education after fifty years, Atlanta University presidential records—John Hope* (Box 70, Folder 2). Archives Research Center, Atlanta University Center.

Hope, J. (1931). *Untitled commencement speech. Atlanta University presidential records—John Hope* (Box 70, Folder 2). Archives Research Center, Atlanta University Center.

Johnson, C. S. (1936). *A preface to racial understanding* (Box 65, Folder 4). John Hope presidential papers. Atlanta University Center Archives Collection. Atlanta, GA.

Jones-Wilson, F. C. (1981). *A traditional model of educational excellence: Dunbar High School of Little Rock, Arkansas*. Washington, DC: Howard University Press.

Morris, V. G., & Morris, C. L. (2000). *Creating caring and nurturing educational environments for African American children*. Westport, CT: Greenwood.

Niagara Movement. (n.d.). Retrieved from http://www.math.buffalo.edu/~sww/0history/hwny-niagara-movement.html

Siddle Walker, V. (1996). *Their highest potential: An African American school community in the segregated South*. Chapel Hill: University of North Carolina Press.

Siddle Walker, V. (2000). Valued segregated schools for African American children in the South, 1935–1969: A review of common themes and characteristics. *Review of Educational Research, 70*(3), 253–285.

Siddle Walker, V., & Tompkins, R. H. (2004). Caring in the past: The case of a southern segregated African American school. In V. Siddle Walker & J. R. Snarey (Eds.), *Racing moral formation: African American perspectives on care and justice* (pp. 77–92). New York, NY: Teachers College Press.

Torrence, R. (1948). *The story of John Hope*. New York, NY: Macmillan.

Conclusion

Honoring a Pedagogy of Caring for Black Males

LISA R. BASS

Caring for students is central to student achievement (Cohen, 2001; Noddings, 1984), student engagement (Wentzel, 1997), and effective school reform (Delpit, 2006; Noddings, 1992, 1994; Shade & Edwards, 1987; Siddle Walker & Snarey, 2004). Therefore, learning the language and culture of caring from multiple perspectives is essential toward understanding the nuances of how Black males care and need to be cared for. This knowledge is especially needed in high-poverty and underachieving populations where change is most needed.

The ethic of care has been studied exhaustively, although not regarding Black males who often lead and attend majority minority schools. This book serves to clarify the lenses through which we view the caring styles of Black men in order to suggest effective caring practices for Black males.

Framing Black masculine caring through the lens of the 'Black male experience' is essential because their life experiences are different. Black males need and express care differently due to societal expectations and negative stereotypes that pervade and even threaten their very existence. Given the known challenges faced by Black males, school teachers, leaders, and community members are charged with being mindful of the these needs so that they can go on to perform to their highest potential.

In this book, we learn that Black men care, but that they care in ways different from the ways in which women care. In addition to the characteristics found in the

Black feminist caring framework Collins, 1989), Black men who care also exhibit characteristics not found in other literature devoted to the exegesis of the notion of caring. The first example of such a theme is "rough love as care," discovered in the Bass study in chapter 1. In this theme, Black men explained the importance of establishing dominance in male-to-male relationships. This is especially true as they negotiate relationships with adolescent Black males. This theme was also alluded to by Dr. Siddle Walker in the foreword. Knowing and understanding this dynamic is important, because not understanding how Black males communicate care to students could cause outsiders looking in to believe that the administrator actually does not like or care for the Black male students or other students the principal feels the need to chastise. Another misperception is that the outsider may believe he, the Black male, is exhibiting aspects of the tough guy, Joe Clark style of leadership. However, there is a difference between unnecessarily harsh leadership, and reaching students through strategic male bonding aimed at leading and motivating them. The second important theme that sets the caring of Black males apart from the caring of other leaders is that they are often "punished" for being seemingly too caring. Since they are expected to be tough, their employers are sometimes disappointed when they emerge as kind and caring or make "soft" decisions based solely on an ethic of caring.

One of the most caring roles assumed by Black males is the role of father. The point of how seriously Black men take the role of fathering is very clearly demonstrated in this book, despite societal perceptions that Black men are absent when it comes to fathering. The theme of the Black man as father is found in most of the chapters, however, Douglas brings this point home powerfully in his very personal account of his experiences of fathering in both his familial and academic contexts.

The need to mask caring was brought out in the Gooden and Spikes study in chapter 2, which discussed the consequences of a leadership style that was "too caring." The Black male principal in this study was placed in a tough school and was expected to use harsh, intimidating tactics as he administered his school. Instead, he was a gentle leader who rejected the notion of ruling harshly and imposing zero-tolerance policies that he knew proved ineffective. These behaviors caused this leader to become unpopular with teachers, and eventually to lose his position. This is why the leaders in the Bass study chose to "wear a mask" and hide their care. They reported feeling pressure to exhibit their leadership as a "tough guy" to maintain their employment. This is a key, because this highlights how Black men often do not feel free to demonstrate care, which adds momentum to the stereotypes that paint Black men as less caring than others. In order to understand Black masculine caring, it is important to recognize that external behaviors exhibited by Black males are not necessarily what they feel. Agosto and Jones also note times when they needed to mask caring so as to not offend others in their immediate environment. Horne further noted the cultural significance of masking care, or cool pose in the Black community.

In addition to caring, we establish that Black males also need to be cared for. Although Black males of all ages are feared and often misunderstood, this does not negate the fact that they need care to survive and flourish in their personal and professional manhood. Ransom and Davis, Beachum and McCray, Agosto and Jones, and Freeland all discuss the need within Black males to be cared for and mentored, and nurtured into becoming the best men and scholars they can become. Beachum and McCray extend Noddings notion that caring is a moral imperative, and note the blatant injustice experienced by Black males as a result of the lack of care they receive in society that can be experienced as anti-Black male.

The Black masculine framework considers notions of spirituality, fatherhood, rough love as care, the importance of caring for Black males, Black males and mentoring, the challenges of Black masculinity, and how Black men wear masks when confounded by the complexities surrounding being a caring Black man in anti-caring institutions. I believe this empirically based framework to be applicable to the ways in which Black boys and men care and need to be cared for; however, I expect this framework to grow and to morph into the ever-evolving realities of Black masculinity.

The purpose of this seminal work was to shed light on the caring nature and styles of Black men. This book is not intended to be an end or even a means to an end on this important topic. However, I would like it to mark the beginning of many conversations on the notion of Black masculine caring, and for these conversations to lead to a continued development of the Black masculine caring framework.

REFERENCES

Cohen, J. (Ed.). (2001). *Caring classrooms/intelligent schools: The social emotional education of young children*. New York, NY: Teachers College Press.

Collins, P. H. (1989). The social construction of black feminist thought. *Signs, 14*(4), 745–773.

Delpit, L. D. (2006). *Other people's children: Cultural conflict in the classroom*. New York, NY: New Press.

Noddings, N. (1984). *Caring: A feminine approach to ethics and moral education*. Berkeley: University of California Press.

Noddings, N. (1992). *The challenge to care in schools* (2nd ed.). New York, NY: Teachers College Press.

Noddings, N. (1994). Conversation as moral education. *Journal of Moral Education, 23*(2), 107–118.

Shade, B. J., & Edwards, P. A. (1987). Ecological correlates of the educative style of Afro-American children. *Journal of Negro Education, 56*(1), 88–99.

Siddle Walker, V., & Snarey, J. R. (2004). *Race-ing moral formation: African American perspectives on care and justice*. New York, NY: Teachers College Press.

Wentzel, K. R. (1997). Student motivation in middle school: The role of perceived pedagogical caring. *Journal of Educational Psychology, 89*(3), 411.

Contributors

Dr. Vonzell Agosto is an associate professor at the University of South Florida, Tampa, in the Educational Leadership and Policy Studies Program. Her research agenda focuses on curriculum leadership related to anti/oppressive education, with an emphasis on race, disability, and gender. She is a co-principal investigator on a federal grant supporting the preparation of doctoral students in the area of special education leadership and policy studies. She currently leads a research project on gender and discipline focused on girls of color across spaces in high school and serves as an educational consultant on schoolwide curriculum improvement.

Dr. Lisa R. Bass is an assistant professor of education at North Carolina State University. Dr. Bass received her PhD in Educational Leadership and Policy studies and Comparative and International Education from the Pennsylvania State University. Her work focuses on education reform, with an emphasis on the ethics of caring and the education of disadvantaged students. An additional research interest is comparative and international education. Her most recent accomplishment is the completion of a co-authored book, *Building Bridges from High Poverty Communities, to Schools, to Productive Citizenship: A Holistic Approach to Addressing Poverty through Exceptional Educational Leadership*.

Dr. Floyd D. Beachum is the Bennett Professor of Urban School Leadership at Lehigh University where he is also an associate professor and program director for Educational Leadership in the College of Education. He received his doctorate in Leadership Studies from Bowling Green State University with an emphasis in Educational Administration. His research interests include leadership in urban education, moral and ethical leadership, and social justice issues in K–12 schools. He has authored several peer-reviewed articles on these topics in many journals. His most recent co-authored book is *School Leadership in a Diverse Society: Helping Schools Prepare All Students for Success*.

Dr. Paul F. Bitting received a PhD in Philosophy of Education from the University of North Carolina in 1985. His research interests include educational foundations, leadership, ethics, moral education, and development, and multicultural and indigenous education. In addition to serving as professor of educational leadership, he also serves as Assistant Dean for Diversity in the College of Education. Dr. Bitting is currently researching the links between traditional philosophy, cultural paradigms, and educational practices.

Dr. James Earl Davis is a professor at Temple University. He received his PhD from Cornell University in Social Policy and Evaluation Research. He was honored with the Bernard C. Watson Endowed Chair in Urban Education. His areas of professional interest include Gender Studies, Sociology of Higher Education, Educational Policy, and Access and Equity. Most recently, he worked on a NSF funded project entitled STEMing the Tide: Exploring Factors Related to Males of Color Interest, Encouragement and Achievement in Mathematics and Science.

Dr. Ty-Ron M. O. Douglas is an assistant professor in the Educational Leadership and Policy Analysis Department at the University of Missouri–Columbia. He earned his PhD at the University of North Carolina at Greensboro. His research explores the intersections among identity, community/geopolitical space, and the socio-cultural foundations of leadership and education, with an emphasis on Black masculinity/families, spirituality, and community-based pedagogical spaces. Dr. Douglas was the recipient of the 2013 Distinguished Dissertation Award by the Critical Educators for Social Justice Special Interest Group of the American Educational Research Association (AERA) and the UNCG School of Education Early Career Alumni Award. His work has appeared in outlets such as *The Urban Review*, *Educational Studies*, *Teachers College Record*, and *Race Ethnicity and Education*. After being awarded a 2015 NCAA Innovations in Research and Practice Grant, Dr. Douglas is currently engaged in a study of Black male student-athletes.

Brian Freeland is a PhD candidate at the University of North Carolina, Charlotte, in the area of Educational Leadership. He has served in the capacity of high school history teacher and in building-level administration for more than twenty-five years. He is passionate about the plight of Black males and has spent a significant amount of time mentoring them informally as well as in formal programs. Most recently, he developed a mentoring initiative that he calls "B-FREE." He continues to be an influential force in the field of education as a scholar, mentor, and practitioner.

Dr. Mark A. Gooden is a professor at the University of Texas at Austin, where he is director of the University of Texas at Austin Principalship Program (UTAPP) in the Educational Administration Department. He graduated with a PhD in Policy and Leadership from the Ohio State University. His research interests include the principalship, issues in urban educational leadership, and legal issues in education. His most recent research appears in *Educational Administration Quarterly*, *Journal of School Leadership*, and *Urban Education*.

Dr. Robert A. Horne, PhD, MDiv, MA, LPC, LCAS/CSI, NCC, is currently an assistant professor at North Carolina Central University. He is a National Board for Certified Counselors Minority Fellowship Program Fellow and ordained minister. He completed his PhD in the Counselor Education program at North Carolina State University.

Amber Jones is a recent graduate of the Educational Studies Department, and a Graduation Generation Fellow candidate in the division of Educational Studies at Emory University and a Graduation Generation Fellow with the Emory University Division of Campus Life. Her research interests include the history of education, African American history, and the educational experiences of African American males. Her dissertation, "Building Men: The Georgia State Council for Work among Negro Boys and the Promotion of Enrichment Programs for African American Boys in Georgia, 1933–37," is a historical case study investigating African American community organizations and their efforts to develop extracurricular enrichment programs for African American males.

Roderick Jones is a doctoral student at the University of South Florida, Tampa, in the Educational Leadership and Policy Studies Program. His expertise is in the area of special education and leadership at the secondary level. His research interests concern the selection and preparation of school administrators, namely, how related decision-making about policies and practices affects diversity in the leadership pipeline serving special and general education. He is currently examining nationwide efforts to prepare special education administrators to address the topic of diversity.

Carlos R. McCray, EdD, is an associate professor for the educational leadership, administration, and policy division at Fordham University. He is the co-author of the books *Cultural Collision and Collusion: Reflections on Hip-Hop Culture, Values, and Schools* and *School Leadership in a Diverse Society: Helping Schools Prepare All Students for Success*. Professor McCray has worked with school leaders and educators in the metropolitan areas of Atlanta, New York City, and London, UK.

Dr. Camille Ransom is a research associate at the PolicyLab at the Children's Hospital of Philadelphia (CHOP). Dr. Ransom received her MSEd from the University of Pennsylvania and her PhD in Urban Education from Temple University. Currently, her research focuses on understanding education outcomes for students in the School District of Philadelphia. Her previous work includes research on out-of-school youth and persistence and engagement in STEM (Science, Technology, Engineering, and Math) subjects for students of color.

Dr. Daniel Spikes is an assistant professor of Educational Administration at Iowa State University. His research interests focus on racial disparities in education and the practices of school districts, schools, and school leaders that serve to perpetuate and/or ameliorate these disparities. Specifically, his research focuses on the following:

- school leadership, in general, with a specific focus on social justice and anti-racist leadership
- pre-service and in-service training of educators on cultural proficiency and/or anti-racism
- urban education
- social justice
- school tracking policies

Postscript A Reflective Essay on B(eing)-FREE

Lesson Learned from Gramp toward Transforming Mass Media Problems into Sustainable Solutions for Black Urban Youth

BRIAN FREELAND

THE PLANTING OF THE "SEED"

Understanding the culture that leads to our growth and development as individuals begins with the positive forces in our lives. Those people who supported us without concern for themselves have been our greatest benefactors, their sacrifices a testament to their efforts to blaze a trail of love, happiness, and success for us. My grandfather, George Freeland, was my first teacher and greatest supporter. He was a man who wanted me to succeed above and beyond his own life circumstances. "Gramp," as I affectionately called him, taught me how to examine life with an eye toward sustainability, although he never actually expressed it in those terms. However, it was implicit in his four teachings, as he encouraged me to value those things that sustain one's life and culture, and instilled in me the following beliefs:

1. Education is a valuable tool.
2. Develop a strong sense of self-awareness, and never allow societal influences to corrupt your fundamental beliefs.
3. Crime is equivalent to slavery, because punishment ends in jail time.
4. Always love and support your family and community.

I have strived to make my grandfather's four points a living reality, for myself and for those in my immediate circle of family, friends, students, and colleagues. Like everyone, I have of course made many regrettable mistakes along the way, but I continue the struggle toward advancing my grandfather's four points to achieve educational advancement for marginalized youth.

These lessons always remain with me. They have been like a boat's rudder, guiding me along a fluid path. I have grown to realize that no one can change the course of greatness that my grandfather planned for me. He has been with me throughout my journey, allowing me to make my own mistakes and learn from them as I move through life. In fact, I could say that our love and relationship had a pedagogical basis; his teachings are ingrained in me, so we are forever inseparable, especially now that I am a teacher. My grandfather was a perfect role model, and he passed his immense wisdom on to me with the love and grace of a master teacher. My grandfather believed in the value of his teachings and many life experiences, and he expected me to follow them. Once, he even taught me with silence, because, though it broke my heart and was a difficult time, his absence from my life for a complete year taught me a valuable and needed lesson.

My grandfather wanted only the best for me, and it was a hard lesson when I realized that not everyone else had my best interests in mind. My grandfather was protective, so as a boy, a young man, and even as an adult, I knew there were some people I could bring around Gramp, and others I could not. He was very concerned with the company I kept, yet he always remained a cordial gentleman in the presence of everyone. Still, when we were alone, I would carefully listen to my grandfather's words of wisdom—and his stories—concerning individual relationships that supported my growth and personal development as a responsible man. My grandfather did not want people in my life who failed to offer me something of lasting, positive value, or who would not add to the rich spring of my knowledge and intelligence. Grace and love, along with proper manners, are the things he wanted me to personify by surrounding myself with like-minded people. Gramp taught me to watch people's actions, first and foremost, and then listen to their words, a lesson I am only now learning to truly appreciate. My grandfather taught me the importance of words, and showed me how they can be transformed into actions that create an atmosphere of success or failure for people. For my grandfather, it was important that I learn to discern the meaning of words, which sometimes greatly impact life's outcomes.

My grandfather used storytelling to communicate his values and lessons, and he was good at it. Gramp told me stories that gave me techniques for dealing with various life situations, although he understood that I would still have to meet my own challenges along the way. My grandfather, the master teacher, would often set up a scenario and ask me to respond to it by providing him with actions I might take in such a situation. I would ask questions and then he would offer his insight and give me the opportunity and time to reflect on his words before I gave my answer. Later, when I began studying Greek philosophy in college, I remember thinking that my grandfather was a version of Socrates, using his dialogic method of teaching. Gramp's unintentional (or maybe intentional!) use of the Socratic method served to shape me as a professional. I love teaching the Socratic method because I had learned and practiced it with my grandfather since my childhood.

In sum, the origin of my social consciousness and my love of teaching began with the wonderful relationship I had with my grandfather. I have never again experienced such joy of learning as I did with my grandfather, and I understand that our special relationship can never be duplicated. I now realize and I am thankful that my grandfather gave me such a wonderful gift to share openly with my students. Teaching is a noble profession that offers people insight about life and prepares them to positively benefit others and our world. I gained the gift of teaching and a love of knowledge from my grandfather George Freeland.

THUGOLOGY: A DEVIANT CULTURAL CONCEPT OF OPPRESSION

If my grandfather were alive today, he would say that the word *thug* means failure for our people, because it destroys families and the love that ultimately supports the Black community. From my grandfather's teachings and wisdom, I developed the term *thugology* to define this cultural concept of oppression. Too many of today's young Black men are unconsciously signing a social contract associated with America's mainstream notions of thugs, resulting in the breakdown of the Black nuclear family, including crime, death, incarceration, and violence that have all claimed the freedom and lives of millions of marginalized young people. The prevalence and effects of accepting such a paradigm supports and causes a number of societal ills, including poverty that produces criminal activity, resulting in crime that is linked to mental, physical, and community-wide destruction of Black urban culture. More specifically, this includes the following issues:

1. The persistent problem of above-average high school dropout rates for Black males.
2. The loss of human and social capital as a result of felony arrest records that impede future job opportunities, which is in part linked to high school dropout rates.
3. Long-term or permanent criminal incarceration that creates a cycle of fatherlessness and perpetual poverty in crime-ridden communities.
4. An inability for families to provide for themselves economically because of felony convictions that make Black males a largely underemployed or unemployed group in America.
5. A lack of available fathers, role models, and mentors for Black male youth.

6. Hip-hop music's validation of irresponsible sexual activity, which can be correlated to the fact that more than 70% of Black women are unwed mothers living below the poverty line in impoverished communities subject to daily crime and violence (Dickerson, 2014).
7. The destruction of neighborhoods and communities resulting from absentee fathers, which results in the formation of gangs who exploit our youth.
8. Illegal activity being valued as an immediate path to economic success rather than the pursuit of educational opportunities as a means to wealth, prestige, economic power, and community building.
9. The mainstream media's negative focus on crime, homicide, incarceration, and violence having diminished social efforts toward finding solutions and improving outcomes for impoverished urban neighborhoods.
10. The lack of love and support for community resulting in the destruction of the nuclear family unit.

These considerable issues and problems require a systematic approach to the formation of initiatives that continually and consciously assess each of these ten factors impeding today's marginalized quality-of-life opportunities for Black young people.

B-FREE: EDUCATION AND EQUALITY TO COUNTER MEDIA AND EMPOWER BLACK YOUTH

Today's mass media serve as a corrosive tool for young men, teaching them behaviors that destroy their quality of life and their opportunities for growth when what they truly need is support and enfranchisement. Over the course of three decades, the mass media and "thug"-centered hip-hop lyricists have placed an emphasis on short-term, high-risk rewards without adequately considering the damage to our communities as a whole (Ball, 2007). The constant and unrealistic attention on criminal behavior as a pathway to economic prosperity has placed millions of Black males in jails and prisons throughout America. Black Americans make up 13% of the U.S. population; 40% of Black Americans are in jail or prison (calculated from Bureau of Justice Statistics, 2009; population statistics are also from Bureau of Justice Statistics, 2009).

Not only is incarceration a tax drain on American society, one which is not socially or economically sustainable, but concerned, progressive citizens understand that we are competing in a worldwide knowledge economy that requires the development of human capital; thus, every time a young Black person is incarcerated in our nation, we fall further behind in the global economic race (United

States Government Accountability Office, 2007). To face these challenges, twenty-first-century thinking now requires that guardians, parents, educators, business leaders, and public officials build sustainable systems that address problems with effective solutions and outcomes.

The social and communal problems in the Black community, as outlined above, must be addressed through education and empowerment. Meeting this need, the Believe in Freedom, Resolutions, Education, and Equality initiative, or B-FREE, is an educational foundation with goals and objectives designed to engage modern youth in a process that creates tangible and sustainable change within Black communities. Specifically, B-FREE is a sustainable movement for marginalized young urban Black males that addresses real community and national issues through educational engagement.

The B-FREE initiative places strong emphasis on participants understanding the language of culture and its power to positively or negatively influence societal outcomes. In a series of interviews, we asked young Black males to identify the major issues facing Black males today. Overwhelmingly, the participants cited stereotypes as a critical problem impacting cultural perception as it relates to Black male youth in America. Interestingly, the participants specifically referred to peer perceptions and stereotypes derived from mass media filtering into their schools and personal relationships. The respondents addressed how they dealt with conflicting cultural concepts such as classroom inattention, the culture of thug or street life, the pressure to dress for peer acceptance without economic resources, disrespect for police authority, gangs, and drugs. Their feedback provided evidence that our young Black men are experiencing marked cultural oppression. Assessing these negative factors, we can surmise that Black males in some social circles of our communities are practicing behaviors that lead directly to crime, violence, and death. Supporters of the B-FREE philosophy believe that open and critical conversations regarding cultural stereotypes and problems afflicting our youth provide opportunities to formulate empowering solutions that address the core issues adversely affecting our community.

REVERSING CULTURAL ABNORMALITIES: TEACHING BLACK YOUTH WITH HISTORY AND MENTORS

Many Black young men interviewed by the B-FREE team revealed marginalized views of themselves and their potential. One young man's assessment of a cultural situation, in particular, was very problematic, but still in line with common perceptions. He insisted that the problems facing Black males had absolutely nothing to do with him, despite admitting that he is, in fact, a contributing member of his community. Then, when asked about the Black graduation rate in his school, he immediately responded that mostly girls graduate but he did not see the point of graduation for him. Regrettably, he did not see how damaging attitudes like his are for the Black community, despite our insistence that strong families and strong communities are built through education. This suggested a serious problem facing our youth in their inability to relate positive outcomes to factors such as education that improve quality of life. Some behaviors that are socially appealing to Black males today are likely to cause cultural problems and hinder building human or social capital in their future communities, as seen in the views of this young interviewee. The strength of most functional societies relies on the positive efforts and collaborative efforts of citizens to develop a promising, productive environment for all community stakeholders (the 2011 Census Bureau Poverty Rate Report shows that Black Americans were hit the hardest at 27.4%). B-FREE teaches participants to view cultural development as an avenue toward improving communities and social relationships.

Overall, the B-FREE initiative is embarking on a journey to empower our young men to improve their quality of life and their circumstances. Team B-FREE recognizes the immense problems facing today's Black males, such as unacceptable high school dropout rates, rising incarceration rates, and homicide rates that are reaching critical proportions. Such societal pandemics must be treated with proactive community action that provides positive outlets where young men can learn to be reflective leaders who address problems collaboratively and find ways to counter adverse societal issues. Team B-FREE will train participants to be agents of change who can recognize negative situations and take positive action to deflect harmful cultural constructs. Our goal is to provide these young men with an opportunity to grow and develop into leaders through face-to-face contact with successful male mentors. Additionally, teaching our youth about the negative historical and societal realities that plague our culture can offer real-world perspective and insight into improving the future of our communities and avoiding their destruction.

The B-FREE initiative emphasizes the importance of rapid, twenty-first-century societal change in which marginalized Black males must engage if they wish to be functional contributors in an ever-changing world. First, Black males have to obtain an education; this begins with earning a high school diploma linked to opportunities for post-secondary economic success. Learning to navigate social systems is also a vital aspect of global awareness. Working in close contact with people to achieve a common goal hones real-world collaborative skills, and marginalized Black males who lack such skills are at a serious disadvantage. B-FREE teaches youth the vital aspects of sustainability beginning with true cognitive awareness of nonconformist behaviors that culturally transform far too many young Black men into impoverished detriments to society. The constant, unrealistic emphasis and attention on criminal behavior as a pathway to economic prosperity has placed millions of Black males in jails and prisons throughout America. If we are to save Black males and our community as a whole, then, we must build sustainable systems that address problems with effective resolutions—immediately.

B-FREE employs an interactive learning approach to development programs that provide participants with a clear focus and goals in an attempt to ensure their academic and social success following high school. Over the course of six weeks during the summer, direction, awareness, and guidance serve as core programmatic values administered by peer mentors who share their personal success stories with the participants. Intellectual engagement and awareness of societal issues is vital to the B-FREE mentorship model, because mentoring young Black males today requires some insight into those negative social pressures and deviant behaviors that have been linked to poor academic performance for young men between the ages of eleven and eighteen.

B-FREE programmatic objectives were designed to encourage participants to place emphasis on academic and social success in the classroom and in school with an eye toward creating a community environment more conducive to fostering increased quality-of-life opportunities.

Objective 1: Identify rising middle school students who demonstrate a need to increase their high school readiness skill set.

Objective 2: Increase comprehensive GPA by 0.05 each grade period until graduation from high school.

Objective 3: Utilize mid-term progress reports, quarterly reports, and semester grades as data points in an attempt to better serve B-FREE participants throughout their high school educational process. We established the following steps to ensure academic and social success in high school that can be utilized to develop sustainable academic and social skills:

Step 1: Focus on classroom tasks and do not be a distraction to the learning process.
Step 2: Use the first twenty days of school to demonstrate a commitment to education.
Step 3: Read and review all course requirements and follow the syllabus daily.
Step 4: Refrain from phone use; absolutely NO SLEEPING in class at any time.
Step 5: Refrain from social partnerships that do not produce positive academic results.
Step 6: Refrain from negative conflicts that may result in physical altercations.
Step 7: Actively participate in school activities that provide positive exposure.
Step 8: Actively seek out positive peer groups and social networks.

Step 9: Seek out academic assistance by utilizing teacher tutorials whenever needed.

Step 10: Communicate academic and social needs with parents, teachers, administration, and B-FREE Mentorship Program staff in the event that problems occur.

Team B-FREE recognizes that collegiate experience may not be an option or a goal for all of our participants; therefore, we also support vocational training and military enrollment as positive outlets toward growth, employment, development, and skill building in an innovative and continuously changing global society.

The philosophy of B-FREE views incarceration as destructive to individuals and to the community as a whole, depleting vital human resources that could be used to generate economic capital that might improve conditions. For example, if we had the millions of young Black males working in our communities and generating an average of $30,000 in yearly income, the economic return would be approximately $50 billion in taxable revenue. Impoverished areas commonly referred to as "the hood" could be transformed into thriving neighborhoods that offered their citizens expanded economic, educational, and employment opportunities that would, in turn, reduce our nation's need for a costly prison industrial complex. Besides the problems associated with incarceration itself, far too many young Black males view joining the criminal culture as a rite of passage when in fact crime only serves to destroy the economic vitality of inner-city communities (United States Census Bureau, 2008). As such, B-FREE teaches that illegal sources of income harm communities rather than empower them with real wealth-building systems. The lure of crime and its immediate gratification has destroyed the lives of too many marginalized American youth, so teaching our participants to evaluate their actions from past, present, and future perspectives helps each young man begin the important process of planning for continued success throughout life.

THE HUMAN CAPITAL CONNECTION: EDUCATING YOUTH ON THEIR VALUE AS HUMAN CAPITAL TO AVOID THE SCHOOL-TO-PRISON AND GRAVEYARD PIPELINES

In the twenty-first century, people are essential assets for business, education, technology, and information systems. The ability to learn faster than your competition may be the only sustainable advantage people have, so investing in people's ideas and learning styles can yield a high return on investment (ROI) for marginalized groups in America. Notably, a 2007 study by the U.S. Government Accountability

Office found that people who live in poverty-stricken areas had fewer life opportunities, in part owing to an inadequate education that further perpetuates marginalization and impoverished circumstances. Thus, B-FREE instills in its participants a strong focus on developing human capital and equipping marginalized youth with the ability to think, respond, and adapt quickly in order to deliver a wide variety of services and products to community stakeholders.

Moreover, the idea of twenty-first-century sustainability mandates that we address real-world problems with impending consequences that threaten the future of our young people's mental and physical well-being. Our youth must be taught to reject behaviors that threaten their potential for improving quality-of-life opportunities. These factors present a major societal problem that is not adequately addressed in the hip-hop culture that is overconsumed by Black youth. The high school dropout rates are directly linked to crime, which increases the incarceration rate and leads to the growth of the private prison industrial complex, and finally results in an enormous burden that prisons and jails place on taxpaying citizens. In addition, Black males have the highest homicide rate in America; the Centers for Disease Control and Prevention (CDC) research findings suggest that Black males' greatest risk factor is death by gunshot (http://www.cdc.gov/violenceprevention/youthviolence/stats_at-a_glance/hr_male.html). More problematically, these murders are predominantly Black-on-Black crimes carried out in marginalized communities that can least afford the loss of human capital. The wealth of any community is in its people, labor, and service, so the murder of a Black person by another Black person creates a loss that is twofold: one dies and the other goes to prison.

In addition to poverty, high incarceration rates, disease, and hip-hop music and its culture also affect Black communities and cause some of the societal ills affecting Black youth. It is important to first note that rap music was originally designed as an avenue for young people to present issues affecting their lives through a musical art form that was relevant to the Black community. Through rap music, socially conscious artists addressed problems facing Black American youth for the purpose of cultural change, social progression, and societal improvement. Hip-hop was originally designed around the concepts of peace, unity, love, work, and having fun. It was creative, fun, and beneficial to the Black community. Afrika Bambaataa, the originator of modern hip-hop, stated that it was "overcoming the negative to the positive" ("Afrika Bambaataa Raps," 2015).

Most certainly there were some instances of early rap music marked by negativity that worked to hurt Black communities. Beginning in 1989 with the hip-hop group N.W.A, the problem has grown immensely. It now seems that popular rap music and hip-hop culture most often serve to exploit and damage our community and especially our children by promoting drugs and violence and equating them with wealth and fame. Socially unconscious "thug" rappers today do nothing more than exacerbate and glorify problems experienced by our youth without providing resolutions, only helping to perpetuate the modern plague on Black youth. According to the CDC, in 2011 homicide was indeed the number one killer of Black men between the ages of fifteen and thirty-four (Centers for Disease Control and Prevention, 2015).

To battle these problems, concerned community members need to work collaboratively, think deeply, and engage in critical conversations that will improve the quality of life for our youth. We must promote the values of education and community involvement, as these are of vital importance if we are to teach our young men techniques that will empower them to remain crime free and build stronger families and communities. Thus, the focus of the B-FREE movement is on educating its participants to better understand how to develop human capital and achieve ROI in Black communities. Principles that B-FREE instills in its participants include the following:

- The ability to learn faster than one's competition as a clear, sustainable advantage, making investment in people, ideas, and education imperative for marginalized groups of people in America.
- A strong focus on developing human capital to equip marginalized youth with the ability to transform and adapt to a rapidly changing globalized economy.
- The ability to think and respond quickly and deliver a wide variety of services and products to community stakeholders for success and sustainability.

Overall, real growth and learning helps students realize their full academic potential beyond what can be determined by standardized testing data. Marginalized youth must be placed on a path toward a sustainable future, and their public school education must provide academic and social training that targets improving their quality of life and opportunities. The No Child Left Behind Act of 2001 (NCLB, 2002), though intended to help students achieve more, has been detrimental to Black youth. Over the course of thirteen years, NCLB has marginalized Black youth by mandating that students be taught and measured through the mechanism of standardized, multiple choice assessments that have not yielded a promising ROI for the lives of marginalized youth (National Center for Fair and Open Testing, 2012.) The challenge today, then, is to effectively utilize the Common Core Curriculum to teach students how to access information in a knowledge economy and achieve success beyond school, which means that educators must rapidly find new ways to collect data and measure student success.

The future demands that we look into our hearts to find the strength to address the wrongs of the past and present to usher in a future that creates a pathway out of poverty for marginalized people. After teaching and learning in urban school districts and community-based organizations for twenty years, I have witnessed firsthand the great wealth that our youth have to offer America's modern global knowledge economy. As a nation, we need their assistance to meet the great challenge of remaining a globally competitive force and close the American achievement gap. Our youth must be taught to focus constructively on efforts that will bring economic sustainability to marginalized groups who have known decades of poverty. Teaching American inner-city youth twenty-first-century skills will enable them to contribute to the economy positively and provide the American taxpayer with a positive ROI. If we provide students with what they need, we will realize what we want—innovation, technological advancements, and future economic security.

GAINING EQUALITY: THE NEED FOR ACCURATE HISTORICAL EDUCATION AND CONSCIOUS ACTIVISM

In the mid-1980s, President Ronald Reagan's administration declared a national War on Drugs; however, that administration then proceeded to cut social education programs designed to teach people about the ills of drugs from the federal budget, relying instead on the "just say no to drugs" program. Unfortunately, this program lacked any real effect as an alternative to the drug culture and economic impoverishment of the inner cities of America. Even more, political officials blamed drugs for factors caused by poverty, such as crime, gangs, and the urban flight to the suburbs. The lack of quality educational programs also failed to transition youth from an industrial economy to the current knowledge worker economy, further damaging Black communities. In retrospect, it also seems clear that the policies of the Reagan administration eroded inner-city social transformative progression by diverting funds from social programs to Cold War initiatives that economically enriched war profiteers at the expense of marginalized American people. All of these factors resulted in stress on inner-city families and consequently weakened the urban family structure. This unfortunate narrative is an example of why a thorough examination of the past is required to avert future problems—because practicing behaviors that destroyed communities in the past will arguably produce the same outcome in the future.

At present, hip-hop thug artists are unwittingly continuing the damage of the Reagan years with their negative messages that divert inner-city youth from focusing on more serious problems plaguing the future of our communities such as crime, incarceration, miseducation, unemployment, and perpetual poverty. Selling drugs is most often, and quite inaccurately, portrayed in hip-hop music as a pathway out of poverty, when in fact it has been a direct pipeline to incarceration and death. Hence, the perception of poor inner-city youth has been shaped by decades of oppressive living conditions that force too many of our brightest young people to think about survivability rather than sustainability. Even more problematic, the recession of 2009 caused American poverty rates to rise to their highest levels in fifty-one years; according to data released by the U.S. Census Bureau (DeNavas-Walt & Proctor, 2014), one out of seven Americans lives in poverty. Higher rates of poverty are often linked to higher rates of crime; if concerned community members do not employ immediate proactive measures to involve our youth in anti-poverty and anti-crime programs, these problems will become plagues. Lessons we teach our youth must serve to protect our progeny from the ravages of criminal proliferation, which will only destroy emerging municipal economies while further marginalizing our youth. America must turn its attention to its urban ghettos and work to transform dilapidated areas into thriving communities, specifically through the development of cooperatives working in conjunction with inner-city youth, administrators, businesses, colleges, universities, professors, schools, and teachers engaged in collaborative learning that advances the development of marginalized youth human capital to improve everyone's future.

Experienced and informative teacher and student voices are essential elements in closing academic achievement gaps. Because teachers work hand in hand with students on a daily basis, they understand first and foremost the teaching strategies and techniques required to improve student learning. They are in tune with and understand the problems that students bring to class on a daily basis. True education involves input from all educational stakeholders, but the source of learning begins with classroom teachers whose insight can offer a wide range of possible community solutions. B-FREE therefore strives to provide an essential outlet for assessing family and community problems while developing solutions that offer educational sustainability utilizing the input of community stakeholders. We seek to develop learning initiatives that produce shared leadership and responsibility, and our goal is positive educational reform that impacts communities through teacher and student preparedness. Serving as an educator for over twenty years, I have always emphasized to my students and colleagues that engaged stakeholder collaboration is the key to real progress toward systemic future change, and I have stressed the following skills:

- **Skill Set 1:** Teach students how to assess their academic skills set to be successful at building learning relationships in their school and community.
- **Skill Set 2:** Employ teacher and peer evaluations of student understanding of sustainable learning initiatives in the global knowledge economy.
- **Skill Set 3:** Provide interactive teaching tools that help students understand how to utilize education as a tool of reflection and problem solving as an essential part of learning.
- **Skill Set 4:** Teach students how to assess their behavior as it relates to improving GPA and creating an atmosphere that promotes good learning

relationships, developing students' soft skills to support academic achievement, social advancement, and increases in human and social capital.

Utilizing these four twenty-first-century skill sets, effective educators working in the school and the community can inspire and uplift students to achieve success and enhance quality-of-life opportunities.

CONCLUSION: SUPPORTING YOUTH GROWTH AND LEARNING BEYOND THE CLASSROOM

Our youth are very intelligent and many view school as a way out of their struggling communities. As such, marginalized youth need to be taught structure and mainstream values in a nonthreatening manner that supports growth and learning that will extend to their communities. In my own educational experiences, I have personally observed many marginalized youth who require structured learning that supports curriculum, but who also need more knowledge and skills that extend beyond the classroom. As the director of the Boys & Girls Club in Syracuse, New York, for example, I was charged with revitalizing a club that no longer served its target membership; young people in the neighborhood would simply not participate because it was unstructured and chaotic. I amended age-group schedules, enforced the rules strictly, and charged my club counselors with using age-appropriate, engaging learning games that could also help members succeed in school. With just a few simple structural changes, the club reached record membership in a short time.

My first teaching assignment is another example of the value of structure. The school population was more than 80% Black, and it was structured in every way to support student learning. The students thrived here, specifically because they knew what was expected of them. These students even went on to help others who lacked the experience of a structured learning environment.

Observing students teaching others how to embrace the learning process is how I designed my classroom pedagogy and my present administrative style. By determining the needs of the students, I have been able to build an educational structure that best supports learning. The B-FREE initiative has grown out of my learning relationships with schools, community organizations, and, most important, marginalized youth who have shared their hopes and dreams with me, and I have come to see clearly the community and social impediments that threaten to halt those dreams. Such engaging critical conversations with youth have provided the foundation and structure for B-FREE. Simply put, I learned how to help youth from the youth, and I have come to understand that it is through engagement with the stakeholders who have the most to gain or lose that we will find solutions to problems and achieve better outcomes. At present, we must pay it forward by cherishing our male children every day.

On December 1, 2011, and again on May 2, 2014, my life came full circle when I became a grandfather. God blessed my son with his own sons, continuing our family name and strengthening our legacy. To a father, sons are much like the sun is to the earth, bringing light and energy with a life force that centers on growing love, forging positivity, and building families. We must avoid the enemies' playground of fear and evil, and the seeds we plant will be free to use the energy of faith, hope, and love that offers divine protection. My goal is to energize and impart knowledge through words, action, and my supportive service toward empowering young Black males' family and community development.

REFERENCES

The 2011 Census. Census.gov

Afrika Bambaataa raps on early hip-hop. (2015, May 7). *Cornell Chronicle*.

Ball, J. A. (2007). Hip-Hop, mass media and 21st century colonization [Weblog post]. *Black agenda report*.

Bureau of Justice Statistics. (2009, March). *Prison inmates at midyear 2008—statistical tables* (revised April 8, 2009). Retrieved from http://www.bjs.gov/

Centers for Disease Control and Prevention. Retrieved from http://www.cdc.gov/ViolencePrevention/index.html

Centers for Disease Control and Prevention. Retrieved from http://www.cdc.gov/violenceprevention/youthviolence/riskprotectivefactors.html

DeNavas-Walt, C., & Proctor, B. D. (2014). *Income and poverty in the United States: 2013*. United States Census Bureau. Retrieved from http://www.census.gov/content/dam/Census/library/publications/2014/demo/p60-249.pdf

Dickerson, J. (2014). The Huffington Post. Retrieved from http://www.huffingtonpost.com/2014/08/05/72-percent-black-fatherhood_n_5648759.html

National Center for Fair and Open Testing. (2012, May). What's wrong with standardized tests? *FairTest*.

No Child Left Behind (NCLB). Act of 2001, Pub. L. No. 107–110, § 115, Stat. 1425 (2002). Retrieved from http://www2.ed.gov/policy/elsec/leg/esea02/107-110.pdf

United States Census Bureau. (2008). *2008 Annual Social and Economic (ASEC) supplement*. Retrieved from http://pubdb3.census.gov/macro/032008/pov/new02_200_01.htm

United States Government Accountability Office. (2007). *Poverty in America: Economic research shows adverse impacts on health status and other social conditions as well as the economic growth rate* (GAO Publication No. GAO-07-344). Washington, DC: Author. Retrieved from www.gao.gov/new.items/d07344.pdf

Index

Achievement gap
  and African American students, 11, 14
  and caring, 11–12, 153
  defined, 27
  and varied discipline measures, 28
  youth helping to close, 171
Adequate Yearly Progress (AYP), 32
Aldridge, D. P., 150
American Baptist Home Mission Society (ABHMS), 145, 151n1
Aquinas, Thomas, 119
Aristotle, 116, 119
Atlanta Baptist College (ABC), 144, 145
Atlanta University, 146, 151
Audi, R., 118

B-FREE, 161–74
Baggini, J., 117
Baier, A., 126
Bailey, D. F., 86
Beachum, Floyd D., 67, 70, 71, 72
Beauboeuf-Lafontant, T., 82
Bell, D., 80
Bennis, W., 123

Bentham, J., 116
Black fathers
  and *culture*, 96–97
  curricular design for, 101–10
  as curriculum, 93–110 passim
  and need for broader curriculum, 97–99
  as *educator*, 93–95
  progressive masculinity of, 99–101
  reading list for, 105
  and new vision of scholars, 95–96
  See also Family unit, Black; Black males
Black males
  and the Black Church, 5–6
  and caring, 1–2, 15, 17, 49, 70, 132–33
  and critique/justice/caring, 66–71
  and depression, 3
  disposability of, 78
  and feminist notion of caring, 14
  and dominant ideologies, 97–98
  as hyper-masculine, 63, 70
  identity, 134–36
  in the media, 2–3, 63, 77–78
  as mentors, 6, 98
  perceptions of, 1–3, 65

as "players," 63
and policing, aggressive, 69
as progressive-regressive, 101, 106, 107, 108, 109, 110
need for role models, 71
as scholars, 65–66
and slavery, 100, 110, 133, 134, 135–36 139
and spirituality and religion, 131–34, 136–39
support networks for, 81
See also Black fathers; Educational leadership, Black males in; Family unit; Students, Black male
"*Black man*," term , 2
Brown, M. C., 98
Bureaucrat-administrator, 30, 34, 35

Care
and the achievement gap, 12
defined, 12, 70
myth of, 121–22
See also Caring; Ethic of care
Caring
"Black feminist," 14
Black masculine, 13
core principles of, 23
devalued, 70
grounded theory of, 23
vs. masculine, 15
and closing the achievement gap, 11–12, 28
feminist
leadership style of, 29
vs. masculine caring, 19
networks, 13
and rough love, 19–20
and spirituality, 18
as standard for, 15
studies of, 14
and education, 3, 4, 12
institutional, 6, 143
practices, intensive, 15
and raising Black males, 5
relational, 12
and student achievement, 23
traditional views of as feminist, 23
womanist, 82

See also, Care; Educational leadership, Black males in; Ethic of care
Carlyle, T., 125
Church, Black, 5–6
Cohen, J., 3
College Board Advocacy and Policy Center, 63–64
Common Core, 170
Cone, J. H., 136
Connelly, F. M., 99
Cook, Coralie, viii, ix
Cooper, Anna Julia, 150
Cose, E., 61
Crisis of the Negro Intellectual, 65
Critical Race Theory (CRT)
and Black male education, 79
care through mentoring, 80–81
and masking mentoring, 81–87, 154
and institutionalized racism, 5
and Black feminist scholars, 46
tenets of, 79–80
"Crucible of Identity: The Negro Lower-Class Family," 99
Cruse, Harold, 65
Cunningham, W. G., 67
Curriculum, Black fathers as, 93–110
Curriculum Integration Project, 30

Dantley, M. E., 93, 95
Davis, Angela, 98–99
Davis, L., 144, 145
Davis-Vines, N. L., 64
Derrida, Jacques, 68–69
DuBois, W. E. B., 59 145, 150
Dyson, M. E., 68

Educational leadership, Black males in
and community ties, 29, 39
and ethic of care, 17, 23
faith and care among, 123–28
and father figure, 18, 85
and need to be needed, 22–23
as role models, 49,
and negative stereotyping, 2, 3–4
placement in schools, 1, 3, 13, 28, 82, 154
and scant studies of men and caring, 14

and special education, 82, 84, 87
and relationship building, 20–21
and "rough love as care," 4, 19–20, 154
and societal expectations, 21–22
and spirituality, 18
style of vs. feminine style, 13
See also Ethic of care; Teachers; Student-teacher relationships
Eisner, E., 93, 104
Equalizer, 2
Ethic of care, 47–49, 115–18
  by African American teachers with African American students, 17, 23, 48–49
  as defined by Nodddings, 47
  and ethno-humanist, 40
  and faith, 117, 123–28
  as traditional feminist construct, 13, 29, 113
  and gender myths, 119–21
  and justice, 117–18
  mentoring as, 78–79
  as moral theory, 115
  research on, 3
  standard for, 15
  and student-teacher relationships, 47–51, 55
  and teacher training, 55
  and virtue ethicists, 116
Ethno-humanist
  vs. bureaucrat-administrator, 30
  and ethic of care, 41
  and focus of, 31, 37

Family unit
  historic African, 100
  Black
    and adoption into, 104–10
    and gangs as, 138
    Moynihan report on, 97
    effect of slavery on, 99
    spiritual/religious view of, 137, 139
    teachers as extension of, 95
    meaning of term, 137
    weakening of, 163, 171
    traditional male role in, 63
Feminist theory
  Black, 1, 13, 46
  and ethical theory, 113, 121, 122, 123, 124

Fenstermacher, G. D., 113, 124
Ferguson, A. A., 51, 105
Framework
  of Black feminist caring, 1, 15, 154
  of Black masculine caring, 4, 13, 15, 23, 87, 155
  CRT as, 79, 84, 87
  of curriculum plan, 93
  ethical, 54, 66, 70
  feminist, 13
  feminist leadership, 13
  of justice, 68–69
  masculine-centered, 13
  of mentoring, 79
Franklin, Jesse, 4, 29–42
Franklin, Robert, 149
Freeland, George, 6, 161–63

Gause, C. P., 95
Gilligan, C. 12, 118
Giroux, H., 78
Gooden, Mark A., 4, 30, 31, 34, 41, 154
Graduation rates, 27–28, 32, 134, 165
Grant, Thomas, 30, 31, 41
Grantham, T. C., 81
Grumet, M. R., 71

Harper, S. R., 62, 63
Harris, S. M., 63
Harro, B., 62
Held, V., 116, 126
Henderson, J. G., 93, 100, 101
Hill-Jackson, V., 52
hooks, b., 47, 61
Hope, John, 143–51 passim
  and external institutional care, 145
  and internal interpersonal care, 144
  and sustainable institutional care, 145–49, 151
  and Black manhood, 149–50
Howard, T., 87
Hume, D., 119

Intensive caring practices, 15
Isom, D., 51, 60, 61

Johnson, C. S., 151
Joseph, P. B., 101, 102

Kant, I., 116, 121–22, 123
Karenga, M., 96
Kincheloe, J. L., 93, 94, 101, 102

Lean on Me, 3
Leadership styles
    and caring, 13
    masculine vs. feminine, 13
    studies of women's, 14, 29–30
Lewis, C., 52
Lewis, C. W., 69
Lomotey, K., 29–30, 34, 36
Lorde, A. G., 110

Males, Black. *See* Black males
Martin, Trayvon, 2, 102
Masculine-centered frameworks and theories, 13
Masking mentoring, 81–87, 154
Mattis, J. S., 138
McCall, N., 61
Media
    on Black man as "player," 63
    influence on Black males, 2–3
    literacy, 95
    and misrepresentation of Black males, 77–78
    and Barack Obama, 77–78
    as corrosive tool, 164
    See also B-Free initiative
Methodology, qualitative, exploratory multi-case study, 15–16
Miller, J. G., 69
Morehouse College, 6, 143– 51 passim
Morrison, P., 62
Moynihan, Daniel, 97, 98–99
Myth
    of care, 121–22
    defined, 120
    of gender, 120–21

National Assessment of Educational Progress (NAEP), 27
National Center for Education Statistics (NCES), 27

Negro Family: Case for National Action, 97
Niagara Movement, 145, 151n2
No Child Left Behind Act (NCLB) 32, 170
Noddings, Nel
    and corrective action, 12, 18
    defining care, 47
    on feminist leadership style, 29
    on relational caring, 12
    and student-teacher relationship, 47–49
Noguera, P. A., 49, 51, 54

Obama, Barack, 77, 109, 138
Oliver, W., 63

Pagels, E., 121
Perry, R. B., 117
Pimentel, C., 80
Pojman, L. P., 117
Plato, 116, 125, 126
Police/policing, 2, 69, 165
Price, T. L., 124
Pritchard, H. A., 115

Rainwater, Lee, 99
Reagan, Ronald, 171
Reference list for Black fathers, 105
"Reformers, systemic," 101
Roberts, M. A., 48, 54
Ryan, J., 66

School administrators, Black male.
    See Educational leadership, Black males in
Schools, urban, high-poverty, 1, 11
    bureaucracy in, 40
    and caring practices, 29
    and community ties, 29, 39
    dress codes in, 37–38
    crisis in, 28
    high-need, 15
    effect of negative mind-set on, 2
    ethno-humanist in, 37, 40
    must shift focus from discipline, 28
    small approach, 33
    See also Achievement gap; Educational leadership, Black males in; Segregation; Students, Black male
"School-to-prison pipeline," 3, 168

Schott Foundation for Public Education, 64
Segregation, 133, 134, 139, 143
Shields, C. M., 70
Siddle Walker, V., 67, 143, 144
Skiba, R. J., 51
Slavery
   introduced Africans to America, 96
   and the Black Church, 133
   and curriculum development, 96, 97–98
   and Black family unit, 110
   and Black masculinity, 100, 101, 133, 134, 135, 139
Smith, V. G., 79
Smith, W., 65
Space Traders, 80
Special education. *See under* Educational leadership, Black males in; Students
Standardized testing, 27, 40, 45, 50, 170
Starratt, R. J., 66, 67, 70, 71
Student-teacher relationships
   and teacher bias, 50–52, 54
   of Black students and Black vs. White teachers, 48–49
   successful models of, 52–54
   future research on, 54–55
Students
   African American/Black
      challenges faced, 27, 31, 71
      and discipline gap, 45
      graduation rates of, 27–28
      and self-definition, 98
      and special education, 27, 28
   Black male
      and need for caring, 4, 49–51, 54
      and discipline gap, 45
      and dropout rate, 45, 78, 163, 169
      early and elementary schooling of, 60–62, 66
      need for positive Black role models, 4–5, 53, 54, 71
      and history of Blacks in America, 69–70
      at intersection of identities, 46–47
      low-income, 11, 47
      and mentoring programs, 54, 55
      and "rough love," 19–20, 154
      in secondary schools, 62–65
      and special education, 45, 50, 64, 65, 78

      and teacher perceptions, 49, 51, 52
   See also Achievement gap; Critical Race Theory (CRT); Ethic of care; Student-teacher relationships; Teachers
Study (current, Bass)
   data analysis and trustworthiness, 16
   implications for research and conclusions of, 23
   methodology, qualitative, exploratory multi-case, 15–16
   participants, 15, 16 *table*, 17–23
   purpose of, 15
   research design of, 15
   and rough love as care, 19–20
   sample and data collection, 16
   significance of, 14
   emergent key themes of, 16–23
   theoretical framework of, 14, 17
Sudarkosa, N., 98, 100

Teacher preparation, 55
Teachers
   and racial bias, 50–52, 54
   and one-caring role, 47–48
   See also Educational leadership, Black males in; Ethic of care; Student-teacher relationships
Testing, standardized, 27, 40, 45, 50, 170
Themes, key, emergent, 16–23
Thomas, D., 51, 64
Thugology, 163–64
Training Day, 2
Tyler, K. M., 4, 50

Utilitarians, 116

Villalpando, O., 79

Washington, Denzel, 2
Watkins, D. C., 3, 96
Wentzel, K. R., 14
Wilson, A. V., 84
Woodson, C. G., 151

ROCHELLE BROCK,
RICHARD GREGGORY JOHNSON III,
& CYNTHIA DILLARD,
Executive Editors

Black Studies and Critical Thinking is an interdisciplinary series which examines the intellectual traditions of and cultural contributions made by people of African descent throughout the world. Whether it is in literature, art, music, science, or academics, these contributions are vast and far-reaching. As we work to stretch the boundaries of knowledge and understanding of issues critical to the Black experience, this series offers a unique opportunity to study the social, economic, and political forces that have shaped the historic experience of Black America, and that continue to determine our future. Black Studies and Critical Thinking is positioned at the forefront of research on the Black experience, and is the source for dynamic, innovative, and creative exploration of the most vital issues facing African Americans. The series invites contributions from all disciplines but is specially suited for cultural studies, anthropology, history, sociology, literature, art, and music.

Subjects of interest include (but are not limited to):

- EDUCATION
- SOCIOLOGY
- HISTORY
- MEDIA/COMMUNICATION
- RELIGION/THEOLOGY
- WOMEN'S STUDIES
- POLICY STUDIES
- ADVERTISING
- AFRICAN AMERICAN STUDIES
- POLITICAL SCIENCE
- LGBT STUDIES

For additional information about this series or for the submission of manuscripts, please contact Dr. Brock (Indiana University Northwest) at brock2@iun.edu; Dr. Johnson (University of San Francisco) at rgjohnsoniii@usfca.edu; or Dr. Dillard (University of Georgia) at cdillard@uga.com.

To order other books in this series, please contact our Customer Service Department:

(800) 770-LANG (within the U.S.)
(212) 647-7706 (outside the U.S.)
(212) 647-7707 FAX

Or browse online by series at www.peterlang.com.

www.ingramcontent.com/pod-product-compliance
Ingram Content Group UK Ltd.
Pitfield, Milton Keynes, MK11 3LW, UK
UKHW022239230426
12048UKWH00018BA/1356